early libertarianism to proud individualism to intrafamily reconciliation to ecumenical cooperation. *Pilgrimage of Faith* is superb institutional history but with distinctly non-parochial appeal. It is a book for anybody who wants to know more about the role of religion in the maturation of democracy.

C.C. GOEN   DOUGLAS R. CHANDLER

DOUGLAS CHANDLER, author, was professor of church history at Wesley Theological Seminary for thirty-four years prior to his retirement in 1973. A New York native, he received his S.T.B. degree from the seminary in 1929, when it was known as Westminster. He has also been a high-school teacher (New York) and a pastor (Connecticut and Maryland). He wrote the sections on the Methodist Protestant Church in *The History of American Methodism,* ed., Emory S. Bucke.

CLARENCE C. GOEN, editor, has been in the department of church history at Wesley since 1960. He is the author of *Revivalism and Separatism in New England,* 1740–1800, and editor of *The Great Awakening,* revival writings of Jonathan Edwards. He is a past president of the American Society of Church History.

Pilgrimage of Faith

PILGRIMAGE *of* FAITH

A Centennial History of
Wesley Theological Seminary
1882-1982

Douglas R. Chandler
Edited by C. C. Goen

Cabin John, Md./Washington, D.C.

Photo Credits

Unless noted below, all photographs and illustrations are from the archives of Wesley Theological Seminary.

Claire Flanders: *frontispiece,* 221   Cameramen, Inc.: 213, 204, 219, 242
Methodist Protestant, 9 November 1898, p. 12; 4, 5   Joseph W. Mollitor: 218
Bruce Reedy: 255   Gene Spurlock: 173   Robert Striar: 209
M. E. Warren: 131, 133, 144, 183, 214, 227, 233, 237, 238, 259
Washington Post: 244   Western Maryland College: 17   Wilson Studio: 71

Library of Congress Cataloging in Publication Data

Chandler, Douglas R., 1901-
  Pilgrimage of Faith.

  Includes bibliographical references and index.
  1. Wesley Theological Seminary—History. I. Goen, C. C. II. Title.
BV4070.W37C48   1984   207'.753   84-1415
ISBN 0-932020-27-5

Design: Lynn Springer
Design Consultant: Chuck Myers
Typography and composition: Options Type Group, Takoma Park, Maryland
Printed by the Maple Press Company, York, Pennsylvania
First Edition, June 1984

Seven Locks Press

Publishers
P.O. Box 72
Cabin John, Maryland 20818

Seven Locks Press is an affiliate of Calvin Kytle Associates

When the question of founding a school for training young men for the ministry in the Methodist Protestant Church was being earnestly debated in the Maryland Conference of 1882, the challenge was forcibly put by the opposition, "What are you going to found the Institution on? Where is your experience, where is your money, where is anything for a foundation?" And the answer that strengthened the hearts of all its friends, was: "We will found it on faith."

Thomas Hamilton Lewis,
first president

WESLEY THEOLOGICAL SEMINARY
Washington, D.C.
1882

Preface

Wesley Theological Seminary, founded in Westminster, Maryland, by the Methodist Protestant Church in 1882, operated for its first seventy-five years on a campus adjacent to Western Maryland College and was called simply by the name of the town. In 1958 the seminary moved to a new campus adjoining The American University in Washington, DC, and took on a new name and character.

Methodist Protestants were a post-Revolutionary group of "reformers" whose advocacy of lay rights and democratic equality in the church hastened the Americanization of Methodism. After organizing as a separate denomination in 1830, they progressed in little more than a century from early libertarianism to proud individualism to intrafamily reconciliation to ecumenical cooperation; and from the time of its founding the seminary was an important institutional expression of that pilgrimage. As the only theological school in The United Methodist Church bearing the Methodist Protestant heritage, the seminary offers a story that may stand as something of a paradigm of the maturing of Methodism in the United States.

When the centennial year of the seminary was approaching, then president John L. Knight urged the Board of Governors to commission a history of the school. They responded affirmatively, and since I had taught Church History here for the last third of the seminary's centennium, they invaded my retirement to place the assignment on me. Writing the history of the school I have loved and served for so many years has been both pleasant and fulfilling, though not without hazards. The temptation either to glorify the past into heroic proportions or to diminish its achievements by contrast with the present is familiar to all who write about institutions dear to their own hearts. Personal memory, moreover, if not subjected to critical historical judgment, can easily invest the past with undeserved significance. I will not claim objectivity, for that would be untruthful—and undesirable as well. I have tried, however, to restrain my bias and to exercise reasonable caution in the construction of this narrative.

The problem of intruding personal memories was most acute in dealing with the last two decades, which could properly be called the most exciting years of the school's century. Historians are customarily cautious—and inept if not—in describing their own times, and therefore I have confined myself to a summary account of the most salient events. I hope that some later historian with a longer perspective may be able to correct my impressionistic survey with a more judicious historical interpretation.

Reliable history, of course, depends primarily on documentary evidence, and fortunately for the present work, abundant records of the seminary's origins and development have survived. In the archives of the school are minutes, diaries, journals, official publications, and private correspondence, all presenting data sufficient to support a comprehensive account of the school's first one hundred years. Although I have drawn extensively on such records, I have kept citations to a minimum, trusting that comments in the text itself are adequate to indicate my sources for the many quotations, paraphrases, and summaries.

Most readers of this book, I presume, will be familiar with Methodist terminology, but for the benefit of non-Methodist readers it may not be amiss to take note here of some common words that Methodists have invested with special meaning. "Conference" is the most common term in Methodist polity. Annual conferences began in 1744, when John Wesley called his lay preachers together for a meeting at which he heard their reports, issued instructions, and gave them their assignments for the ensuing year. Their appointed fields of labor were called "circuits" (later "charges," and now "appointments") and were always determined by the conference. Such meetings became an annual practice, and in due time Wesley's pattern of organization was transplanted to America. Methodist preachers met in Philadelphia to form the first annual conference in America in 1773. As the church grew, other annual conferences were organized on a regional basis, and in 1792 all the preachers came together in a General Conference that was to meet every four years. In 1812 the General Conference became delegated and thenceforth consisted of delegates elected from all the annual conferences. From its inception, the General Conference has had full legislative power over all connectional matters for the entire denomination. All the conferences are now composed of elected lay and ministerial delegates in equal numbers. An "area" is analogous to a diocese, the region administered by a bishop, and may include more than one annual conference. "Districts" are administrative subdivisions of an annual conference, and "district superintendents" (formerly called "presiding elders") are ministers appointed by the bishop to oversee the churches and pastors within these smaller territories. *The Book of Discipline* (as it is now called) contains decisions of the General Conference by which the whole denomination is governed. Issued quadrennially since 1792, with revisions and additions as necessary, it remains the authoritative constitution of the denomination. This summarizes the organizational development of mainline Methodism, but most of the bodies that separated from the Methodist Episcopal Church retained the same pattern by organizing their own conferences and drawing up their own constitutions and books of discipline.

Two persons whose lives were inseparable from the school for well over half a century, though now departed, lived to contribute much to this book. Dorothy Elderdice, daughter of the seminary's longest-serving president, preserved and collected her father's papers and wrote his biography. Montgomery J. Shroyer, professor of New Testament for forty-two years until his retirement in 1961, knew intimately and reported faithfully on the school's early life, its goals and ideals. I have had the benefit not only of their collections of papers and other memorabilia but of many hours of their personal reminiscences.

It is a pleasure to recognize the generous cooperation of those who have made my task so rewarding. Roland Kircher and his staff in the seminary library were unfailingly helpful, and it would be impossible to find more willing and efficient assistance. Claudia Steinbruckner, Gracemary Snyder, and Mary Twomey responded cheerfully to every request for aid. Susan May promptly located every item I asked for and discovered several I had not known about. Virginia Hamner typed the manuscript as a labor of love. Emily Chandler listened to the whole story many times, by turns appreciative, critical, and corrective. John E. Bevan, Heather Faulkner, and Laurence H. Stookey read the typescript and offered many wise suggestions for improvement. Clarence C. Goen prepared the work for publication and patiently shepherded it through the press. Grateful recognition is also due Jane Gold, an extraordinarily meticulous copyeditor at Seven Locks Press. For all of these fellow laborers I am grateful.

Douglas R. Chandler
Advent 1983

Contents

1

From small
beginnings

For more than half of its first century Westminster
Theological Seminary enjoyed the distinction of being the only
seminary of the Methodist Protestant Church. This singular-
ity the school lost in 1939, when it became one of ten
theological seminaries of The Methodist Church—a church
where, some said, anything small was suspect. Westminster
Seminary had then only forty-five students and a full-time
faculty of four. But being small had never been a heavy cross
for Methodist Protestants; their origin and subsequent career
as reformers and radicals had inured them to minority status.
Upon uniting with the northern and southern wings of
Episcopal Methodism in 1939, they could relax, gratified to
see many of their formerly disturbing reforms accepted as
prevailing Methodist practice. To understand the heritage of
the seminary, it is necessary to know something of the
character of the denomination that founded it.

Protest against episcopacy:
a new church

The Methodist Protestant Church originated as a separation
from the Methodist Episcopal Church in protest against the
aristocratic control of bishops. Organized in 1830, it was
known during its first two years as "The Associated Methodist
Churches." Unofficially Methodist Protestants were called
"Radicals," "Reformers," or "New Side Methodists." For
more than forty years prior to separation they had been try-

ing to introduce more of American democracy into the Methodist Episcopal Church. That church, created by Wesley's preachers in America at the Lovely Lane Church in Baltimore at Christmas 1784, seemed oblivious of lay members' rights. Reflecting John Wesley's unabashed Toryism, Francis Asbury's autocratic disposition, and the conservatism of ministerial tradition, the episcopal structure of early American Methodism incorporated few of the ideas of representative government then current. Asbury clearly tried to accept the "American cause," but he was uneasy with the novelty of voting in church affairs. He always feared defection among Methodists on the issue of episcopal authority and his own exercise of it. Moreover, it seemed to him risky to increase representation in church conferences and to give a voice in church government to more than the itinerant clergy. Very few political theories, Asbury thought, carry over well into church government. "Here," he wrote, "are some similitudes of form but not of nature." Civic governments, for example, should change their elected leaders from time to time; spiritual governments should not. In church governments, since they are spiritual, "one election to [the bishop's] office is sufficient during life."[1]

To such assumptions of clerical authority John Wesley had given clear endorsement. Referring to John Locke, he once mused that if the right of choosing governors belongs to every partaker of human nature, then it belongs not only to men but also to women, and to those under twenty-one, and to those who have lived threescore; "but none did ever maintain this nor probably ever will."[2] Wesley wrote to John Mason on 13 January 1790: "As long as I live the people shall have no share in choosing their stewards or leaders among the Methodists. We are not republicans and never intend to be. It would be better for those who are so minded to go quietly away."

But laicism was spreading, and American Methodists "so minded" would neither go away nor remain quiet. Robert Strawbridge, an Irish local preacher in Maryland, ignored the Wesley-Asbury prohibitions and on his own authority gave the sacraments to his followers with unordained hands. When Strawbridge died an untimely death in 1781, Asbury wrote: "I am inclined to think the Lord took him away in judgment because he was in a way to do hurt to his cause.''[3] A decade later the itinerant elders in conference had no patience to wait for God to act in such a way again; so when one of the traveling preachers (James O'Kelly) tried to appeal his appointment, the conference voted him down and added to the *Discipline* a warning:

> If a member of our church shall be clearly convicted of endeavoring to sow dissentions [*sic*] in any of our societies, by inveighing against either our doctrines or discipline, such person so offending shall be first reproved by the senior Minister or Preacher of his circuit; and if he afterwards persist in such pernicious practices he shall be expelled [from] the society.[4]

Jesse Lee, the first American Methodist historian, observed in southern local preachers (who were unordained) an "uneasy and restless Spirit" arising from the contention that they "ought to have a seat and vote in all our conferences" and that "there ought to be a delegation of lay members." When the preachers complained that taxation without representation was as wrong in churches as in nations, the elders replied that Methodists did not tax anyone and therefore representation was no issue.[5] In 1816 the local preachers petitioned the General Conference for membership and the right to vote. They were refused, although at that time they outnumbered the itinerant elders three to one.

But preachers in conference could not silence the calls for reform. The reformers' ideas deeply affected the life and structure of many local churches, reflecting, especially after 1812, the new vocabulary of political democracy: constitutional procedures, voting rights, representation, rotation and short terms in office, and the whole concept of "the common people" participating in their own government. In American Methodism such ideas set laity and unordained preachers against a power elite composed of bishops, presiding elders, and itinerants.

By 1820 the reformers had a battle cry: "election of presiding elders." These dignitaries, now called district superintendents, were traditionally appointed by the bishops to assist in overseeing the subdivisions of the annual conferences. The General Conference of that year degenerated into bitter conflict with many days of angry debate, political maneuvering in and out of sessions, and hot-tempered personal attacks from both sides, all ending in failure for the reform movement. Then followed a decade of noisy internal strife. Partisan societies often met boldly in Methodist churches. A reform literature appeared. *The Wesleyan Repository and Religious Intelligencer,* founded in 1821 and edited by an able Philadelphia layman, William S. Stockton, became in 1824 *Mutual Rights,* and after 1831 *The Methodist Protestant*. Pledged to free and open debate, this journal appeared to conservatives as extremely dangerous, and its discovery in a preacher's home made the possessor at once an object of suspicion in his annual conference.

Eventually, almost inevitably, came the expulsions, beginning in 1827. Reform conventions quickly followed, called by those expelled and by their angry supporters who withdrew to join them. In Baltimore, the storm center, the reformers bought an Episcopal church building (St. John's), where, in November 1830, forty-nine ministerial and thirty-four lay delegates representing conferences and churches from Alabama to Canada organized a new denomination—the Methodist Protestant Church. Almost all the reform demands were written into its constitution: the election of presiding elders, lay representation in all conferences, local preachers' rights, abolition of the episcopacy, the right to appeal appointments, and safeguards on trials and appeals of ministers and members.

The names of these stormy advocates of "members' rights" became household words among Methodist Protestants. Upon the founding of the seminary in 1882 and long afterward, their pictures looked down from hall and classroom walls. There were Nicholas Snethen (1769-1845), Asbury's one-time "silver trumpet," eloquent and able though shrill at times, who became the "father of lay representation"; Alexander McCaine (1768-1856), author of an exhaustive treatise with the somewhat hissing title, *The History and Mystery of Methodist Episcopacy;* Asa Shinn (1781-1853), orator, editor, and theologian; Cornelius Springer (1790-1875) from Ohio; Dr. Samuel Jennings (1771-1854) of Georgetown, DC; and Francis Waters (1792-1868), lawyer, college president at the age of

Nicholas Snethen (1769-1845) was "the first advocate of reform . . . the ablest of all the Reformers" of his day. As a delegate to General Conference in 1812, he took a leading part in the debate over the election of presiding elders and declared that "he would never again appear in a General Conference unless sent there by a vote of both laymen and preachers." Chosen president of the Convention of Reformers in 1828, he is properly termed "the Father of Methodist Protestantism."

twenty-six, and the one who proposed the word "Protestant" instead of "Representative" in naming the new church.

The list of founders is long and would be out of place here, but Thomas Hewlings Stockton (1808-1868) should be remembered as one of the most impressive exemplars of the Methodist Protestant heritage.[6] For several generations ministerial candidates read and spoke of him with awe. Stockton balanced beautifully on the thin line between orthodoxy and nonconformity. Even more prolific than his father, William S. Stockton, he was editor and chief contributor to the church's journals. In some twenty other publications he sent forth poetry, sermons, treatises on reform views, and essays on literary and moral subjects. He published the hymnbook of 1837, and from 1839 to 1858 he launched and edited at least five religious periodicals. In 1846, when elected a delegate to the World's Convention of Christian Protestant Ministers meeting in London, he first planned to attend but then refused when he learned that Universalists and Unitarians were not invited because they were not considered "Christian ministers." In 1849 he was elected president of Miami University at Oxford, Ohio, but declined the position because of his primary commitment to preaching and religious journalism. He also rejected a Doctor of Divinity degree offered to him by Gettysburg College. He was twice chaplain of the United States Congress, 1833-35 and 1859-61, and in 1863 he delivered the prayer at the National Cemetery at Gettysburg preceding Lincoln's historic address. Twice, once in Philadelphia and again in Cincinnati, he resigned his pastorate in order to organize "societies of brotherly love" on John Wesley's idea that small groups within the church would quicken its spiritual life. Throughout his career Stockton was moved by two deep convictions: equality of ministers and laity, and equality of races. He clearly reflects the best in the Methodist Protestant tradition.

The reform ideas were not difficult to understand. Ministerial candidates, who learned them in the prescribed Course of Study preparing for ordination, saw them as biblically warranted and socially desirable features of church life, while church members read them repeatedly in their denominational papers. In the seventieth anniversary issue of *The Methodist*

Thomas Hewlings Stockton (1808-68) was widely regarded as "the most eloquent preacher the Methodist Protestant Church ever produced." He also did extensive work as an author and editor, leading Methodist Protestants to name their publishing house the Stockton Press.

Protestant for 9 November 1898, thirty-two large pages are filled with reform history, biographical sketches of nearly forty reform leaders, and articles on liberty and equality in the churches. The embellished cover boldy reasserts the historic three-line motto of the reformers:

Mutual Rights—Liberal Methodism
A Church Without a Bishop in a Country Without a King
Free Grace—Free Speech

At the bottom of the cover is a scroll containing the words, "One is your Master, even Christ, and all ye are brethren" (Matt. 23:8). The whole concludes with *"Fides, Libertas, Amicitia, Praecipua Animi Humani Bona Sunt."* It would be hard to find a more graphic declaration of Methodist Protestant principles than this 1898 poster-cover of their Baltimore weekly.

The ministerial course of study

Methodist Protestants provided for ministerial education through a "prescribed course of reading" printed with their first *Constitution and Discipline* of 1830. Candidates were expected to "read, or consult carefully . . . as far as may be practicable" some thirty books grouped into three "classes," or years. Particularly important were the Scriptures and the *Constitution and Discipline* of the Methodist Protestant Church. Also emphasized were John Wesley's *Sermons* and *Notes;* Paley's *Horae Paulinae, Natural Theology,* and *Evidences of Christianity;* Prideaux's *Connections;* Fletcher's *Checks to Antinomianism;* Butler's *Analogy of Religion;* Watt's *Improvement of the Mind;* Hedge's *Logic;* Jamieson's *Rhetoric;* Campbell's *Lectures on Ecclesiastical History;* Mosheim's *Ecclesiastical History;* and Rollin's *Ancient History.* Other works on the list were Clarke's *Commentary,* Milton's *Paradise Lost,* Hannah Moore's *Works,* and some guides to grammar and pronunciation which "should always be kept ready at hand." Instruction on ancient nomenclature could be found in "Walker's *Key* to the proper names which occur in the scriptures."

Responsibility for supervising the trainees was assigned to the annual conferences. The Maryland Conference took an initial step in 1829, appointing a committee "to examine the qualifications of candidates for the ministry and for ordination [and] to prepare a course of reading and study for such candidates." The members of this committee were Alexander McCaine (scholar and polemicist), Frederick Stier (itinerant preacher and pastor), and James R. Williams (self-taught in Hebrew, Greek, Latin, and French, and also the author of the denomination's first history, a textbook used for forty years in the Conference Course of Study). The Maryland Conference published its own list of sixteen titles, which included most of the works emphasized by the 1830 *Discipline* plus Magee's *On the Atonement* and, "if convenient," Brown's *Philosophy* and Blair's *Rhetoric and Lectures.* At the end of the list was a note: "The committee beg leave to say, that a regular and attentive perusal of the foregoing works will more fully enable the junior preacher to discharge his public ministerial duties than the use of books of *skeletons* or sketches of sermons."

Following the example of the Maryland Conference's more realistic demands, the list of required books in the 1834 *Discipline* was somewhat shorter. Nineteen titles were prescribed, ten in preparation for a license to preach and nine more for ordination. Forty-three books were added, "recommended by the ministers of the Methodist Church as a suitable collection" and probably intended as a starter for the preacher's library. The whole regimen of reading and study in the Methodist Protestant *Discipline* differed in only one respect from that in the *Discipline* of the Methodist Episcopal Church: the despised titles by Nathan Bangs and John Emory defending episcopacy and the old authorities were replaced by the works of Nicholas Snethen, Alexander McCaine, and Samuel Jennings, the foremost Methodist Protestant apologists.

In 1858 the *Discipline* ordered examinations to be given in several subjects: Bible doctrines, systematic divinity, common English studies, composition (an essay or sermon), the Christian sacraments, church government, Bible history, and general history. These examinations, the directive cautioned, were "to be strictly Biblical, requiring the candidates to give the statement of the doctrine and the Scripture proofs." Each annual conference appointed a committee to examine the students under its care. The examining bodies went under various names, such as "Committee on Itinerancy and Orders," "Faculty of Instruction," or "Committee of Examination." A report from North Carolina's Committee on Itinerancy and Orders, 1891-92, illustrates how such supervision operated:

> We recommend the promotion of Brother J. G. W. Holloway to the class of the second year with requirement to review Binney's Compend.
>
> Brother J. S. Stowe passed an approved examination on all studies of the first year, excepting Binney's Compend, and we recommend his advancement to the class of the second year.
>
> W. C. Lewis failing to arrive in time for examination on all the studies is permitted to enter the class of the third year, to be examined on Butler's Analogy, Logic, and Watson's Institutes, first and second parts and prepare a sermon on Apostasy.
>
> J. D. Williams was promoted to class of the second year and required to submit a sermon on Repentance.

The Maryland Conference regarded its responsibility for ministerial training with utmost gravity. Each year the Faculty of Instruction gave detailed reports listing all the required books, the examiners, and the grades earned by each student. A typical notice read:

> The Faculty meets Tuesday before Conference at 3 o'clock P.M. to examine students and at 7:30 P.M. for business. . . . Correct answers to two-thirds of the questions asked will be required to pass a candidate either for the itinerancy or into any class of the course, or for orders. Two-thirds [correct] will be marked 70. All questions answered [correctly] or less three, will be marked 100, and all receiving 100 will be so reported to the Conference.

In 1882 the examiners reported favorably on the cases of John M. Gill, Hugh L. Elderdice, and James H. Maynard, who "were all marked 100 in all the studies upon which they were examined." That same year the conference added Homiletics to the first-year program in the Course of Study, directing that the textbook be *The Theory of Preaching* by Austin Phelps and that B. F. Benson be the examiner. The report stated also that "all students in the Preparatory Department will be required to prepare a synopsis of the New Testament, of at least twenty pages of letter paper." The same requirement respecting other parts of the Bible was imposed on first- and second-year students, while "students of the Third Year will be expected to furnish proof of careful study of the whole Word of God in a paper of not less than the number of pages above named."[7]

The financial assistance needed for the candidates was as great a problem as courses of study and examinations. On 19 January 1866 some "ministers and members" gathered in Springfield, Ohio, called by some of their number who were "impressed with the inadequacy and inefficiency of our Annual Conference arrangements to sufficiently advise and assist young men who might desire to enter the ministry, and [concerned] that there was no channel through which the whole church could unite in assisting her sons in obtaining an education for the work of the ministry." This group proceeded at once to organize a Board of Ministerial Education, to draw up a constitution and bylaws, to elect officers, and to raise funds. Long, detailed, and carefully prepared reports to the General Conference confirm the remarkable work of this group. Its records were accurate and its requirements specific. Every ministerial candidate was expected to answer before the annual conference several questions about personal religious experience, motives, morals, conduct, and debts. Each promised to withdraw from the denomination "in an orderly manner if his theology changed" and "to refrain from the use of tobacco, wine and all intoxicating liquors." Frequent inquiries and reports determined the candidate's eligibility to borrow from the board's funds, as well as his fitness to seek ordination. The board's report of 1884 summarizes nearly two decades of its labors: "83 young men have received aid; 55 of these are now engaged in work for our church; 10 have united with other denominations; 5 have died; 10 are engaged in other business; 3 have made shipwreck of faith." By 1897, 262 young men had received aid totaling $109,000 in the thirty years of the Ohio board's existence.[8]

College theology for ministers

By the middle of the nineteenth century Methodist Protestants, like other churches in America, were experiencing increased pressures for a better educated ministry. Heirs of the
pietist tradition, they felt the age-long tension between heart
and head, piety and intellect. In 1855 the *Western Methodist
Protestant* appealed for a learned ministry. While conceding
that a college education should not be required, the author
of the appeal nevertheless declared:

> To set an individual to preach the gospel who is a log-
> gerhead...is abominable....We have every means to
> educate our ministers and if they will not be educated they
> should stay at home, on their farms or in their
> shops....Why can not a minister of letters be as spiritual
> as one who is ignorant?[9]

By 1880 all Methodist Protestant regional conferences were
urging (but not requiring) college training for their ministerial
candidates. But the language of the 1881 report of the North
Carolina Committee on Ministerial Education reflects a linger-
ing ambivalence:

> It is our opinion that a scholastic and theologic education
> should go together. But we cannot point out the bounds of
> either....Our fathers went before us without a standard
> or a measure of either scholastic or theologic attain-
> ment...and no one will cast a stone at their learning or
> theology, power or success. Therefore we do not feel it to
> be our imperious duty to say more than that any education
> that will give to the Church of God a ministry of able, liberal,
> and manly characters is quite sufficient for the demands both
> of Church and Society.

Nevertheless, the denomination was busy founding colleges.
There were now Yadkin in North Carolina (established 1861),
Adrian in Michigan, and Western Maryland at Westminster
(both established 1866). Three more western colleges opened
later: Westminster College in Texas (1895), Kansas City
University (1896), and West Lafayette College in Muskingum,
Ohio (1900). All these institutions advertised "departments"
or "schools" of theology.

The professor of Theology at Western Maryland College for fourteen years (1868-82) was Augustus Webster, pastor of St. John's Methodist Protestant Church in Baltimore. A friend described him as standing "erect in the pulpit and when the full, resonant tones of his melodious voice echoed in melting pathos over spellbound congregations. . .[there were] exhibitions of power akin to apostolic times." Little is known of the content of Webster's courses except what can be inferred from the titles of the books he assigned. The college catalog of 1869-70 lists these as Gesenius's *Hebrew Grammar,* Watson's *Theological Institutes,* Prideaux's *Connections,* Mosheim's *Ecclesiastical History,* Powell on *Succession,* Edwards on *Baptism,* and Miller's *Clerical Manners and Habits.* In addition to meeting Webster's expectations, ministerial candidates through the 1870s were also required to recite daily "to the President on such theological text books as have been prescribed by the Board of Trustees." The president referred to was the Reverend James Thomas Ward, and the books prescribed were all drawn from the Course of Study in the denomination's *Constitution and Discipline.*

The number of theological students in the college varied from six to thirteen, and they seem to have enjoyed some status of dignity and respect on the campus. Ten members of the class of 1880 included some who went on to distinguish themselves in the ministry. At the end of their four years together, they celebrated with a "public entertainment" in the Methodist Protestant church in Westminster, described by "Spectator" in *The Methodist Protestant* for 19 June 1880. The "exercises" included a variety of orations and musical numbers by the graduates. The class president, John M. Gill of Northumberland County, Virginia, spoke on the Christian ministry; Edwin A. Warfield of Urbana, Maryland, sang a solo; and William W. Dumm of Johnsville, Maryland, delivered a sermon on "Paul's Defense before Agrippa." Warfield read Derzhavin's "Ode to God," and Hugh L. Elderdice of Burrsville, Maryland, contributed an original poem entitled "Sowing and Reaping." The reporter observed that Elderdice's "poetical taste is excellent, and few of his age can surpass him." At the end, "Spectator" added that the class had "established a theological library at the College and they respectfully invite contributions to it." The reporter hoped piously that when students returned to the college in September, some "theological boys would be among them with quickened desires to be instrumental in leading many souls into the fold of Christ, washed and sanctified, out of every kindred, and tongue, and people, and nation."

Three members of this 1880 class in Theology from Western Maryland College went on to graduate study. Warfield entered the Westminster Theological Seminary (which opened two years later) and became its first and only graduate in 1884. William Kirk was one of six graduates of the seminary in 1885. Elderdice completed the conference Course of Study and then broke precedent by going to Yale Divinity School, from which he was graduated in 1890. The other members of the class prepared for conference membership and ordination in the more usual way by completing the Course of Study and passing the examinations administered by the faculty committee of their annual conference. This last process was normal among all American Methodists until well into the twentieth century.*

After Elderdice became president of Westminster Seminary (in 1897), he used to say that the seminary's founders "were not Fathers and Elders of the church but only beardless boys." By "boys" he meant the theological students at Adrian and Western Maryland colleges who decided to force the issue of theological education on the church. In 1880 they prepared a petition for publication in the denominational press. In their earnestness the students wrote more brashly than some of their elders thought proper. They began with some strongly worded "whereas" paragraphs about an age which "demands a ministry liberally educated" and about their church not providing such education "as sister denominations do." They then stated their blunt resolution that "we unite in presenting these facts through the Church papers, and in petitioning the officials of the Church, and, indeed, the whole membership . . . to establish a satisfactory Theological Department in each Col-

---

* In 1940 the Methodist *Discipline* provided that graduation from a theological seminary could be accepted in lieu of the Course of Study, but not until 1956 was a degree from both college and seminary made the standard of admission to all annual conferences.

lege under the management of the Faculties . . . and that We, as Theological Students preparing for the Ministry of Christ in the Methodist Protestant Church, are determined to do all within our power to place ourselves on an equal footing with the Ministry of other churches and ask only equal advantages.''

Many agreed with the students and saw nothing offensive in their bold appeal. But not Edward J. Drinkhouse, the conservative editor of *The Methodist Protestant.* Using his editorial page to put "the boys" in their proper place, he complained that their petition did not come from "persons entitled to demand" but from students—and in threatening language, at that. Their warning that "unless we furnish such schools our students will go to other schools and come back— if they do not change their minds" rankled him, and he told his readers: "There is a class of men in the Methodist Protestant Church, lineal descendants of the sufferers of 1828, who instinctively resent any sort of threat, whether issuing from the smoke and thunders of lofty assumptions, or garlanded with the sweet familiarity of enthusiastic appeal." Furthermore, he added, these ministerial students were indebted to the denomination's Board of Ministerial Education for their college training, and if they "declare they will go to Yale," then "let them go to Yale. But before they go, let them pay us back what we have spent on them." The disgruntled Drinkhouse spoke for a passing generation, however; his editorial was already out of date, as events in Maryland were about to show.

By 1880 Maryland Methodist Protestants, aware of the theological school impulse in other American churches, were thinking of their Western Maryland College as the logical place for their own school of theology. An early proposal came from James B. Walker, speaking for the Conference Board of Ministerial Training. In *The Methodist Protestant* of 17 April 1880 he announced plans for a separate building to house theological students at the college.

> Every room in the College building must be held for those who can pay the regular College charges. . . . We have been compelled to provide rooms for the theological class outside of the college building. . . . A large brick building has been procured near the College to accommodate over

twenty students. . . . It will be ready for our use by September next . . . . The rooms are each to accommodate two students and each one is to pay our landlord one dollar per month, or ten dollars per year.—But these rooms must be furnished [with] a carpet, bed, table, washstand, stove, etc.—all that would be needed would not, perhaps, cost over $60—we especially solicit the cooperation of pastors and our lady friends.

Walker's plan was apparently premature. Separate housing for theology students at Westminster was not provided until two years later, and then it was in a building housing a new independent seminary.

Meanwhile, the venerable Augustus Webster, commuting from his Baltimore pastorate, continued to lecture at the college on the Trinity, Original Sin, and Redemption. In the spring of 1881 the college petitioned the Maryland Conference for some "early provision to be made to teach systematic theology." There was rising concern that the more able students, "ambitious" to study theology in a scholastic setting, might seek their education in other institutions. Should this happen, "there is danger of losing them [from] the ministry of their own church." The college anticipated that the desired courses could be offered on its campus "with but little additional expense." The conference responded to the petition by approving a motion, made by L. W. Bates, "that Dr. J. T. Murray, Rev. P. L. Wilson and Dr. Charles Billingslea be a committee to mature some plan by which systematic theology may be taught the graduates of Western Maryland College who are preparing for the Christian ministry and report the same to the next session of this Conference."

The conference met next in March 1882 at Broadway Church in Baltimore. On the fourth day the committee reported, recommending that a Department of Theology be established at Western Maryland College, that a minister of the conference be designated as the principal, that members of the college faculty, "as may be available and as may be necessary, give instruction in the several branches of the schedule of studies adopted . . . and, if practicable, that the Pastor of the Methodist Protestant Church in Westminster be included in the Faculty, that the Principal be appointed at this session of the Conference and, [when] confirmed by the Trustees of the College, he shall at once enter upon his duties, organize a faculty and commence the course of instruction in the Department of Theology (in the College) at the beginning of the Collegiate year in September." A part of the report asked for financial support from the "College Collection," as well as for pledges of ten dollars each from one hundred persons for the present year, and expressed a desire that "the students in Theology should as soon as practicable be accommodated in a building separate from and contiguous to the College [as] a Divinity Hall."

This report of Murray, Wilson, and Billingslea was supported by Western Maryland's president, James Thomas Ward. He told the conference that fourteen college students were studying to be ministers of the gospel and that they had been pursuing the studies of the college curriculum in literature, science, and the classics. Ward testified that "our experience . . . has convinced us that it is utterly impracticable to carry students through even the most limited theological course with any satisfactory degree of success at the same time that they are pursuing the regular College course." He called for a separate college department for theological study in which the regular program would be "subordinate and not as now the principal one pursued." There is no mention in the conference records for 1882 of any disapproval of these plans to separate the theological education of ministers from the main college curriculum. Probably few realized that the "department" they were approving would be born as an independent institution and grow into a major free-standing seminary.

Thomas Hamilton Lewis and the new seminary

The Maryland Annual Conference of 1882, in accepting the report of its special committee on ministerial education, had little difficulty deciding who should be "principal" of the proposed Department of Theology at Western Maryland College. Although a nominating committee went through the motions of presenting four names, seventy-eight of the eighty-four votes cast were for Thomas Hamilton Lewis (1852-1929), the bright and handsome pastor of the "Mother Church" of Methodist Protestantism, St. John's in Baltimore, and son-in-law of President Ward.

Lewis plunged immediately into his new assignment, ready with all the energy, enthusiasm, and vision that the project required. The college was completely cooperative, and President Ward did more for his son-in-law than simply cheer from the sidelines. In May the college offered the theological students free dormitory rooms, free tuition for college classes, and free board, washing, heating, and lighting. But from the outset Lewis had something more in mind than a department in the college. He asked for an independent institution, a separate school of theology, and the college trustees promptly provided five acres of land and borrowed $2,500 for a building.[10] The seminary catalog printed that summer promised that the building "now in course of erection will provide Library, Recitation and Lecture Halls, as well as commodious apartments for the residence of students [and] will be ready for occupancy in September."

This was much more than the Maryland Conference had authorized, but Lewis's explanation at the next session was typically confident and persuasive. The conference fairly hummed with pleasure. "We heartily endorse the action of the Principal," they said, "in departing from the line of procedure. . . passed at the last session of this body. . . as it was altogether impracticable to establish a Department of Theology in Western Maryland College." The conference expressed gratitude for the fifteen students already enrolled and for "the receipts from tuition fees [which] have met the current expenses, the salary of the Principal excepted." An appropriation of $1,200 was recommended for Lewis's salary and house rent. Three ministers and two laymen appointed by the Maryland Conference and two ministers and three laymen appointed by the General Conference were "to constitute. . . the Board of Governors of the Westminster Theological Seminary of the Methodist Protestant Church, located at Westminster, Carroll County, Maryland." Lewis was asked to remain as principal "until the contemplated Act of Incorporation and the election of a President. . . by the Board."[11] But Lewis was already acting "presidential," and

Thomas Hamilton Lewis (1852-1929) was elected in 1882 as the "Principal of the School of Theology" to be established at Western Maryland College. He soon founded the Westminster Theological Seminary as an independent institution and served as its first president 1882-86.

with characteristic independence he changed his title to president even before incorporation was secured on 8 April 1884.

From the historical paragraph in the seminary's first catalog, one might conclude that the school "had its inception" in a committee, a resolution, and a Maryland Annual Conference decision. But it owed its origin equally to the man who was its organizer and first president, Thomas Hamilton Lewis. Some said that, like the Hebrews in Egypt, he "made bricks without straw," but Lewis put it another way. In his Inaugural Address, delivered at the first commencement in 1884, he said:

> When the question of founding a school for training young men for the ministry in the Methodist Protestant Church was being earnestly debated in the Maryland Conference of 1882, the challenge was forcibly put by the opposition, "What are you going to found the Institution on? Where is your experience, where is your money, where is anything for a foundation?" And the answer that strengthened the hearts of all its friends, was: "We will found it on faith."[12]

Faith there was, and little else, but it was a faith well supported by his own clear thinking, administrative skill, boundless energy, and almost unlimited self-assurance.

Thomas Hamilton Lewis was born in Dover, Delaware, on 11 December 1852. After his father died in 1853, the family moved to Maryland. He graduated in 1875 from Western Maryland College and two years later married Mary Ward, daughter of its president. Always afterward Ward called him "my son." Lewis served two brief pastorates—Cumberland, Maryland, and St. John's in Baltimore—and took post-graduate studies in Hebrew and Syriac at The Johns Hopkins University. Although he was only thirty years of age when he was chosen to organize theological instruction at Western Maryland College, he proved to be more than equal to the task. He was president of the seminary for four years, 1882-86, and the manner in which he discharged that responsibility presaged a long career of high honors and distinguished leadership in the church.

In 1886 Lewis became president of Western Maryland College, exchanging offices with his father-in-law, who had been president of the college for eighteen years and at the age of sixty-six wanted what he hoped would be less demanding work. Lewis served as president of the college for thirty-four years. During two of those years (1902-04) he added to his duties the presidency of the denomination's Adrian College in Michigan. The Adrian trustees, desperately in debt, had called for someone "with skill, tact and unbounded hope and energy" to save their school from closing. Lewis went "back and forth every two weeks between Western Maryland and Adrian without expense to Adrian save his traveling expenses and necessary extra assistance in the President's office at Western Maryland."[13] After a brilliant administration Lewis resigned from Western Maryland College in 1920 and was then elected president of the Methodist Protestant General Conference, a position he had held once before for a four-year term. He died in 1929.

People thought of Lewis as "Mr. Methodist Protestant," and for half a century he qualified for the title. Few church officials have been more popular or in more demand. Even in the mid-twentieth century some still remembered his commanding presence, handsome face, squared jaw, and flashing eye. Long remembered too, and often quoted, were his sermons and addresses, particularly those inspired by his beloved Methodist Protestant principles: equality of clergy and laity, Methodist union, racial equality, and "the good life."[14] Occasionally his championship of representative government within Methodism and his disdain of episcopacy made him seem abrasive until his sly humor was detected. In a favorite analogy he ridiculed the autocratic polity of Episcopal Methodism:

> If the President of the United States (Bishop) were elected by Congress for life, and if the President appointed the Governors of States (Presiding Elders) and if the Governors recommended to the President the appointment of County Sheriffs (Pastors), and if the Sheriffs appointed or nominated the County Commissioners (Quarterly Conference) and if the Legislature (Annual Conference) were composed of the Sheriffs and Governor and elected one half of the members of Congress (General Conference) and a convention (Electoral Conference) of delegates chosen by the County Commissioners elected the other half of the members of Congress, we would have a civil government exactly like the government of the Methodist Episcopal Church. But no one would call this a representative government.[15]

Lewis loved an audience and knew how to orchestrate a supportive response. In 1908, at the General Conference of the Methodist Episcopal Church in Baltimore's Lyric Hall, he spoke on Methodist union. Comparing his small denomination to "little Benjamin," he concluded:

> Brethren, is the little child to lead the great hosts of divided Methodism? We dare not ask it as an honor, but if it be required of us we bring all our treasures and lay all our identity upon the altar as a sacrifice; or [if] we may but beat a drum or carry a flag while Judah and Ephraim once more march on to the same music of peace, joyfully we will say Amen, God wills it.[16]

The Christian Advocate reported that "the audience arose and waved their handkerchiefs amid great applause and singing."

Lewis opened the seminary in the fall of 1882 with fifteen students and two faculty members besides himself. The first catalog lists him as principal and professor of Biblical and

19

Historical Theology. President Ward came from the college to teach Systematic Theology, and the Reverend Joshua Thomas Murray took time from his pastoral duties in the local church to lecture on Pastoral Theology. Lewis announced that "provision had been made" for someone to teach New Testament Greek and Exegesis. This probably refers to James W. Reese, who taught at the college; although he regularly "heard recitations," he was not formally listed as a member of the faculty until 1886.

In the seminary's early years nearly all the teachers besides the president were members of the college faculty, retired ministers, or pastors of nearby churches. A prototype of the teaching pastors was Joshua Thomas Murray, D.D. (1830-99). He had had more than thirty years in the ministry at almost every kind and size of church—Harper's Ferry, West Virginia; Pipe Creek, Maryland; Philadelphia; Baltimore; Washington, DC; and Newark, New Jersey. When the seminary opened, he was the appointed pastor of the Methodist Protestant church in Westminster, and in 1886 he served briefly as editor of *The Methodist Protestant.* He therefore was qualified as well as convenient for the chair of Pastoral Theology. The Maryland Conference had directed that this teaching responsibility be assigned to the town pastor, even though that meant frequent changes in the chair because of shifts in pastoral appointments. After Murray became president of the conference a year later, John David Kinzer (1841-1911) came to the Westminster church and to the course in Pastoral Theology. Like Murray, he was regarded as prepared for such teaching by many years as a successful pastor.

In the first catalog President Lewis advertised the advantages of the seminary's location. Only thirty miles from Baltimore, with good train service, the county seat town of Westminster was "high and healthy," rural and prosperous, and providentially free from the "immoralities" of the city. Widely known for its attractiveness, the campus offered an eastward view overlooking the town and a westward panorama of fertile Carroll County farms rolling toward distant mountains. The seminarians soon fell naturally into the habit of calling their slope "Seminary Hill," and the college—though occupying much of the same hill—seemed not to object. "Contiguity to the College," wrote President Lewis, made it possible "to give to theological students all the advantages of association with professors and students of liberal culture [in addition to] the lectures, recitations and apparatus of the Collegiate establishment." There would also be "opportunities for evangelical labor" in conducting religious services at the college, Lewis added, while a large and flourishing Methodist Protestant church in the town, along with numerous other churches in the surrounding area, "will give frequent occasion for the exercise of young men in the work of the pulpit."

The calendar for the first year (1882-83) was brief:
September 5, Tuesday . . . . Entrance Day
September 6, Wednesday . . . . Introductory Lecture
December 21, 22 . . . . Examination of Classes
December 23-31 . . . . Christmas Holiday
January 2, Tuesday . . . . Beginning of Second Term
April 23, 24 . . . . Final Examinations
April 26, Thursday . . . . Public Commencement

On the Saturday before Entrance Day Lewis took the train to Baltimore to preach his farewell sermon at St. John's. Returning on the Sunday afternoon train, he completed plans for the school's opening. Entrance Day went mostly as scheduled, but there was some unanticipated confusion. The college opened the same day for its sixteenth year, and because its Ward Hall was under construction, the campus was cluttered. Carriages, lumber wagons, carpenters, masons, students and their parents—all had to make the best of it together. Complicating everything was what many believed to be a risky decision by the college to become "a school for both sexes in separate departments." The separation of men and women, to be reassuring, had to apply to all students on campus, including those at the seminary. Every area, even walkways and common rooms, was to be carefully designated as to who could use it and when. President Ward confided to his diary on 18 August his appreciation of a suggestion from "son T.H.L." for solving a problem with respect to the college book room: "two rooms so arranged that male and female students can be furnished [with books] separately."

The seminary building—still being called the School of

21

The first building, erected in 1882, served the seminary until 1887, when an addition at the rear provided a significant expansion of the facilities.

Theology—was not quite ready that first week, but some students had already arrived because the catalog had announced that it was "of the greatest importance that students be present at the opening of the term." By week's end there were fifteen young men on campus: one "Graduate with a Collegiate degree and entering for the Degree Bachelor of Divinity," ten "Collegiates, pursuing a course in College and residing in the Seminary for Lectures, Reading and Special Studies," and four "Special students. . .taking a course for immediate preparation for the ministry." After the Introductory Lecture by Lewis, classes settled into a regular schedule. Lewis began his lectures on Biblical and Historical Theology, while Murray came up the hill from his church study to tell the students how to preach and make pastoral calls.

The Public Commencement scheduled for 26 April 1883 could not be held because there were no graduates until 1884. But in that year a three-day program made for a gala occasion. On Sunday, 4 May, there was an "Annual Sermon" by Lucius Bates; on Monday an "Anniversary of Theological Association"; and on Tuesday an inspection by the Board of Visitors and the spring meeting of the Board of Governors during the day, and in the evening the Public Commencement. Incorporation proceedings had been completed one month previously, so Lewis was now legally the president of the seminary. He took advantage of the occasion to deliver his Inaugural Address. It had the kind of vigor and confidence his audiences were beginning to expect and admire. At the climax of his address he declared, "We have concluded our calculations, we have determined our bearings, we have made our chart, we have come to our first commencement, and our future is to work out our present plans."

The one graduate of that first commencement was Edwin Alonzo Warfield of Urbana, in nearby Frederick County, Maryland. He had graduated from Western Maryland College four years earlier. After receiving his seminary degree he became pastor successively of several Maryland and Virginia churches, as well as professor of Ecclesiastical History (1886-88) and of Hebrew (1888) at his theological alma mater. He earned a Ph.D. degree at Yale in 1904 and two years later returned to Western Maryland College to teach English for fifteen years. The quaint obituary written by his friends for the conference records describes him as "polished in manners, amiable in disposition, genial in spirit, tender of heart, faithful in friendship, a gentleman of the old type of gallantry, a scholar of the old school of classics."

A flexible course of study

At the outset of his presidency Lewis bravely announced, "Our method has been and will be *to adjust the studies to the student* and not to insist on universal compliance with an inexorable curriculum." This intention had little to do with course content or even with the subjects taught. As "progressive" as he may have sounded, Lewis was at heart a traditionalist. In his Inaugural Address he voiced his contentment with the old doctrines and the old methods. "Permanence, not progress," he said, was his primary concern for the students' learning. Any "adjustments" in the program would be determined by each individual's previous preparation and by the amount of time one could give to study.

In its desire to make its resources available to as many students as possible, the seminary offered during its first year a short course called the "Conference Course." Every annual

23

conference desperately needs preachers, Lewis explained, "and it is the object of this course to equip in the shortest possible time a force of young men for immediate work." The course was to run for six months, from September to March. How successful it was is hard to discover; there is no mention of it after the first year of the seminary's operation.

Except for the short-lived experiment with the Conference Course, the seminary designed its curriculum for applicants who held a baccalaureate degree from a recognized college. But since such applicants were few in number and the educational backgrounds of other prospective students varied widely, it was necessary to offer several different programs of study. The "Graduates," those holding the A.B. or equivalent, were offered a two-year course of study leading to the Bachelor of Divinity degree. The "Collegiates" were for the most part ministerial students at Western Maryland College who were admitted to the seminary on examination; some of their seminary credits could apply toward the A.B. degree at the college, but if they completed seminary studies without graduating from the college, which they might do in two years, they were awarded only a diploma from the seminary. Then for students with no college experience, some with less than a high school education, there was a program called variously "Special" or "Introductory," which might prepare them to join an annual conference and be appointed to a parish. Although in 1891 "ability to enter the Freshman class of a college," as determined by an examination, became an entrance requirement—a stipulation that almost closed the school—at the outset the seminary took very seriously its responsibility for the Special students: "They will be received, and such studies assigned them as may be, in the judgment of the Faculty, best adapted to fit them for the Ministry in the time allotted to them for preparation." The non-college students who remained for the full course received a "Testimonial of Graduation," while those who left earlier received a certificate for the work they had done.

All students, regardless of their condition of admission, had to wrestle with the same subjects: Hebrew Language and Literature, New Testament Exegesis, Systematic Theology, Pastoral Theology, and Historical Theology. English was an additional requirement for the Introductory group. All students read (or tried to read) selections from Genesis, Ruth, Jonah, the Psalms, and Isaiah in Hebrew; and portions of the Gospels, Acts, and various Epistles in Greek. Systematic Theology included such courses as Compendium of Theology (an introductory survey), Christian Evidences, Existence and Attributes of God, Original Sin and Redemption, and Morals and Institutions of Christianity. There were also Scripture History, Sacred History, The Church to the Tenth Century, The Reformation, History of the Modern Church, History of Methodism and the Methodist Protestant Church, Homiletics, The Christian Pastor, and—far from least—The Discipline and Institutions of the Methodist Protestant Church. The second catalog labored the obvious: "All students of the Seminary will be required to devote some portion of their time to reading."

What was taught in these courses of the early years was determined for the most part by two considerations. The first was the "old classical tradition" in which the president and most of the professors had been trained. This tradition aimed at familiarity with ancient languages (particularly the biblical languages), philosophy, theology, and history, together with the rudiments of English, science, and mathematics. Second was the Wesleyan Methodist inheritance in theology, Christian experience, and church polity. In this last, of course, a careful distinction was drawn between Wesley's ideas for Methodist organization and the corruption of those ideas by Episcopal Methodism in America.

There was little or no problem in selecting basic books for the courses. These were all named quadrennially in the *Discipline* of the church and in the Maryland Conference Course of Study. All who applied for conference membership and ordination, even the seminary's graduates, had to be examined on these books by the conference's examining committee. (In 1899 President Elderdice persuaded the Maryland Conference to accept graduation from the seminary in lieu of the conference examinations, but this exemption did not apply to proficiency in Hebrew, Greek, English, and Elocution.) Some of the titles were hardy perennials: Binney's *Compendium of Theology,* Butler's *Analogy of Religion,* Watson's *Theological Institutes,* Barrows' *Sacred Geography and Antiq-*

25

uities, Miller's *Christian Ministry,* and Powell on *Succession.*
Miley's *Systematic Theology* and Broadus's *Preparation and
Delivery of Sermons* were welcomed as soon as they appeared.
Paley, Prideaux, and Fletcher were let go—reluctantly, no
doubt, for had not Wesley and even Asbury approved and used
them? Mosheim's *Ecclesiastical History* could go too, but with
less hesitancy; Wesley had said that Mosheim was only "as
lively as the nature of the subject will bear," and Asbury had
thought him "too dry and speculative." Fisher's *Church
History* was far better.

All the courses were required, none elective. When students
chose to come to Westminster, they elected the Westminster
curriculum. The subjects announced in the early catalogs
remained fixed for decades. On Wednesday afternoons there
was drill in Hymns and Scripture Reading, and on other days
Impromptu Debate, Literary Culture, Practice in Parliamentary Rules, and drill in Vocal Music. President Ward's diary
entry for Monday, 2 October 1882, describes the routine of
instruction: "Pastor Murray...hears the recitations in
'Homiletics' regularly twice each week at the School of
Theology; son T.H.L. [Lewis] oftener those in Hebrew and
Church History and Biblical Introduction, [college] Professor
Reese (at his home) thrice a week in Greek New Testament,
and I as often (at the School) in Systematic Theology." A week
later Ward wrote, "This morning [I lectured] to theologues
before assigning first lesson in Wakefield's *Complete System
of Christian Theology*."

Each year Lewis and Ward brought to the campus a dozen
or so special lecturers whom they regarded as able to stimulate,
inform, and advise the students on matters somewhat marginal
to the regular courses but still important. The lecturers were
usually ministerial members of the Maryland Conference in
nearby pastorates, visitors from other states, missionaries, or
representatives of denominational agencies. There were
Lawrence W. Bates on "Exhumed History of the Methodist
Protestant Church," Henry C. Cushing on "The Ethical and
Aesthetical in Relation to Christianity," E. R. McGregor on
"Palestine in the Time of Christ," A. D. Melvin on "Revivals
and How to Promote Them," and David L. Greenfield on "The
Preacher in His Study" and "The Preacher in His Pulpit." Ward

lectured frequently on "Famous Preachers and Their Methods," while others from the college discoursed on their favorite themes. Visiting lectureships declined about 1890, possibly because of Ward's less aggressive pursuit of them, and were revived by President Elderdice after 1897.

One sentence in the second catalog (1883) refers to the school's facilities: "A building has been erected for the use of the Seminary with special adaptations and provision for its work." Pictures show a plain three-story building, neatly gabled, with three large chimneys. The third catalog discloses that the "special adaptations" were rooms for recitation, chapel, and the library; there were "also rooms sufficiently large" for double occupancy by students. The total cost of the seminary's property was reported in 1885 as $4,000 with a debt of $1,300. Reports from the Board of Governors show occasional improvements: a porch across the front and a chapel "neatly fitted" in 1891, a steam-heat furnace costing $425 in 1892, and electricity and a bathroom in 1900 when Mt. Lebanon Church "contributed $26.00 for two iron tubs."

Each student was to pay one hundred dollars per year, which would cover all charges: board, washing, fuel, room, servant's attention, tuition, and other necessary expenses except books and light. Books were available for purchase "at clergyman's discount." Residence rooms were heated and provided with bedstead, mattress, wardrobe, toilet, table, lamp, and chairs; but students furnished their own bedclothing, pillows, and towels. Married students could rent houses in town for six to twelve dollars per month. Unmarried students took their meals at the college, registered as "table boarders." They had to bring their own "fork, spoon and napkin-ring plainly marked with their name."

These directives changed very little in the Lewis and Ward years, 1882-97. By 1891 the cost for the entire year had gone up to $135 "exclusive of books and light." Books averaged from five to ten dollars a year. Students unable to remain the full year could receive some refund for board but not for room or tuition. In 1894 "loans without interest" became available from the denomination's Board of Ministerial Education "to an amount not exceeding one hundred dollars a year, to be repaid after entering the ministry, at the rate of ten per cent

Small Beginnings

27

of the salary received each year until the whole amount is paid." The catalog describes the process of obtaining a loan and urges pastors and churches to help young men who show promise for ministry but at the same time to be careful to "satisfy themselves of the fitness of the candidates."

A presidential exchange

Ward and Lewis exchanged offices in 1886, and the new arrangement pleased everyone. At sixty-six years of age Ward was finding the burdens at the college too heavy. Raising money was becoming increasingly difficult for him, while student discipline, anxious parents, repairs for old buildings and contracts for new ones were leaving only skimpy fragments of time for his precious lectures in Theology. He said he wanted "a lighter work," and he sought it in the seminary. Meanwhile, "son T.H.L." was exhibiting far more energy than a few theology students and some classes in Hebrew could consume. Ward's fondness for his son-in-law and pride in his achievements were evenly matched by Lewis's love and admiration for "dear Mary's father," and so the transition went smoothly for both men and their institutions.

In 1882, when James Thomas Ward became professor of Systematic Theology in the new Westminster Seminary, he had been president of Western Maryland College for fourteen years. Adding a seminary class in Theology did not increase his labors by very much, for he had been teaching the subject in the college for years. During Lewis's four-year presidency at the seminary, Ward went daily for his class; and after exchanging offices with his son-in-law in 1886, he continued his lectures in Systematic Theology for ten more years until his death. No one doubted that he was the one best qualified to guide young ministers through Watson's *Institutes,* Fletcher's *Checks,* and Butler's *Analogy.*

Ward was born in Georgetown, DC, on 21 August 1820. He studied at Columbian College (now The George Washington University) and at Brookeville Academy in Montgomery County, Maryland, and then "pursued theological studies" with Augustus Webster and Andrew Lipscomb,

Methodist Protestant ministers in Maryland. There is a hint of some family affluence in what a friend wrote for his obituary. After telling of Ward's conversion at the age of thirteen, his ordination, and his entrance into the itinerant ministry of the Methodist Protestant Church, the writer described the church of that time as "scarcely advanced beyond its infancy, an ecclesiastical experiment in Methodism, with only a few church buildings, no parsonages, poor, with nothing to attract in all it had except a pure gospel under the auspices of American and Scriptural ideas of government." Into this church, the friend observed, Ward came "out of that elegant city home" to be the assistant preacher at Pipe Creek (in Carroll County, Maryland). He was then twenty-one years old.

Ward served other assignments at Williamsport and Cumberland in Maryland; Washington, DC; and Philadelphia, Pennsylvania. He wrote and published a few articles, some in a series called "Letters from the Highlands," in *The Columbian Fountain,* a temperance journal which he sometimes co-edited with his minister father. His other writings include "Fifty Short Letters to Save Souls" and "How to Study the Bible," plus a popular *Daily Manual for Bible Reading* (Baltimore, 1894). Ward said that for many years he "subordinated all other studies to that of the Bible, the Book above all." Characteristically, he insisted that Bible study required reverence, prayer, and the spirit of docility—qualities by nature his own. That he was impeccably orthodox goes without saying; college and seminary trustees would never have tolerated anyone suspected of a "modernist" thought. As German Higher Criticism began to infiltrate American theological schools, people who knew Ward said that "he was higher than the higher critics." He was mild-mannered and soft-spoken, with scholarly inclinations and habits, and a pulpit style described as "plain, practical and intensely earnest." There is a gentle sadness in the memorial verse he wrote when one of his daughters died at the age of four:

James Thomas Ward (1820-97) was president of Western Maryland College 1868-86. Father-in-law of Thomas Hamilton Lewis, he exchanged offices with Lewis in 1886 and served as president of the seminary until his death. Lamenting that students were so "uninstructed in English" that they were "dazed at the contemplation of Hebrew and Greek," he sent many of them back to the college and nearly emptied the seminary.

> E'en for the dead I will not bind
> My heart to grief; for is it not as if
> The rose that climbed my garden wall
> Had bloomed the other side?

President Ward's most curious (and laborious) work was his collection of more than one hundred neatly handwritten notebooks, small and stitched, containing his own somewhat sermonic biblical commentary interspersed with relevant clippings from his wide reading. He began this project in 1853 while he was pastor in Philadelphia and some time later wrote for it a descriptive title page:

> J. T. Ward's Alphabetical, Literary and Biblical Register of Extracts, Abstracts, Notes and References, the whole constituting a GENERAL INDEX AND COMMON-PLACE BOOK of such items (selected and original) as he may deem worthy of preservation in this way;—designed to promote his improvement in knowledge and virtue, and his usefulness as a man, a Christian, and, particularly, as a Minister of the Gospel of Christ.

More informative is Ward's diary, which he kept diligently for many years. Bound volumes running from 1868 to 1888 are in the Western Maryland College library. They contain summaries in a spidery hand of each day's doings, particularly family life, with frequent references to "my dear wife" and "our dear children," and in nearly every paragraph there is some proud mention of his son-in-law, Thomas Hamilton Lewis. The diary also reveals that the college always took precedence over the seminary in Ward's concerns.

Disappointments crowded the years of Ward's seminary presidency, and he soon lost the strength to cope with them. The heaviest burden was his reluctant acceptance of the fact that his ideas of a graduate school of theology were unrealistic. The students who came, with very few exceptions, were completely lost in the courses, entirely unable to grasp the subject matter before them. Complicating matters was their insistent claim that they were "called to preach"; and Ward, like John Wesley before him, felt duty bound to test their claim by insisting on thorough preparation through diligent study. The faculty supported him without hesitation and cooperated in suppressing every tendency to lower curricular requirements. James M. Reese, a Western Maryland College professor who taught Greek at the seminary from 1886 to 1903, became so agitated at a proposal for excusing some students from his classes that he flatly refused to discuss the matter. No one was to be graduated and sent into the ministry without a knowledge of the biblical languages. Consequently, no one was graduated for two years before Ward's death nor for two years afterward.

When Ward died in March 1897, many expected that the seminary would not long survive him. Indeed, no catalog was published for 1896, Ward's last year. A candid explanation of the difficulties appeared in that year's report of the Board of Governors. They supported Ward unanimously and outlined a heroic attempt to salvage what they could from an impossible situation:

> After years of observation of the practical results of the Seminary arrangements . . . it was no longer deemed wise or expedient to put into the Seminary youths who were untutored in English and whose minds for lack of training, were unprepared to profit by the Seminary course. In general those who were sent to us would have found a more fitting place in a grammar school than in a Theological Seminary,

In 1888 the seminary boasted twenty-one students (of whom thirteen are pictured here) and three professors under President Ward. Ward is seated at the center; at his left is James M. Reese, and to his right are Joshua Thomas Murray and Edwin Alonzo Warfield.

dazed at the contemplation of Greek and Hebrew verbs. In consequence they came out of the school without proficiency in their own tongue or any other, and quite as little in theology. . . . To correct this evil, it was determined to raise the standard of requirements for those who should be admitted. It was certain that this would exclude for a time the majority of the candidates. These were to be put in the College classes until duly prepared for the Seminary course. As a consequence, during the current year all of the candidates for the ministry have been in the College. . . . Thus it may take two or three years to demonstrate that this year of inaction will have resulted in a much better equipped class of young men in our ministry.

The report was frank enough to add what many were reluctant to accept:

The President of the Seminary, as well as the Board of Governors, realizes that the institution needs a more vigorous and enterprising management; and he is ready at any time to give place to one who has the requisite qualifications. We need for President a man of vigor and with talent for affairs combined with requisite theological and literary qualifications and he to be aided by competent teachers.

One year later, in 1897, the board found their "man of vigor." He was the Reverend Hugh Latimer Elderdice, graduate of Western Maryland College and of Yale Divinity School, and pastor of the Pocomoke City Methodist Protestant Church. Elderdice was to be president of Westminster Seminary for the next thirty-five years.

Miracle and sacrifice: the Elderdice era

In the spring of 1897 the Board of Governors recognized that they must either "make the Seminary a success or abandon it." Yet notwithstanding the school's precarious situation, they could be hopeful.

> We have a good start. We own five acres of land . . . [and] a good building, with accommodation for 20 students. The building is suitably furnished and heated by steam. We have an invested fund of $3,200 . . . twenty-five hundred dollars of this amount bequeathed to us by Brother E. J. Hill, late of Washington City. The Board has realized the necessity of a more energetic conduct of affairs and has arranged accordingly for the services of Rev. H. L. Elderdice as President and Rev. B. F. Benson for the Chair of Systematic Theology.[1]

President Elderdice, in his thirty-five-year tenure, was to become literally the savior of the seminary.

Man of Vigor

Hugh Latimer Elderdice was born in Carlisle, Pennsylvania, on 24 July 1860. The family lineage was Scotch-Irish, the family religion Covenanter Presbyterian. Family conviction was declared in the Protestant baptismal names of the father, James Martin, and his three sons: James Luther, John Calvin, and Hugh Latimer. Their strong belief in equal rights turned them to the Methodist Protestant Church; and Hugh Latimer, along with his father, his uncle John, his brother James, and his nephew Charles, all became ministers in that denomination.

Hugh Latimer Elderdice (1860-1938) was president of the seminary for thirty-five years, 1897-1932. He saved the school from dying and established it on a firm base of support.

Hugh Latimer attended Rainsburg Male and Female Academy in Pennsylvania, then came to Western Maryland College. After graduating in 1880, he completed the Conference Course of Study and then enrolled in Yale Divinity School. Two summers of his Yale period he spent as a missionary for the Congregationalists in northwest Minnesota, where he organized a Congregational church—an experience that gave him a lifelong affinity for the Congregational way. He had been licensed to preach during his last year in college, and his excellent academic record, complemented by perfect grades in the Maryland Conference Course of Study, outweighed any suspicions about his Congregational connections and made him a most welcome candidate for the ministry. He did not receive his Yale degree until 1890 because his last year there was interrupted by his father's death. He went home to be with the family (a stepmother, two half brothers, and a sister) and to supply his father's pulpit. Upon being ordained in 1885, he was appointed at once to Broadway Church in Baltimore. There he demonstrated the "vigor" for which he was to become known in the denomination. Visitors to the church wrote admiringly of the energetic young pastor and his efficient direction of a growing congregation with a crowded Sunday School.

While at Rainsburg Academy Elderdice met Annabel Smith, and she waited for him—not always patiently—until his school days were over. They were married in time to enjoy together the new parsonage at Broadway. A daughter, Dorothy, was born on 7 April 1892, and three weeks later came Elderdice's next appointment—to Pocomoke City, another thriving Methodist Protestant parish far down on Maryland's Eastern Shore. There a son, Hugh Latimer, Jr., was born on 7 December 1895. The family thus numbered four when Elderdice's invitation to Westminster came in April 1897.

It was a crisis year for the seminary. President Ward had died in March and was resting in the Westminster cemetery. The faculty was demoralized, the students discouraged. Upon appointing Elderdice as president, the Board of Governors had to ask the Maryland Conference to guarantee the seminary an annual allowance of $1,800 for salaries: $1,000 for Elderdice and $800 for Benson. An additional $700 would come, they hoped, from contributions from other annual conferences, particularly the New Jersey, North Carolina, West Virginia, and Pennsylvania conferences. Western conferences were "off limits," being claimed by Adrian College for support of a proposed theological seminary in Michigan.

Everyone obviously was expecting the young president to work some kind of miracle. Elderdice knew he was starting at the bottom. His daughter, Dorothy, recorded his recollections of arriving at the school.

> It might seem that a great honor was being conferred upon him; actually he was being handed a job nobody else wanted. How often have I heard him say that when he arrived in the bleak, forbidding seminary building, there were only five students and they were packing to leave. But he persuaded them to stay.

The following year ten students enrolled. The Board of Governors agreed to cancel all tuition charges because the president promised to solicit scholarships himself, an agreement he carried out faithfully and successfully for years. He persuaded various churches to repair and refurnish the students' rooms, and by the next year several rooms bore the names of the contributing churches: Howard Chapel, Salem, Trinity, Libertytown, Central, Alnutt Memorial, Starr, and Cecil Circuit.

Elderdice's annual report to the Board of Governors on 10 May 1898 summarized the accomplishments of his first year on the job. He had arrived on 26 April 1897 and persuaded the five students to continue their studies until the end of the term, 4 June. "No commencement exercises were held for the reason that there were no graduates and the newly appointed teachers had not had time to prepare a creditable program." He had painted the building, landscaped the grounds, and erected several outbuildings, paying for the improvements through personal appeals to individuals and churches. "The third floor of the Seminary is unfurnished but with your permission I shall visit some of the churches of the Maryland District [Conference]—and any other District to which I may be invited—during this vacation and appeal for money to furnish [the third-floor rooms] on the Room Plan."

One item barely mentioned by the new president in his first report attracted the board's attention: "an attractive and comfortable house" built for the president during the year had cost $2,426.77. "The money to build it was drawn from the endowment fund," the board noted, "and interest on it will have to be paid annually, to the current expenses of the Seminary." But Elderdice simply added the amount to his fund-raising goals, and in due time the loan was repaid.

Visiting the churches to solicit support for the seminary was a constant and demanding necessity. Elderdice did it the year around and drafted the faculty for it on their summer vacations. He made every lecture and sermon an opportunity for receiving an offering and urging pledges to the seminary. When pastors demurred because of a conflict with their own financial campaigns, Elderdice would quickly propose a more convenient date for his visit. The Board of Governors noted in 1898 that the president had "spent most of the Sabbaths of the year...preaching for the pastors and collecting money," and as a result had received $358.51 from "patronizing Conferences" outside of Maryland (North Carolina, West Virginia, New Jersey, and New York), and $777.35 from the churches in the Maryland Conference. Still due were pledges totalling more than one thousand dollars. If these are paid, the board predicted, "we will be able to meet our obligations [which] will fully justify the wisdom of the new departure made a year ago [to engage more vigorous leadership]."

Notwithstanding the difficulty of keeping the school functioning, academic standards tightened perceptibly during Elderdice's early years. In 1897 the Degree students were promised the Bachelor of Divinity (B.D.) after two years of rigorous post-A.B. studies and the presentation of an acceptable thesis on a substantial theological topic. The Graduates were admitted if they were ready for the junior year in college, and after studying for two years and passing a comprehensive examination, they were granted a certificate. The non-college course, now called "English" because it did not require the biblical languages, was open to those who could pass a high school equivalency examination. Students in the English Course studied the same subjects as the Graduates, except for the languages, and those who completed the two-year course received an English Course certificate. In Elderdice's second year those without a college degree had to be ready at least to enter the sophomore year in college and were required to study three years in the seminary and present an acceptable thesis before they could qualify for the certificate. Such standards were practically impossible to maintain consistently, however, and the catalogs for the early years of the twentieth century betray some waffling on the lowest educational achievement that might qualify an applicant for admission to the non-college course, called the Diploma Course in 1904 and afterwards.

In the early years of the seminary, as in most other American theological schools of the nineteenth century, first-year students with at least two years of college were admitted as juniors. This was the case even for those who held a degree from an accredited college. After a year of successful study they were advanced to the senior class, and upon completion of a further year of study and a thesis, they were graduated. This pattern of entering as juniors, studying full time for two years, and then graduating prevailed at Westminster until 1904. But by that time many students were finding it difficult to complete the requirements in two years, and those in between the junior and senior classes were beginning to be called "middlers." The catalogs of 1905 and 1906 no longer referred to "two years of successful study," but simply advised post-A.B. students that "after the completion of the course of study" and the presentation of an acceptable thesis, they would be awarded the B.D. degree. Most students could complete the program in three years, however, and in 1907 the middle year was formalized. The catalog of that year spoke of "the three years' course of study," and thereafter the class years were referred to regularly as junior, middle, and senior.

The curriculum established in the early years of Elderdice's administration held, with minor adjustments in standards and requirements, until 1923. In that year the seminary announced four separate programs, introduced some new degree nomenclature, and, most significantly, stated explicitly that the school was "open to men and women" who wished to prepare themselves for the Christian ministry. What had been called the Graduate Course (for college graduates only) now became the Degree Course; it required three years of study, including the biblical languages, and a senior thesis for the Bachelor of Divinity degree (B.D.). The new Graduate Course became an advanced program with three possibilities for those holding the B.D. degree: thirty-two additional credit hours plus a thesis would lead to a Bachelor of Sacred Theology (S.T.B.); thirty-two credit hours plus a thesis and a comprehensive examination would lead to a Master of Sacred Theology (S.T.M.); and sixty-four credit hours plus five years' experience in ministry, two comprehensive examinations (one written, one oral), and a thesis would lead to a Doctor of Sacred Theology (S.T.D.). The somewhat illogical scheme of awarding a second baccalaureate as an advanced degree was abandoned in 1925, when the seminary's first degree was changed to the S.T.B. (granted for ninety-six credit hours of post-A.B. study and a thesis), and the S.T.M. was abandoned. (In 1934 the S.T.D. quietly expired and was replaced by a revived S.T.M. program, which flourished until a major overhaul of the curriculum in the 1960s.)

The other two programs of 1923 were called "Diploma" and "Special." Earlier both terms had referred to non-college persons studying at the seminary. Now the Diploma Course differed from the Degree Course mainly in not requiring the biblical languages; students admitted to this program were expected to perform at the level of college graduates in three years of study and to write a thesis in order to receive a diploma. The Special Course, as redefined in 1923, was offered to a limited number of college graduates who because of other pursuits could not take the regular course of study, to wives of ministerial students, and to other persons wishing to train for Christian service—what later would be called "lay ministry." Each Special student received a certificate noting the work he or she had completed. These four courses of study held, with minor modifications in specific requirements, until after World War II.

The charter of incorporation put the seminary under the supervision of the General Conference of the Methodist Protestant Church through a Board of Governors consisting of three ministers and two laymen elected quadrennially by the Maryland Conference and two ministers and three laymen elected quadrennially by the General Conference. But the board was usually far behind the scenes of planning and action, being content to let President Elderdice run the school. Some of the governors had been "founding fathers" of the seminary; and all of them, though lacking the kind of formal education that it furnished, believed in its importance for the future ministry of the church. Elderdice often wrote their reports for them, as well as his own, but they trusted him and were gratified by what he was doing to put the school on a sound academic and financial footing.

Elderdice's vigorous leadership inspired board members to help the school in other ways, too. Dr. Joshua Webster Hering, treasurer of the board from 1883 until his death in 1913, was a man of many gifts and talents. Westminster physician-banker, trustee and treasurer of Western Maryland College, superintendent of the Westminster Sunday School for twenty-five years, delegate to General Conference and once its president, state comptroller, state senator, and Public Service Commissioner, he came annually for fifteen years to lecture to the students—gratis—on topics related to "the preservation of health." Hering would talk on "Ministerial Hygiene," "Voice Production and Preservation," "The Care of the Body," or "The Pastor's Relation to Civil Law." He established in 1899 the first prize for proficiency in Hebrew (won the following year by Charles Edward Forlines). Interdenominational

39

fellowship appealed to Hering too, so annually he invited all the clergy of the town, Roman Catholic and Protestant, to his home for dinner. Thomas Murray, a Baltimore attorney, wrote to Elderdice in 1914: "I recall . . . once using a Latin quotation in the presence of Dr. Hering [and] he reproved me with the plain English quotation: 'A little learning is a dangerous thing.' "

President Elderdice could always count on the Mathers of Westminster for encouragement and support. T. W. Mather was a valuable member and treasurer of the board for ten years and George K. Mather was secretary-treasurer for nearly a quarter of a century. Mather's store on Main Street was a Westminster tradition, and residents without conscious effort linked the name with the Methodist Protestant Church and the Westminster Seminary. George Mather was as good at gardening as at merchandising, and he gave time and talent to landscaping the seminary grounds, transforming the whole campus more than once by his gifts and generous labors. Dr. Charles Billingslea, a Westminster dentist, was a faithful supporter from the beginning; although he was never a member of the board, he was on the first committee in the conference that recommended the founding of the seminary, and he remained ready to help whenever Elderdice asked him.

The first president of the board, Lawrence Webster Bates, held that office for eighteen years until his death in 1901. Born in 1819 to a Quaker family in Burlington County, New Jersey, he began to serve churches in the Maryland Conference in 1840. His name and presence always prompted thoughts of dignity, sound learning, orthodox preaching, and tireless pastoral labors. He was elected delegate to every General Conference from 1862 to 1896. Gettysburg College honored him with a Doctor of Divinity degree in 1868. During Ward's last four years as president of the seminary, Bates taught Historical and Pastoral Theology, and Elderdice persuaded him to stay on after 1897 to lecture on the same subjects as emeritus professor without compensation. When he died in 1901, he was not replaced.

Building the faculty

Death was the usual termination of tenure for the faculty during the seminary's first half-century. Benjamin Franklin Benson, appointed the same year as Elderdice, taught Systematic and Practical Theology for the last five years of his life. Having been a pastor for over forty years in Virginia and Maryland, he is another example of the seminary's dependence on self-educated scholars with wide practical experience. At the time the seminary began, he was vice-president of Western Maryland College and thus was convenient as well as qualified. A tireless student, sometimes tediously orthodox, he had a "peculiar mental habit . . . a well-nigh slavish devotion to details," which led him to build every lecture in slow steps to its logical conclusion. Those who knew him said that a part of his creed was "a place for everything and everything in its place," and that both his home and his classroom exhibited this passion for order. His health failed in 1901, and in August of that year he wrote to Elderdice from Crumpton, New Jersey: "I am thinking of a short stay on the seashore, probably at Ocean Grove [a Methodist encampment]. . . . I linger on the edge of collapse. . . . Can you deposit in the U. N. Bank some money for me?" Elderdice promptly sent him a check for $70.83, his salary for July. Benson barely held on through another year and died peacefully on 30 November 1902. The last paragraph of his will reads, "I leave my Oxford Bible, over which my soul has shouted a thousand times, to my greatly beloved daughter, Lida. Amen."

Upon Benson's death, Elderdice saw an opportunity to "reconstruct" the faculty. James M. Reese, an Episcopalian professor of Greek at the college, had been teaching the seminarians New Testament since 1886, supplementing his college salary by $200 a year for four or five recitations a week. In May 1903 Elderdice wrote to Reese:

> The death of Dr. Benson has made necessary a reconstruction of the Faculty. . . . It is a source of keen regret to the Board that it can not afford to solicit your valuable services for next year. A vote of highest appreciation of your teaching in the Seminary is hereby extended.

Probably this abrupt termination of his service was unwelcome to Reese. A marginal note on Elderdice's copy of the letter reads, "Sent check for $50.00; he returned voucher without a word."

The "reconstruction" which Elderdice had in mind was the appointment of two new professors, Henry Caleb Cushing to teach Systematic and Practical Theology and Claude Cicero Douglas to teach New Testament. Cushing was sixty-five years old, superannuated and living on his farm in Sudley Springs, Virginia. He had served nineteen pastorates in his fifty years of ministry, and now as a venerable patriarch he was enjoying a well-earned reputation for scholarship and theological acumen. Elderdice said that Cushing "kept abreast of the current literature in the theological world and was able to analyze and classify the latest books." It would be perhaps an understatement to say that he was theologically conservative. "He had no patience," Elderdice observed, "with the destructive critics." There was a quiet strength in Cushing's tall, dignified presence. His white hair, solemn countenance, and squared jaw emphasized by a jutting white beard spoke of no sympathy with "modernism" but of absolute fidelity to "the faith once delivered to the saints."

According to custom at the time, Cushing's "contract" consisted of a letter from President Elderdice.

> Dear Dr.—Can the Board of Governors secure your services in the Seminary next year on the following conditions: 1) To teach Systematic and Practical Theology—or any other combination of theological studies exclusive of Hebrew and Greek. 2) To give about three hours service every day except Saturday and Sunday . . . . 3) The salary to be $200 for the scholastic year. Of course, the value of your work is not represented by this sum. Our only hope is that with the aid you receive from the Superannuated Fund and the income from your farm, this additional $200 will enable you to live in comfort, and at the same time give to your Church the ripeness of your Christian experience and the wisdom which comes with age.

Cushing's reply was immediate.

> Your proposition comes to me as the call of Providence. My wife and I have been discussing the possibility of making a change of residence and we had reached the conclu-

sion that Westminster would suit us best if we could make both ends meet financially. So it is with great satisfaction that I give an *affirmative* answer.

This arrangement followed a pattern already well established. During its first twenty years, the seminary drew many of its teachers from the ranks of retired ministers and experienced pastors who came on a part-time basis. Murray, Kinzer, Mills, and Greenfield taught Pastoral Theology while they were pastors in the Westminster church; and Bates, Benson, and Cushing rounded out their many years of pastoral service by a few less strenuous years of teaching in the seminary. The president, however, was not entirely happy with such makeshift arrangements, and after Benson died—notwithstanding the offer he was making to Cushing—Elderdice told the board that the seminary could no longer "make a nest for a minister who has outlived his usefulness in the pastorate. We cannot afford to seem to make a comfortable berth for any man, who in the natural order of events, will soon enter the rank of superannuates." But at the same time, the board, and Elderdice too, had little inclination to disregard "the wisdom which comes with age." Besides, Cushing was able, scholarly, respected—and available for $200 a year. His presence graced the seminary classrooms for five years, and everyone was satisfied with his teaching.

Along with Cushing, Elderdice was able to get what he had long wanted, a young full-time teacher. Claude Cicero Douglas, a 1901 graduate of the seminary, was named professor of Hebrew, Greek, and Historical Theology in 1903. He was from West Virginia, and this supported Elderdice's oft-repeated advertisement that the seminary was not limited to a local Maryland constituency. But Douglas was unable to come immediately; on 31 December he wrote the president from Morgantown, West Virginia, that he was shipping his books by freight but would "not be able to enter [the] classroom until January. . . . Thank you very much for your kindness in offering us your home till we secure a place to stay. Mrs. Douglas is not very well." Douglas arrived in due time, however, and his teaching proved to be eminently satisfactory. Eight years later Elderdice was still pleased with his choice, as his correspondence shows:

[Douglas] is married, has three children, the oldest a boy of nineteen. He is forty-five years old. He led his class at Western Maryland College all the way. Graduated as valedictorian, took two Gold Prizes, graduated from the Seminary at the head of his class [and] so impressed the Faculty that at the first vacancy he was elected to fill it. The college gave him the M.A. in 1904, offered him the D.D. in 1909 which he refused because of modesty.... He is competent, thorough and entirely conscientious.[2]

In addition to teaching a wide variety of courses, Douglas was expected, as were all other professors, to spend much of his time in the summer raising funds—to "shake the bushes," as the students put it. His first summer had discouraging days as he tried to find money to build himself a faculty residence in Westminster. From Pennsboro, West Virginia, he wrote to Elderdice: "I preached at 3 points yesterday and secured only $12.58....Perhaps you had better send me a little money if you can." He remained at Westminster until 1914, when further graduate studies and the West drew him ultimately to a professorship in the Maclay College of Theology at the University of Southern California.

Another Westminster alumnus from West Virginia followed Douglas as professor of New Testament Greek and Exegesis. Warren H. Hodges, a graduate of the University of West Virginia, had shown such promise and proficiency by the time he graduated from the seminary in 1911 that when Douglas resigned, Elderdice invited him to take over the teaching in New Testament. Hodges stayed only five years. In 1919 he left, explaining (as Elderdice reported) that his resignation was "not because of any dissatisfaction with his treatment or surroundings, but because it is his deep conviction that his field is the pastorate rather than the Professor's chair." After a dozen years as pastor in Maryland, Virginia, and Delaware, Hodges moved to Seattle, Washington, and served churches there until his retirement in 1945. He died in 1954.

By 1905 it appeared to Elderdice that money might be found for one more faculty member. Cushing was no drain because of his retirement pension; he would remain until 1908, the year of his death. Hering and Lewis were lecturing gratis on Health and Christian Evidences respectively, and Miss Nannie Lease was being borrowed from the college for instruction in Elocution. The president's salary together with that of Douglas came to less than $2,000. When Elderdice learned that Charles Edward Forlines had resigned from his position at Adrian, where he had been for two years as dean and professor of Philosophy and Theology, he promptly offered him the chair of Theism and Historical Theology. Elderdice had been watching this student from North Carolina and knew of his impressive record as an honors graduate from Western Maryland College in 1897 and from Westminster Seminary in 1901, and he saw in him qualities that he admired and the seminary needed. He wrote to every member of the board, obtained permission to engage Forlines "at a salary of $500 and board, a total of $590," and was immensely gratified when Forlines accepted. A few months later Elderdice reported to the board:

> The Professor has more than justified my expectations, filling with peculiar fitness the chairs of Theism and Historical Theology and lecturing on the Bible as a textbook. He has been very popular with the students and as he rooms in the building [Forlines was unmarried], his presence has been helpful both to them and to me in my frequent absences.

Forlines was to teach at Westminster for thirty-eight years and to serve as president from 1935 to 1943.

It was never easy for Elderdice to find the money for even these few faculty additions. Sometimes a little bargaining with the college helped to make a few dollars go a long way. In 1906, when Western Maryland was looking for a professor of Philosophy, Elderdice offered his newly acquired Forlines for six periods during the first term and twelve periods during the second and third terms. "Prof. Douglas of the Seminary and myself will add to our work some of the branches now taught by Prof. Forlines. . . . In return the College is to pay to the Seminary $200 and to furnish board for Prof. Forlines." This arrangement raised Forlines's salary to $600 and saved the seminary $190, though at the expense of an increased work load for Douglas and Elderdice. But notwithstanding a few complications in the transaction, the two schools and presumably the men involved seem to have been satisfied.

Competition with Adrian College in Michigan for church funds, while inevitable, was usually free from bitterness or tension. This good will is illustrated in the circumstances by which Elderdice brought Harlan Luther Feeman (1873-1957) to the seminary faculty. Feeman, born in Illinois, was a graduate of Adrian College and Drew Seminary. He had been head of the Department of History and Economics at Adrian, and president of the theological seminary there for the two years of its existence. In 1911, when Adrian Seminary closed, Elderdice invited Feeman to come to Westminster as professor of Biblical and Practical Theology. For six years Feeman taught at Westminster, then went back to Adrian College, where he was president for twenty-three years. He claimed some credit for steering one of his "theological boys" toward Westminster, an action that put the seminary heavily in his debt. Writing to Dorothy Elderdice in later years, he revealed his little ploy.

> I heard Montgomery J. Shroyer was lining up for Hartford [Seminary]. . . .I felt he was a choice student and an important man for [our] Seminary and I laid myself out writing not only a letter of some length but one aimed to break through his fences. He came to Westminster. He was a prince of a student. Your father fell in love with him. Shroyer made a good record in Hebrew and I imagine before he was ever out of Seminary [your father] had fixed it in the laws of the "Medes and Persians" that Shroyer would some day be on the Faculty and it came to be.

During the years of World War I the seminary had only three full-time teachers besides the president. While Feeman taught Biblical and Practical Theology, Elderdice could limit himself to Hebrew Language and Literature. Hodges had New Testament Greek and Exegesis, and Forlines had moved into Systematic Theology. Feeman's departure in 1917 made necessary some shuffling of assignments, a common procedure throughout the seminary's first half-century. Hodges took over Biblical Theology and Elderdice reclaimed Pastoral Theology. But Elderdice had to report to the Board of Governors that "because of the president's frequent campaigns he has not been able to cover all the work of that department, so he has called to his aid men who could give a series of lectures on Pastoral Theology, Clerical Manners and Morals, Social Service, and

In 1908 the full-time faculty consisted of President Elderdice (seated, left) and three professors. Henry Caleb Cushing is seated on the right, while the two look-alikes are Charles Edward Forlines (left) and Claude Cicero Douglas.

Foreign Missions 5 [lectures] each, except 10 for Social Service." What was really needed, Elderdice reminded the board, was another professor, and he hoped that such a person might come from the Midwest. But "in view of the unsettled condition of the financial world, due to the war, it would be uncertain whether we could pay his salary; indeed, we have no assurance of the present corps of teachers being paid all promised them."[3] Elderdice could take a leap of faith when it seemed warranted, but in 1917 the times demanded caution.

The two men who came most frequently to lecture in "the practical field" were David Lee Greenfield (1848-1917) and Edgar Thomas Read (1874-1947). Greenfield, pastor of the Methodist Protestant church in the town, joined a venerable line of teachers in Pastoral Theology. With more than forty years of experience in many churches, he was a recognized scholar, disciplined in the writing of sermons and—although the term "pastoral counseling" had not yet entered the theological vocabulary—sensitive to the spiritual needs of his parishioners. It is easy to see why Elderdice thought him well qualified to teach young ministers how to preach, pray, and make pastoral calls. Greenfield lectured to classes at the seminary from 1909 to 1915.

Read also came in 1909, and he remained for twelve years in an adjunct role. For two years after Feeman left, the catalog named Read professor of Pastoral Theology, but for the most part he simply continued as a visiting lecturer, coming from his pastorates in Baltimore, Westminster, Easton, and other Maryland towns. His personal library was said to be the largest in the Maryland Conference, and his literary interests were displayed in the titles of his lectures: "Christ in Poetry," "The Preacher and the Novel," "Emerson and His Friends," "Poets of Faith," "The Old Testament Interpreted by the Poets," "The Bible and Shakespeare," and "Some Great Teaching Books" (e.g., *Les Misérables, A Tale of Two Cities, Vanity Fair, The Scarlet Letter, Dr. Jekyll and Mr. Hyde*). Read stressed devotional literature and for many years wrote "The Quiet Hour" page of *The Methodist Protestant Recorder,* a feature widely copied by other periodicals for a national readership.

Montgomery J. Shroyer

After Feeman's resignation in 1917, Elderdice had only two full-time professors besides himself: Hodges and Forlines. The United States had entered World War I, and in November 1917 Elderdice described its effect on the seminary for readers of *The Methodist Protestant Recorder.*

> In spite of military calls to which several college graduates harkened, who had planned to enter the Seminary, we opened our fall term with the same number of students as we had when we closed last spring and others are booked to enter in the next term . . . a notable triumph in these days when so many of our educational institutions are losing heavily, some reporting a loss of 50% in enrollment. It is also gratifying to report that in spite of the abnormal raising of funds for the Red Cross League, the Liberty Loans and the Y.M.C.A. campaigns our people are liberally responding to our appeals for funds. . . . On every side the high cost of living, the scarcity of labor and the general conditions demanding economy and sacrifice, keep us in strenuous toil. Yet our faith is firm, our hope is bright, our determination is grim, our morale among professors and students is all that could be desired in a "school of the prophets."

Although the war did little direct harm, it did delay the appointment of the next professor. As patriotic duty pressed its insistent demands on all Americans, Elderdice took leave in the summer of 1918 to work for two and a half months under the Religious Committee of the National War Work Council of the Y.M.C.A. As Religious Work Secretary, he was stationed at Camp Merritt, New Jersey, in a ministry his daughter described as "one of the great events of his life." Reflecting on it later, Elderdice recalled that the thousands of recruits at Camp Merritt waiting for embarkation were

> eager for the sympathetic word and responsive to the gospel appeal. This chance for only one shot makes the Y.M.C.A. speaker more concerned to do his best. Result: perpetual revival. Many a time I have seen a modern Pentecost, men standing by the hundreds to confess Christ and sign the war roll of Christian soldiers.[4]

Like most of the other religious leaders of the United States in that period, Elderdice was convinced that the crusade against the Central Powers was a holy war, and he did not question the fusing of patriotic fervor with Christian devotion.

Returning to his presidential post in the fall of 1918, Elderdice found influenza raging on the seminary campus. It was necessary to suspend classes for several weeks and to turn the seminary building into an infirmary. In mask and gown the president nursed at night, while others managed the day shift. The school greeted the Armistice in weakness and solemnity but with gratitude.

As the epidemic subsided, Elderdice resumed his most pressing duty, finding an addition to the faculty. He had long wanted a scholar from the Midwest, and now he set his sights on the young man whom Feeman had earlier steered to Westminster. Montgomery J. Shroyer (1888-1981) of Indiana graduated from the seminary in 1915 with an impressive record. Determined to make his ministry genuinely pastoral, he accepted appointment to a rural Indiana parish, where he served faithfully for three years. In 1918 he entered the Army chaplaincy. He expected overseas service, but Armistice Day found him still in Pittsburgh. Elderdice located him there through information from Marie Noble, a Western Maryland graduate from Maryland's Eastern Shore, whom Shroyer had married the previous year.

It took six months to persuade Shroyer to accept. He not only wanted certainty about the decision, but he also needed to obtain an early discharge from the Army. Finally in June

1919, at Shroyer's request, Elderdice sent him a written description of the faculty position and the terms of the seminary's offer. He would succeed Warren Hodges as professor of Biblical Theology and possibly move into New Testament Greek the second year; the seminary would provide summer study leave at full salary to prepare for the teaching of Greek, paid summer vacations of a month or six weeks, and a salary the first year of $1,500, "$200 to be paid by the use of a house and garden and $1,300 in money." The proposal concluded with a stipulation: "You will be expected to visit churches or Conferences in the interests of the Seminary, with traveling expenses paid, or if not so employed, you may be called upon for some office work when not on vacation." The offer was accompanied by a letter which Elderdice suggested Shroyer show to his commanding officer:

My dear Chaplain:

Ever since you were a student in the Westminster Theological Seminary I have had my eye on you for a Professorship in this institution. The hour has now struck for me to call. I do so for the following reasons:

First: Professor Hodges . . . resigned last month to return to the pastorate and a successor must now be found.

Second: You have peculiar qualifications, intellectual, social and spiritual, which eminently qualify you for this position.

Third: You are a young man and it is highly desirable that our new Professor be young so that he may grow up with the institution.

Fourth: From every point of view, personal, geographical and denominational, you are the one of the entire Church to whom I can look to fill the bill; and I assure [you] that if you fail me I know not where to turn.

I hope your Commanding Officer may decide that it will be "for the good of the service" to discharge you, and that you may be willing to heed this call of your Church to this large field of service. I hope I may soon have a favorable answer.

Captain Shroyer's reply came four days later. "I have shown [the commanding officer] your letter. . . . He has given me the assurance . . . of a discharge on or before September 1st. . . .

50

I hereby accept your offer to a professorship in the Seminary beginning September 30th, 1919."[5] Elderdice was jubilant. "Your acceptance makes us all happy here," he wrote back. "I am sure you will also be happy . . . and happier the longer you remain." Shroyer remained for forty-two years until his retirement in 1961—the longest tenure in the seminary's history.

When he first came to teach, Shroyer said he did not feel competent to take over New Testament Greek and Exegesis, but he would take Beginners Greek and New Testament Theology. Part-time help for the Greek classes came from a Presbyterian, Dr. James Fraser, Princeton graduate, ex-president of New Windsor College and pastor of the New Windsor Presbyterian Church, six miles away. After two years Fraser's Greek duties were shifted to Herbert Taylor Stephens (1864-1929). Stephens, born in Ohio, a graduate of Adrian College and pastor for a brief time in the Pittsburgh Conference, yearned to teach; and his brother, who was chancellor at Kansas City University, had appointed him to the faculty there. In 1921 Elderdice joined Albert Norman Ward, president of Western Maryland College, in inviting Stephens to come to Westminster. For eight years Stephens divided his time between the college, where he taught Philosophy, and the seminary, where he offered courses in Theism and New Testament Exegesis. The students respected his scholarship, pedantic as it was, and slept quietly through his dull lectures.

Only diffidence accounted for Shroyer's hesitation to teach Greek and Exegesis, but before long he was offering these and other subjects as well. In some catalogs he is listed as professor of Biblical Theology and Christian Sociology, and in others his name appears with World Religions and Rural Church. He confided later that he "qualified" to teach the last-named subject by taking a summer course at Purdue University. His real love, however, was the New Testament, and in 1929 he went to Yale on a two-year leave of absence to work toward a Ph.D. in that subject. He received the degree in 1935, becoming the first full-time professor in the seminary to hold an earned doctorate.[6]

Shroyer pioneered at Westminster a more critical and discriminating study of the Bible, yet he would have disclaimed any such distinction. Methodist Protestants, like so many other evangelicals of the early twentieth century, were vigilant defenders of "divine inspiration" and "scriptural infallibility" and resisted any scholastic assault on the Bible as the Word of God. Shroyer, however, could not resist pointing out various inconsistencies, contradictions, and mistranslations. This, when noised abroad, made for some uneasiness throughout the denomination, a feeling possibly increased by Shroyer's pointed applications of biblical ethics to society and contemporary life. He never missed an opportunity to teach what the Bible was really saying about sin and salvation, at the same time enlivening his classes with homespun vignettes, country colloquialisms, and modern parables. Sometimes he would comment jocularly on the seminary Nativity plays—on "poor Joseph" standing at one side in the manger scene like a puzzled stepfather, or on the "co-ed angels" borrowed from the college with no scriptural warrant for female angels. And where can anybody find in the Bible that there were *three* wise men, or that they came to the manger? Shroyer told his class that when Moses struck the rock for water, "he clobbered that rock." The class laughed lightheartedly but remembered the sin of anger. Shroyer's erudition was never stuffy. He was a true scholar and his detailed knowledge of Greek gave him confidence in his interpretations. Once, when teaching the Book of Revelation to an adult church class, he lost patience with the recommended textbook. "To keep from losing my mind," he told the class, "I went back to the Greek text of Revelation and worked through it to see what it was all about. I can understand the [Bible's] Greek better than the author's English."

Shroyer's pulpit prayers, unlike those of many others, were unmistakably addressed to God. He liked the Psalms for praying, and he had a gift for putting the Old and New Testaments together in a contemporary setting.

> I have found strength in that marvelous Psalm, the 27th. . . .
> I have found a prayer in that Psalm the depth of which I
> have been unable to fathom: "Show me thy way, O Lord,
> and lead me in a plainly marked path because of mine
> enemies." I say I have not been able to explore it fully but
> I have strange intimations of paths which God might point

Montgomery J. Shroyer (1888-1981) was still a lively teacher in 1961, the year of his retirement.

out when enemies surround us. He himself has taken some strange paths in the face of the world's terrible sin and hatred. His Son took a strange path we now call the "via Dolorosa." And when we pray it might just come about that God would show us a good path, a path of peace, for our stumbling feet.

So when he prayed in wartime for American soldiers, worshipers were sometimes startled when he went on to pray also for the "poor lads" of Germany, Russia, Korea, and Vietnam, and for "God's little ones whom we have bombed in Hiroshima and Nagasaki."

Shroyer was baptized a Lutheran, ordained a Methodist Protestant, and called to serve a Congregational church while he was a graduate student at Yale. He was equally at home with Quakers, Baptists, Presbyterians, Roman Catholics, and Jews, and in fact seemed unaware of any human barriers, religious, national, social, or political. He agreed completely with the Westminster Church of the Brethren in their rejection of war and commitment to Christian servanthood in the world. He joined every anti-war demonstration he could, stood in vigils protesting the manufacture of nerve gas at Camp Detrick in nearby Frederick, and supported conscientious objectors in the student body by going to court in their defense and writing to them in prison. Scholarly competence, human compassion, puckish humor, and many more qualities graced the forty-two years that Shroyer taught at the seminary. It is not too much to say that his long and productive tenure, spanning the period from the middle of the Elderdice era to the new beginning in Washington, symbolizes the decisive way by which President Elderdice turned the seminary around and set it on a course of enlarging usefulness to the church and the world.

'Miss Dorothy'

Employed as a part-time teacher of Oratory in 1914, Dorothy Elderdice could not have imagined that at age twenty-two she was beginning more than thirty years of "tenured" service to her father's school. He told her, "I'll let you get in on my reputation but you'll have to get out on your own." Many years later she claimed "the all-time record among

53

Seminary faculty members for shifting from part-time teaching to no teaching to full-time teaching and then back again.'' In 1914 she had just graduated from the Emerson College of Oratory in Boston. After teaching for three years, she returned to Boston for a year of study at the Leland Powers School of the Spoken Word. Summarizing her subsequent career, she wrote:

> In the fall of 1918 I came back to the Seminary with a requested change in my title, teacher of Public Speaking—putting in more hours this time. In 1921 I accepted a position as full-time teacher of Speech and Dramatics at Idaho Technical Institute, Pocatello. Between that year and 1927 I studied in New York, worked at the Church of All Nations, and spent two years in West Palm Beach, Florida, as city Dramatic Director. I returned to the Seminary in 1927, gradually going into full-time teaching through the 1930s when we had a fully developed department of religious drama and speech, with incidentals such as Story Telling and Recreational Leadership.

On campus she was universally known as ''Miss Dorothy,'' a traditional title of respect accorded to southern ladies. When she returned in 1927, her father's earlier aversion to ''plays'' had subsided and he asked her to initiate a course in Religious Drama. She began at once to make plays and pageants a prominent feature of seminary life. Her first play was *Jehovah-Jireh,* a dramatization of Abraham's sacrifice of Isaac. Her role as director was interrupted by pneumonia, but from her sick bed she was able to advise about props and costumes. ''On the night of the performance,'' she said, ''the students raised the shades in the Seminary chapel so that I could see the light . . . and follow the action in my mind's eye!'' During the following summer (1928) the students in the Leadership Training School (a summer program of study for lay people) presented her arrangement of *David and Jonathan,* staged on the lawn. A singing procession started at the seminary ''porch''; the king and his court came from the president's house, and ''David killed Goliath back of the house while the mob shouted to tell the audience what was happening, as in a Greek chorus. Finally David emerged bearing a huge papier-mâché head we had gotten from a Baltimore costumer.'' Later

54

that summer the class learned with some surprise that one of their textbooks considered the story of David and Goliath "too blood-thirsty to be dramatized." But Miss Elderdice simply shrugged. "The warning came too late," she said; "the deed was already done."[7]

For ten years religious drama flourished at the seminary. Miss Elderdice taught play production and directed the students in plays of many kinds. There were *Everyman, The Traveling Man, He Came Seeing, Hachi-no-ki* (a Japanese "noh" play), and many oft-repeated favorites, such as *The Bishop's Candlesticks, The Servant in the House, Ba Thane, The Finger of God,* and *The Terrible Meek.* She also designed a portable stage, which enabled her student troupe to take their plays on tour. But the drama program ran into difficulty in 1937. In Miss Elderdice's view, that turn of events resulted from an accreditation visit to the seminary. "The august gentlemen who go around accrediting institutions," she explained,

> decided that too much time was being devoted to dramatics and the Seminary should emphasize music instead. So in 1937 I was asked to give part of my time to the library and part to speech, with perhaps one or two courses in speech and religious drama—but no more touring plays. I was, however, permitted to present our Outdoor Nativity from 1930 until my resignation in 1950.

But the real catalyst of change was probably the shock of her 1937 production of *Ten Nights in a Bar Room*—in the seminary chapel, no less. At the end of that play, Mary Scott Forlines, former preceptress of the college and now the wife of the seminary president, stood up in the audience to lament the desecration of the chapel, indeed of the whole of Seminary Hill, by such an unseemly performance. Miss Elderdice was stung. After 1937 she limited her teaching to the classroom with only occasional extensions, though the catalog continued to describe her course as a "history of the church and drama, the modern church play and pageant, [with a] study of setting, costuming and lighting, [and] production of a workshop play by the class." Her Advanced Drama included "production of plays in nearby churches . . . where each student is required to direct one play during the year." In 1941 she added

Dorothy Elderdice directed the annual nativity pageant in the 1930s and 1940s. Professor Shroyer teased her about using female angels with no scriptural warrant.

a course in Radio Speech that offered "practice in the preparation and presentation of radio scripts [with] broadcasting over station WFMD," the local station. Although she resigned as professor of Speech in 1950, she was listed as instructor in Religious Drama for four more years.

Under Miss Elderdice's direction all drama at the seminary, with rare exceptions, was designed to proclaim a moral message, usually of world peace and racial equality. This was especially true of the annual Nativity Pageant. Begun in 1930 and repeated every December until 1951, this "medieval miracle" required for its production a Nativity Guild of students and faculty, and there was annual excitement over

Miss Dorothy drew on all available resources to stress the universal significance of the birth of Christ. Her title for this scene was "Christmas Greetings from China," and the Chinese actor was enlisted from a neighboring town.

the casting for leading parts. During much of December the seminary halls were a shambles of wiring, lights, properties, costumes, and stage materials; but somehow the spectacle of the event on a wintry, starlit night compensated for the chaos. The pageant spread across the whole front façade of the seminary building with lighting, amplification, recorded music, and tableaux which simulated famous artists' portrayals of the Annunciation, shepherds and sheep, royal magi, and the manger scene. Angels leaned from the windows with harps and trumpets in a blaze of light, while "Gloria in Excelsis" rang over the town from the tower. For a climax, people of all nations, races, and ages crowded about the Christ-child on the seminary steps in a testimony of love and good will. People wondered how Miss Dorothy could discover and bring together so many representatives of different nations and races from the town and county.

Until she died in 1979, revered and loved at the age of 87, Dorothy Elderdice's whole life centered around her Westminster home and her father's school. In addition to her classes in Speech and Drama, she was the seminary librarian for over a decade and office secretary to her father for more weary years than she liked to recall. She directed the Westminster Community Players from 1934 to 1941. She wrote and directed many pageants for Easter, Christmas, the Western Maryland College centennial, the nation's bicentennial, and the fiftieth anniversary of the Women's International League for Peace and Freedom at The Hague in 1965. She seemed to be incapable of recognizing boundaries, whether of race, religion, or nation; and she succeeded at times in changing Westminster Seminary's somewhat narrow parochialism into a compassion that was worldwide. She marched for civil rights and for equal rights for women. She openly criticized the Vietnam War. Racial equality, open theaters and restaurants, world peace, and international understanding were all on her agenda for energetic, tireless action. When some Jehovah's Witnesses came to her door, she welcomed them, listened respectfully to their recordings, accepted their literature, served them tea, and sent them out loaded with peace pamphlets, civil rights tracts, and other brochures in support of her own cherished causes. Foreign students at both the college and seminary made her home theirs, and she supported and sponsored them as "my international family." Indomitable to the end, she smiled at watchers around her deathbed and said cheerfully, "Tell all my friends I'm having a glorious passing." After her death, an annual Elderdice Peace Week was inaugurated at Western Maryland College to honor "in perpetuity, alumna Dorothy Elderdice, a respected proponent of peace and civil rights."

One more professor joined the faculty during Elderdice's presidency. Fred Garrigus Holloway, a graduate and fellow of Drew University with exceptional gifts and skills in languages and literature, came from his pastorate in 1928 to teach biblical languages, relieving Elderdice of the Hebrew classes. Four years later Holloway became president of the seminary. But all the succeeding years would remain the legacy of the Elderdice era and of the man who practically incarnated the seminary—at least in the mind of the denomination that maintained it—for more than a third of a century.

In 1932, the last year Elderdice (center) was president, the full-time faculty consisted of Fred G. Holloway and Dorothy Elderdice (standing), plus Charles E. Forlines (left) and Montgomery J. Shroyer.

3

Hugh Latimer Elderdice:
the man at his post

Thirty-five years of Westminster Seminary history, as made and recorded by President Elderdice, can be found in his office correspondence—thirty-five letter-file boxes of just about everything that crossed his desk: office memos, book orders, and appointments; student inquiries, applications, admissions, and rejections; requests from married students for housing and jobs for their wives; letters official, personal, and sometimes "confidential"; orders for coal, repairs, furniture, fertilizer, and building supplies; disputes over bills for electricity and plumbing; faculty selection, remuneration, and teaching duties; reports to and from the Board of Governors; scholarship bequests and disbursements; notes on contributions from alumni, friends, and churches; and a hundred other things. Apparently he destroyed no correspondence intentionally. All letters received were filed alphabetically, by years, with his reply sometimes in carbon or more often scrawled on the back. He wrote in at least one margin, "I did not reply to this foolish letter." He was the president, and no detail was too small to be considered his responsibility. He was also the registrar, director of admissions, chief fund raiser, recruitment agent, bookkeeper, treasurer, superintendent of buildings and grounds, director of counseling, and field work supervisor. As need required, he was professor of Hebrew, Historical Theology, or Practical Theology. And sometimes, he noted with amusement, he was the janitor. In all of his capacities as administrator, builder, teacher/counselor, public speaker, and moderate churchman, he placed the stamp of his own character indelibly on the institution he did so much to save.

The administrator

During Elderdice's entire time as president, the administrative load never lessened. In 1924 Crates Johnson, editor of the denomination's Sunday School publications, invited him to contribute a weekly page to *The Teacher's Quarterly*. Elderdice declined, listing some of his "prior assignments":

1. President of the Westminster Theological Seminary.
2. Treasurer of several funds that are continually calling for more cash.
3. Secretary of the Board of Governors.
4. Field agent for the collecting of money for [a] new Parsonage now being erected.
5. Solicitor-General for Scholarship, Endowment, Library, and Current Expenses.
6. My own stenographer and my own typist for one and all of these and several other interests.

At the end of the letter Elderdice added, "I am confident that after reading the above you will want to take up a collection to hire me some kind of help."

He apparently forgot to tell Johnson that he was also the registrar, director of admissions, and scheduling committee. One alumnus recalled the summer morning in 1926 when he came to the president's office to apply for admission the following September. He found a gracious welcome and was duly enrolled subject to receipt of his transcript of college courses. Upon learning that the young man was to be a commuting student-pastor, Elderdice asked, "I am making up the schedule for the fall, and do you wish to say what days of the week would be most convenient for you to come?"

Finding the money for salaries, scholarships, and operating expenses was always difficult and often discouraging. Elderdice wanted all professors to be remunerated fairly, yet he was impatient with outside agitation on the matter of faculty salaries. He silenced one inquirer by telling him it was the board's policy and desire to increase salaries "whenever the prosperity of the Seminary would justify such increases and they have always done so on their own initiative. . . . The best service you can render in this matter is to do nothing and say nothing."[1] Elderdice admitted that on the subject of ministerial remuneration he had "an old fashioned view."

> A man called to preach will go where God calls regardless of the exact amount stipulated as salary. . . .If you have it all figured out you are walking by sight and not by faith. While we are to use common sense in preparing to meet our financial obligations to self and family, we must leave the good Lord a margin for his Providential care.

Scholarships were particularly important, for they determined the number of students that could be admitted. Elderdice wrote unceasingly to his board members, asking in nearly every letter for a hundred-dollar tuition scholarship. Those who could not contribute were asked to find someone who could, and most of them either paid up or found a substitute. Every catalog until 1948 printed in bold type: "NO WORTHY MAN IS EVER COMPELLED TO LEAVE THE SEMINARY BECAUSE OF INABILITY TO PAY ALL HIS EXPENSES." This was a promise hard to keep, but it was kept. In 1930 Elderdice wrote to a young applicant: "In my thirty years as President I have never known a student to be obliged to leave because of a lack of funds. I am convinced that if the Lord has called you to preach the way will be open for you to do so." A similar logic appeared in his appeals for scholarship money: "If God has called this young man we have an obligation to pay his tuition." Elderdice's endless correspondence on this matter was matched by miles of travel. His rule was to accept only traveling expenses, nothing for preaching or lecturing. "No begging—but if I preach on a Sunday [I] receive a voluntary collection for the Seminary. . . . I am traveling in the interest of the Seminary and do not feel justified in visiting any place unless I can make it tell for my work."

In 1901 the seminary had only six scholarships to offer. By 1903 Elderdice could report a surplus of $300 which he had deposited as a scholarship fund in the Westminster Savings Bank at 3.5 percent. In 1911 this fund amounted to nearly $4,000, in 1922 $9,000, and in 1932 $18,587. The bank weathered the depression of the 1930s, and there is no record that the seminary lost any of its money due to bank failure.

Dispensing these meager amounts was a responsibility as serious as it was happy. If Elderdice had faith in a prospective student, he pressed him to come. To one he wrote:

> I like the ring and tone of [your letter] and am sure that a way can be found to put you thru [sic]. If you are willing to do your part be assured that we will do all we can to help you out. Come ahead with your $40 and try it for a term at least. We will make up the lack of funds.[2]

To another:

> If you arrive with $100 to your credit I think we can see you through the year all right. Your Seminary expenses will be $50 plus about $10 for books. If you need it I will give you enough money to pay your rent for the year; and if you still find yourself short I will make an additional donation. So come on and trust the good Lord to take care of you here.[3]

There are scores of letters like these in the Elderdice File.

No impecunious applicant received a better offer than Raleigh Hunter, a former student in North Carolina who had had to withdraw from the seminary because of inadequate resources. When he inquired about returning, Elderdice wrote:

> Glad that you still desire to [re-]enter Seminary . . . and finish your course. Sorry to learn of your financial difficulties. Why did you not let me know all this long ago? I might have been in a position to have helped you some. I . . . will gladly do all in my power to help you come next year. So I make this promise: A gift of $150.
>
> | | |
> |---|---:|
> | You owe a balance of | $36.41 |
> | Seminary Bill for next year | 50.00 |
> | Books | 14.00 |
> | Rent | 50.00 |
> | Total due Sept. 1914 | $150.41 |
> | To be paid by Raleigh Hunter | .41 |
> | Balance due Sept. 1914 for year 1914-15 | $150.00 |
> | To be paid by Elderdice. | |
>
> This leaves you only forty-one cents to raise, plus your living expenses. Your rent may be more than $50 and your books may be less than $14; but I will stand good for $150, free gift.[4]

Some of the available scholarship funds came with conditions attached. The redoubtable Drinkhouse had left a portion of his estate to the seminary to be used for student aid, and every recipient had to sign a pledge ''to abstain from the use of intoxicating liquors as a beverage, from the use of tobacco in all its forms, and from the use of narcotics not prescribed by a physician.'' The second prohibition went further than the Methodist Protestant *Discipline,* which did not forbid the use of tobacco. Smoking, in fact, was not uncommon among ministers of the denomination; the seminary's first president, Thomas Hamilton Lewis, had been known to enjoy an occasional cigar. But Elderdice stood with Drinkhouse on this point, and having no wish to encourage his church's toleration of tobacco, he sometimes warned prospective students that smokers should expect no financial assistance.

The students needed not only scholarships; they needed employment as well. The catalog was encouraging: ''Vacant pulpits and charitable institutions offer remunerative labor for vacation [while] Conference Presidents and Charitable Institutions frequently call for the service of needy and deserving students.'' Finding such ''remunerative labor'' was one of Elderdice's heaviest tasks. He looked upon this as a duty that came with his job, and he gave to it hours of correspondence and consultation. In fact, the presidents of the various annual conferences and their appointing committees gave over the task of student church appointments to the seminary president, accepting his assignments without question. On his part, Elderdice was always careful to seem to defer to conference authority.

For many years it was almost impossible to find denominational support for Westminster Seminary beyond the borders of the Maryland Conference. After all, the idea of the seminary came to fruition in that conference, and since Methodist Protestant schools in Michigan, Kansas, and Texas were at times desperately in need of funds, solicitations and drives from the East were usually regarded as unwarranted intrusions. This feeling diminished, however, with the growing respect for ministerial education and with the recognition of Westminster as the denomination's only theological seminary.

In 1922 Elderdice reviewed a quarter of a century of his administration with ''the note of a Silver Jubilee.'' In 1897 the Maryland Conference had provided nearly all of the money necessary for maintaining the school. Only four other conferences had contributed, and the total of their gifts came to less than one hundred dollars. But, Elderdice observed with evident satisfaction,

> since we are not to despise the day of small things we must place them on the roll of honor: Maryland $1,389; New Jersey $36; North Carolina $26; New York $13; and West Virginia $1—total $1,465. One by one other conferences rallied to our support...until today all of our 27 conferences share the financial burden of the Seminary and the sum total received this year...amounts to $5,820... exclusive of $7,112 from the students.

By a nice balance of miracle and sacrifice these amounts kept the property in good repair and paid the salaries. In addition, reported Elderdice, scholarships had been collected "from liberal laymen and generous churches" totaling $35,000 for the twenty-five years. And the endowment, he added, came to "a grand total of $12,762."

It was now time to move the seminary out of its Maryland matrix into the sphere of full denominational support. For twenty-five years Elderdice had chafed under the old 1884 charter, which provided for a Board of Governors consisting of three ministers and two laymen elected quadrennially by the Maryland Conference and two ministers and three laymen elected quadrennially by the General Conference. By 1922 it was clear that the school had outgrown all provincial boundaries, so the board petitioned the Maryland legislature for a charter change which would require that all its members be elected by the General Conference. This was granted, and Elderdice in his elation remembered to include in his report a "grateful tribute to the honored Mother of us all—the old Maryland Conference...for founding, nurturing and largely supporting this institution for two score years." But now, he added, the new charter "makes the Seminary a strictly denominational institution, and the one common center to which all the hosts of our Israel may rally."

The builder

Elderdice began building as soon as he entered office, and by the time he retired in 1932 the campus in Westminster had reached its full development. In his first summer, 1897, he

The original building of 1882 was expanded in 1887 (center section) and again in 1907 (rear wing). The whole structure was demolished in 1920 to make room for a new building of Tudor Gothic design.

completed what he called a "cottage" for the president but which the Board of Governors described as "an attractive and comfortable house." Ten years later a new wing was built onto the seminary building, providing a chapel, more space for the library, and rooms for twenty more students. The total cost was $4,483, part of which came from a Silver Jubilee Fund; the remainder was borrowed from endowment funds. Next came two faculty residences: the North Carolina Cottage in 1911 and the West Virginia Cottage in 1914. They were named for the annual conferences that gave the money to build them, largely as a result of appeals made during personal visits by

The addition of 1887 provided space for a chapel. On the walls were no icons of classical Christianity but pictures of the founders of the Methodist Protestant Church. The Greek inscription, translated, reads: "Ready always with an answer" (I Peter 3:15).

the president and various professors. Charles E. Forlines, who was from North Carolina, spent many weeks canvassing his home conference for funds to build the house that was to be his residence for many years. Each cottage cost about three thousand dollars.

The new seminary building of 1920 was Elderdice's largest and most impressive building achievement. In 1916 he told his board that he thought the old building was unsightly and that its "barn-like look" was a discredit to the church. The president applied to the General Conference, which met that year in Zanesville, Ohio, for permission to launch a campaign to raise $50,000 for a new building. But Western Maryland College was into its Golden Jubilee Campaign for $50,000, so Elderdice "stepped aside and gave the right of way to the College." But by February 1918 the way was clear for the seminary to launch its campaign. The architect selected was Paul Reese of Westminster, a Western Maryland graduate whom Elderdice had known since childhood. In a letter of reference Elderdice once recommended him as "competent...affable, attractive, and an entertaining conversationalist...a gentleman in every respect. I understand he has occasionally gone on a spree but so far as I know he is now steady and entirely reliable."[5]

Reese's designs delighted all who saw them, and general enthusiasm for the task managed to survive even the distractions, disasters, and high prices of World War I. In 1919 the president reported: "In cash and in subscriptions we have gone 'over the top' in our $50,000 campaign. Immediate building being prohibited by postwar conditions, I have been depositing the cash at 4%." The contractor, Charles B. Hunter, had wisely begun to purchase materials before prices climbed any higher, and during the winter of 1918 he had laid by a considerable stockpile of lumber, bricks, and cement. The old building was razed in the summer of 1919, and the new one begun at the same location on 26 September. Dorothy Elderdice described the ground-breaking:

> My father dug the first shovel full from the northwest corner, Dr. Forlines from the northeast corner and I from the southeast corner. The President spoke these words: "This ground is broken for the new building of the Westminster

Theological Seminary, for the Glory of God, for the advancement of the Kingdom of Christ on earth, and the theological prosperity of the Methodist Protestant Church.''

With seminary classes crowded into what space was available at the college, there was a rush to complete the building in time for the opening of the next school year. Paul Reese having moved away (to Charleston, W. Va.), a new architect, Charles Anderson of Baltimore, came to direct the work. Miss Elderdice followed the details of construction:

> The President of the Seminary appeared as a day laborer in overalls. Likewise Dr. Forlines and Prof. Shroyer.... T. W. Mather, chairman of the Building Committee, was available at any hour.... Small strikes were met by discharging the strikers; and threatened strikes on a larger scale were prevented by increasing wages before the time came to strike. The building contains the best materials and workmanship, and architect Anderson declares that this building could not have been built in Baltimore this summer.[6]

The building was not ready for use until 26 October, which delayed the opening of school for the fall semester. Even then the seminary had to borrow three lecture rooms from the college. But Elderdice could capitalize even on frustrating delays. He wrote to a waiting student, ''This would be a good time for you to make a little spending money.'' And to other students he wrote that all the money in sight had been spent ''and I am borrowing $16,000''; they should therefore ask for an offering from their local churches or friends to help furnish their rooms.

Dedication Day came at last on 17 December 1920, and the president pronounced it ''the most notable day in the history of the Seminary.'' Delegated representatives from other seminaries, distinguished guests, a colorful academic procession, imposing speeches, and all the accompanying festivities brought gratifying accolades from many sources. The building towering from its hilltop location was immensely impressive. Ornate by later standards, its Tudor Gothic style pleased the eyes of that generation. Elderdice expressed thanks for ''an architectural gem, beautiful for situation, and the glory of the whole earth, so far as the Methodist Protestant Church covers

The new building of 1920 gave the seminary more space and grandeur. The inscription over the entrance—in such ornate Gothic capitals that it was sometimes mistaken for Hebrew—reads: "BLESSED BE THY COMING IN AND BLESSED BE THY GOING OUT." The uppermost room was called "the tower room" and was used for prayer and meditation. The cross on the top pinnacle stirred considerable controversy among Methodist Protestants.

the earth'' (cf. Psalm 85:2). The cost of the new building came to $115,000. On the day of dedication a debt remained of $30,000, which was at once retired by gifts from individuals and representatives of five annual conferences—Maryland, Ohio, North Carolina, Pittsburgh, and Eastern—and by the Board of Education of the denomination.

One feature of the new building provoked controversy: the cross on the tower seemed to some a Roman Catholic symbol, the use of which might be expected of Methodist Episcopalians but never of Methodist Protestants. Elderdice defended his architect in the matter, trying to allay prejudices and explaining carefully by tradition and doctrine the symbol's rightful place over a school of theology. But the debate lingered long. Four years after the dedication of the new building, a contributor sent a small check for a new residence for the president. "Please use the enclosed for the 'Preacher's Home,' " she wrote, "with this proviso, however: that you do not have a cross placed on top of it. As an old Methodist Protestant [I think] it savors too much of Roman Catholicism though Methodists have a better right to its use I will admit." Elderdice patiently sought to mollify her with a repetition of his stock arguments.

First: It was placed there by a Methodist Episcopal minister in honor of his father who was a Methodist Protestant preacher—James Thompson, a contemporary of your father and my father.

Second: It is not the Latin Cross of Roman Catholicism but the Celtic Cross of other religious denominations.

Third: Long before the Papal Church the Cross was the symbol of Christianity . . . .

Fourth: "When I Survey the Wondrous Cross" was written by Isaac Watts, the father of English Hymnody.

Fifth: A Christian older than the oldest Methodist wrote: "God forbid that I should glory save in the cross of our Lord Jesus Christ."

Elderdice could never have dreamed that a similar controversy would develop in protests against the college's removal of that same cross in the 1960s.

In comparison to the old building and its crowded quarters, the new building was palatial. It afforded four large classrooms, a library, chapel, and president's office on the first floor. On the second and third floors were students' rooms. At the top of a narrow stairway was a central "tower room" with a panoramic view across Carroll County's hills to the distant mountains, a room reserved for use as a sanctuary for private prayer and meditation. Later, library stacks would expand to the basement, which they would have to share with a ping-pong table and the vice-president's office. But for now, people marveled at the new building as a place where fifty students could be comfortably housed and educated, and probably no one dreamed of the overcrowding that later growth would bring.

All this English Gothic dignity gave the old presidential "cottage" next door the appearance of pathetic shabbiness. Its unsightliness was matched by its inadequacy. In 1920, the year of the new seminary building, Daniel Baker gave the president $500 toward a new home and Elderdice deposited it as seed money. Two years later the Maryland Conference authorized a campaign for the project, ordering special offerings on the first Sunday in May and stating optimistically that "if 2,520 churches responded with only $5 per church the result would be $12,600." Elderdice was embarrassed. "That would furnish a palace,'' he protested. But 1922 was his ''Jubilee Year,'' and as the campaign gained momentum, the Board of Governors ''directed that an architect be employed to draw up plans for a new home for the president to cost not less than $12,000.'' The Silver Jubilee offering was a disappointment, and Elderdice recovered from his embarrassment sufficiently to ''grease the wheels'' a little. ''After a year of waiting,'' he wrote, ''I discovered that if this volunteer method were to be the plan, the house would not be erected in my lifetime.'' So he began personal solicitation and recommended ''that money for the house be taken from the Endowment Fund

In 1922 Elderdice permitted—then encouraged—construction of a new residence for the president. Completed in 1924, it bespoke a quiet dignity commensurate with the elegance of the new seminary building nearby.

on the ground that it will be a permanent investment.'' Dorothy Elderdice remembered the course of events:

On April 9, 1924 we moved out of our old rattletrap house with its leaky roof and creaky doors and shed no tears over its demolition. It was rather a lark to be camping out in the Seminary building while our beautiful new home was going up. On May 15 my mother dug the first shovel of dirt and by November 17 we moved in the new house. My father's ''palace'' that was to cost an extravagant $12,600 actually ran to $25,000 by the time the new shrubbery and cement walks had been laid. It was all paid for by 1926. And what a joy it was! Now we had plenty of room for seminary festive [and official] occasions.

The seventh and last building that Elderdice put up was another faculty residence. He broached the project to the board in a way that both illustrated his decisive leadership and revealed the state of the seminary's finances in the midst of the depression. On 30 March 1931 he wrote to each governor:

> Dr. Shroyer will return next Sept. from his two years of absence, studying at Yale. Professor Holloway has been occupying his former home—the West Virginia Cottage. This means that we need to build another cottage for one or other of these men. Are you willing to authorize the committee on Investments, or the Officers of the Board of Governors—the President, the Treasurer, and the Secretary—as an Executive Committee, to proceed with this enterprise?

> We have $18,000 of the Endowment Fund in Bonds, and in the Westminster Savings Bank we have over $12,000. From this Bank we could draw enough to build and have several thousand dollars remaining.

> It has been our custom to use Endowment money for all our buildings of Residence, and the rental value which helped pay the salaries of the occupants has been regarded as the equivalent of interest. If you approve of this proposed action please send your vote immediately for if we are to have the house ready by Sept. 1, we must hasten to give the contract.

All the board members promptly voted "yes." The house was completed in the summer of 1931 and was ready for Shroyer when he returned from Yale. There was no need to borrow from endowment funds, since the $7,000 it cost came from the Pittsburgh Conference as "a memorial to the life and work of Herbert Taylor Stephens," who taught at the seminary from 1921 to 1929. The house was known as "The Pittsburgh Cottage."

Homes for faculty members, made possible by designated gifts from churches and annual conferences, lined the lower edge of the Westminster campus. The "Pittsburgh Cottage" was built in 1931 as a memorial to Professor Herbert Taylor Stephens.

The teacher/counselor

When *The Methodist Protestant* asked President Elderdice in 1901 to write an article on "What a Young Minister Ought to Study," he complied with an essay that illumines both his own theological and scholarly interests and his intentions for the seminary during the thirty-five years of his administration. He wrote first on "General Studies" and began with history, biography, travel, exploration, and discovery. Then he urged reading in modern science and philosophy.

> He who is content to end his studies with the scientists of forty years ago may be complacent but he is not critical nor well-informed. Whether you accept or reject the theory of evolution is not the question; the question is: do you know what that theory is? . . . It is not enough to be familiar with Socrates, Plato, Descartes, Spinoza, Locke, Hume, Leibnitz, Kant, Fichte, Schopenhauer, Hegel and Comte; we need the later views of Porter, Ladd and James.

Next came poetry with comments on sixteen poets from Milton to James Whitcomb Riley. Then political economy:

> Is legislation for the individual or for the corporation, has Capital divine right and Labor none and is commerce to be crowned king? When the preacher can discuss all social problems in the language of "the shop" both the capitalist and the laborer will fill his pews. Without turning the pulpit into a political rostrum or posing as a sensationalist, the minister may find in his Bible a panacea for the aches and ills of modern social and civil life.

Elderdice concluded the section on "General Studies" with a plea for ministers to study art: "Possibly no general study is more neglected by the ministry." After alluding to Delaroche, Claude Lorraine, Turner, Rembrandt, Ruysdael, Millet, Diaz, and Daubigny, he declared that "Christianity has always welcomed art to the altar and the hearth except in the day of Puritan supremacy, when, in the words of Lowell, 'They turned beauty out of the meeting-house and slammed the door in her face.' "

The section of his essay on "Special Studies" rested on the premise that the minister "must be a Biblical Specialist," and to achieve this end, Elderdice suggested books for the young

72

minister's library. Those who had attended the seminary had seen them all. Under "Exegetical and Expository" were Lange's *Commentary* "for comprehensive, dogmatic and practical treatment"; Keil and Delitzsch on the Old Testament; *The Expositor's Bible;* Meyer on Romans "for keen grammatical criticism," Godet on John "for critical and spiritual excellence," Lightfoot on Galatians ("an elaborate work"), and Perowne on the Psalms ("the best published"). Then he added, "If you are not afraid of the International Critical Commentary under the editorship of Briggs, Driver and Plummer you will have the latest if not the most conservative treatment of the Bible . . . by different writers, foremost among modern scholars of the liberal school." He also noted two Bible dictionaries: "Conservative is Smith [and] in sympathy with the Higher Criticism is the late work edited by Hastings."

Only Neander and Fisher were named for Church History, along with the mandatory accounts of the Methodist Protestant Church by Bassett and Drinkhouse, and of the Maryland Conference by Murray and Lewis. One sentence under "Doctrinal" listed without comment the systems of Dwight, Hodge, Watson, Wesley, Pope, and Miley. Also named were Hengstenberg's *Christology of the Old Testament,* Dorner's *Doctrine of the Person of Christ,* and Hagenbuch's *History of Doctrine.* Biblical Theology received a few descriptive words: Ochler on the Old Testament is "comprehensive and prolix," Schultz "exhaustive and radical," Bennett "brief and conservative."

> A. B. Davidson's work when complete will be the best. On the New Testament Adeney has a modest work and Stevens has a more ambitious volume; the works of Wendt, Beyschlag, and Holtzmann are worthy of reading if not acceptance.

Devotional suggestions were limited to *Pilgrim's Progress, The Reformed Pastor* by Baxter, *The Imitation of Christ* by Thomas à Kempis, *The Tongue of Fire* by Arthur, and "the recent writings of F. B. Meyer."

Elderdice concluded with a long paragraph headed "Miscellaneous." In this he put "all Methodist Protestant publications not already specified," the works of Henry Drummond, Conybeare and Howson on Paul, Green's *Old Testa-*

ment Introduction, the Koran, and representative writings of "the three schools now struggling for the ascendancy in religious thought: the Keswick School with such leaders as F. B. Meyer and G. Campbell Morgan . . . the Critical School as represented by Driver and Briggs, and the Conservative School represented by the old Princetonian who clings to traditional views of the Bible and the Church." A conspicuous footnote announced the opening of the seminary on 23 September and advised that "its curriculum contains the best course of study for candidates for the ministry."

This lengthy article is not as comprehensive as it might seem on first reading. It is, in fact, puzzling because of its failure to mention any work dealing with pastoral ministry. The seminary curriculum certainly included appropriate reading in pastoralia, but it took another query to draw a bibliography out of the president. In 1926 a new professor of Practical Theology in the Lutheran Seminary at Gettysburg wrote to ask Elderdice, by now a veteran teacher in that field, for advice. His first question was, "What text books do you use?" Elderdice gave a summary list:

> Broadus on the Preparation and Delivery of Sermons, Dean Brown on the Art of Preaching, Phelps on the Theory of Preaching, Johnson on The Ideal Ministry and the Christian Preacher by Garvie, History of Preaching by Dargan and Broadus, Brastow on The Modern Pulpit, Gladden on The Christian Pastor and the Working Church, The Work of the Pastor by Erdman—and scores of others. Most of the work is done by lectures and blackboard drill in Sermonizing.

A second question, "Do you use the case method?" received the simple answer, "Yes." Question three, "How do you keep in touch with the churches in your territory?" brought the reply, "a. By Conference Presidents, b. By pulpit committees of local churches, c. By personal correspondence with the pastors." To the fourth question, "Do you supervise the preaching done by students in neighboring churches?" Elderdice responded, "We drill them in class room and Chapel before [they go] to their churches, quiz them on their return, and are influenced by criticisms from local parishes in which they have preached." Elderdice's short description of his tools and methods was doubtless of limited help to a beginning professor, for he was obviously answering in haste, but his letter does afford some insight into how he went about the teaching task. Other clues come from his book orders for his classes and the library, which show a serious intention on his part to keep pace with the best and usually the most recent works in all the subjects of the theological curriculum.

From his students (and they were "his") Elderdice demanded complete dedication, total honesty, and hard work. If they exhibited these qualities, he usually gave them passing grades. Failures he handed down more often for iniquity than for incompetence, believing that the churches would suffer less from conscientious, hard-working pastors, however dull, than from bright ecclesiastical manipulators. Except for his classes in Hebrew, he usually taught by lecturing. As a teacher he had one single aim: to make good ministers of his students. They read his assignments, took copious notes, copied his blackboard outlines, laughed at his jokes, prepared for exams, and stood always in awe of his commanding presence and erudition.

In the early years of his administration Elderdice encouraged almost all applicants to come to the seminary. He especially wanted college graduates for the Degree Course, but those with less preparation were welcome into the other three courses according to their qualifications. Even so, a few applicants had to be turned away. Once, when answering a letter of inquiry from a man who had only six years of elementary schooling and whose writing suggested near illiteracy, Elderdice resorted to a kindness that was almost devious. The man was not a Methodist Protestant but a member of the Methodist Episcopal Church; and seizing on this, Elderdice replied, "We never proselyte. You should apply to Drew."

In 1917 an applicant wrote that he would be twenty-one in June, that he had completed the eighth grade in the state of Kansas at thirteen, that he had spent four months in an accredited high school studying German, ancient history, algebra, and rhetoric, and that he had then received eight months' training under a private teacher in modern history, rhetoric, geometry, and agriculture. He now held a degree from Chillicothe (Missouri) Business College, where he had studied "Bookkeeping and Stenography with [other] studies in Spelling, Arithmetic, Grammar, Typewriting, Parliamentary Law, Common Law, Salesmanship, Stenotypy, Stocks and Bonds and Banking, Rapid Calculation, Correspondence and Penmanship.'' The young man concluded, ''I intend to become an evangelist.'' Elderdice's reply illustrates his admissions policy.

I have just received a letter from Rev. J. H. McCraken of Wilmington, N.C. and on the basis of his splendid endorsement [of you] and your letter...I am willing to make you the following offer:

1. You may enter next September without examination, our Junior [first-year] Class, and after three years of successful study we will graduate you with a diploma, but not a degree. The degree is given only to students who enter with a degree of some College.

2. We will furnish you board, laundry, furnished room, light, fuel and janitor's attention for $186 a year.... Your books will average from ten to fourteen dollars a year....

3. The rooms are assigned in the order of application...and I will take pleasure in reserving for you a desirable room.

When Elderdice could influence an applicant to complete a college degree before coming to the seminary, he was always pleased. But so urgent was the need for pastors that the Board of Education of the denomination was glad to accept seminary-trained persons whether or not they had studied at any college. There was the ever-springing hope, rather vague at times, that the young candidate would earn a college degree later, and a few did. But Elderdice was sometimes dubious. In 1926 he wrote to the president of the Board of Education, Dr. Frank Stephenson, that a young man from Cambridge, Maryland, had entered Western Maryland College, was frightened at the threat of some student hazing, became unhappy because he would have to do extra work to compensate for deficiencies in his high school commercial course, and so ''got homesick and went home.'' Now he was applying to the seminary and wanted a loan of $200 from the board. Elderdice analyzed the case:

Here is a young man shying [away from] college because of his fear of hazing and because he has to do some extra work. The Seminary is in a delicate position: If we admit him it will look like the Seminary is a dumping-ground for men not nervy enough to take the college when they have a chance. On the other hand, if we turn him down his pastor and church may give the Seminary "Hail Columbia" for not admitting a godly young man called to preach the Gospel.

Elderdice obviously hoped that, in this case at least, the Board of Education would insist on "college first," but in that he was disappointed. College preparation for seminary studies did not become mandatory until a quarter of a century later.

Elderdice maintained his presidential dignity with an easy grace, so that it never stood in his way when students needed his help. When they were sick, he nursed them and carried food to their rooms from his home next door. He reported news to their concerned parents, made their appointments with doctors, and found substitutes for their parish duties. Few seemed hesitant to ask him for help. Once, shortly after commencement, a new graduate wrote:

Dear Dr. Elderdice: Will you please go up to my room and look under the mattress. You will find a pair of trousers which I was pressing and which I forgot. If you will mail them to me I will send you the postage.

The president noted in the margin, "Sent Parcel Post." One anxious mother wrote to ask if her son was doing well, if he was studying and obeying the rules, and if he had remembered to change to his winter underwear because he caught cold easily. Elderdice replied reassuringly that he had talked with the lad. "I expressed myself rather sharply and he promised to go to his room and [don the warmer underwear]."

One delicate problem Elderdice faced in his first decade was keeping the seminary men off the part of the college campus occupied by the women students. This seems to have worried the seminary more than the college. In November 1904 Elderdice prepared a long statement which he read in chapel, repeating the rules and sternly demanding obedience. He prefaced his remarks with a description of the close friendship between the two institutions and the responsibility the seminarians should feel as the college students' "religious leaders."

Mingle with them as much as you can, cultivate their confidence and when the time comes for special revival work, you may have the first rich fruit of the Christian ministry.... And so, in order that there may be no possible mistake in the future as to your rights and privileges on the forbidden ground, I notify you that it is never to be used simply for your personal pleasure nor as a convenient shortcut during prohibited hours. It may be used under the following circumstances: 1. In going to and from meals, 2. In going to and from Chapel and Y.M.C.A. meetings, 3. At night and when roads are snowbound.

A marginal note said, "Submitted to Dr. Lewis [president of the College]...who gave his approval." An additional note read, "Later Dr. Lewis—without consulting me—gave permission to married men living downtown to use the girls' side constantly."

But supporters of the seminary wanted eternal vigilance over the students, and Elderdice tried to oblige until college officials took the matter out of his hands. In 1906 he noted:

I rebuked J. D. Smith for walking down town yesterday via the front of the College. He replied that the leading members of the [College] faculty had given him permission to walk in the middle of the public road—newly made. This was not my understanding but if the Faculty of the College has so ruled I'll say no more about it.

Elderdice kept his word, and thereafter the college made the rules. In September 1906 President Lewis and Vice-President McDaniel gave a summary directive from the college, which Elderdice posted under the heading, "Seminary Student Privileges on the Grounds Appropriated to the Young Ladies of the College."

1. The Seminary students are permitted to go to and from the Seminary to the Dining Room direct by the entrance next to the Seminary.

2. The Seminary students may cross the grounds in front of the Main Building to reach the Boys' Walk in going to and from town, chapel or Alumni Hall only after 7 P.M. Care must be taken that there is no interference when the Young Ladies are assembling or going to and from chapel and Alumni Hall.

3. The Young Ladies' Walk from the Porch to the Arch is never to be used by the Seminary students.

4. In the event of snow-bound roads the Seminary students are to have the use of the College paths.

The most vigilant guardian of the proprieties in male-female relationships was Mary Scott, preceptress at Western Maryland College after 1900. Miss Scott was much disturbed when one of the seminary students, who traveled to Baltimore on weekends, wrote to one of the young women of the college without her parents' permission. Scott complained to Elderdice. He called the man in, lectured him roundly, and extracted from him a promise to desist or at least to ask the woman's parents for permission to take such a liberty. Then he wrote reassuringly to Scott, who in turn thanked him for his help in what she felt could have become a serious problem. In 1908 the preceptress married one of the seminary professors, Charles E. Forlines; and after he became president of the seminary in 1935, she was hostess for all social affairs in the president's house. In her entertaining one may be sure that the "proprieties" were always carefully observed.

In 1923 two women were admitted to the seminary as students, and one of them, Maybelle May Shaffer from Indiana, in 1926 became the first woman graduate. In his 1927 report Elderdice admitted, "I was slow to open the doors of the Seminary to women but the result of our first experiment is that I am eager for more." He said that women students "demonstrated the truth that 'it is not good for man to be alone' even in the sacred halls of a Theological Seminary," for the men so improved their "speech, attire and conduct that I have eliminated from our curriculum that ancient classic: Miller on Clerical Manners and Habits." Elderdice was evidently trying to season a heavy report with a light word. He was more forthright in 1926 when answering an inquiry from a prospective student in New Jersey. He wrote that the seminary admitted women to the Degree Course if they were college graduates or to the Diploma Course if they lacked a college degree, and that they were free to "enter any field of Christian service, including the ministry." He then added:

> My personal opinion is that as a rule woman's normal work is in the home and not in the pulpit. There may be notable exceptions to this rule. If she prefers to work outside the home then some kind of special service, missionary activity, or religious education would be preferable to the official ministry.

The following year Elderdice was in London and went to Guild House, where he heard the renowned Maude Royden preach. To his daughter Dorothy he wrote, "I admit [she] disarmed some of my prejudice against women preachers."

No problem seems to have been too great for Elderdice's counseling skills, or at least he never backed away from an unpleasant situation. Some cases were difficult, others delicate, and some merely vexing; but he duly recorded them all in the "office file." Once, when a married student confessed that he was living in adultery, Elderdice summarized the substance of his dealings with the man in Hebrew characters, a transliteration which guaranteed confidentiality and kept the scandal from the channels of gossip. To another student he wrote, "I thank God for your strong animal passions," and then lectured him sternly on self-control. When one Sally wrote to him about a student who had expressed his love for her but seemed to have no serious intentions (he "falls in love with every girl he meets"), Elderdice noted: "I immediately called on him in his room. . . . His foolishness over women makes him not only a laughing stock but extremely offensive—I have come to regard his case as hopeless."

A wide variety of matters demanded his attention. A cheating problem disturbed him greatly, as did student delinquencies in financial obligations. He felt duty bound to exercise paternal control over students' comings and goings. A Maryland pastor once asked him, "Will you give Brother Charles Elderdice [the president's nephew] permission to leave the Seminary to fill my [preaching] appointment in Bel Air Wednesday night?" The answer was negative. "Brother Charles Elderdice has just this hour returned from North Carolina and has been absent since last Thursday and there are other reasons why he can not go." In 1904, when students complained about meals in the college dining hall, as they often did, Elderdice posted a stern warning: "I notify you that it is against the rules for any Seminary student except married men to take their meals downtown. You can stand it for a while yet, I am sure. It may be good to have a taste of the heroic if you are 'to endure hardness as a good soldier.'" When a student wrote to him at tedious length asking about the relative advantages and disadvantages of some churches he thought were "open" to him, Elderdice replied with barely veiled sarcasm: "Since you assure me that you are following the directions of the Holy Spirit in looking for new fields and are not influenced by worldly ambition or the prospect of higher salary I have no more advice to give."

Some of the students thought Elderdice was excessively vigilant over their manners, speech, and general deportment, since he never lost an opportunity to remind them of their ministerial calling and of the dignity and graces that should accompany it. One day a student referred carelessly to the apostles as "those fellows," whereupon the president rebuked him with a ten-minute lecture on the proper vocabulary for sacred subjects. But he was also skillful in teaching the amenities. In the president's home students experienced the meaning and methods of gracious hospitality as Annabel Elderdice served tea or lunch or supper to many a lonely young man. One gray November day a first-year student brought his new bride to visit his classes and mustered enough courage to take her to the president's office for an introduction. A few moments later Elderdice made a quick trip across the yard to his home, returned, found the couple in the library, and said, "Mrs. Elderdice would be pleased if you could join us for lunch after your next class." The noon hour following gave to the young couple a bright memory of a cheerful fire, sparkling silver and china, and warm friendliness—all creating what Marylanders like to call "a feast of reason and a flow of soul." The parsonages of many graduates reflected in years afterward the graces observed in visits to the parsonage at the seminary.

Annabel Elderdice was hostess for many guests. Dorothy Elderdice recalled that the Board of Governors formed an important part of her parents' circle. They were often "dropping in" to show their friendly interest. The big dinner for them at noon on the day of commencement had to be planned "for twenty or more guests, depending on how many wives decided to come at the last minute." On such occasions, George Bell, "the venerable and beloved janitor, would don a white coat to play butler." Walter Sims followed Bell and was the dependable custodian of grounds and buildings for twenty-five years; he too could put on the white coat whenever the occasion required it. The whole seminary community appreciated both of these men and cherished fond memories of their faithful service.

Except in the family and among a few friends, the president was always "Dr. Elderdice." A nephew's letter begins "Dear Uncle Hugh," and one friend of many years wrote to him as "Dear Lat.," but such informalities were rare. As he walked down Main Street, his black hat, black suit, cane, and white mustache advertised the quiet dignity of a "gentleman of the old school"—a description he liked to apply to others when expressing his approval. But dignity never obscured the kindness in him nor limited the pleasure of his company. People crossed the street to greet him, and every shop and store and office welcomed his visits. His gentle jokes seasoned wise counsel, and genuine sympathy softened every reproof.

The lecturer and preacher

President Elderdice became the most celebrated lecturer and preacher in his denomination. More "itinerant" in his extensive travels than any pastor in the itinerancy, he did not always need or want a new message. If he deemed a sermon or lecture effective, he would repeat it, in some cases many times, and many of his more popular deliverances acquired a wide notoriety. *The Methodist Protestant Recorder* of 23 September 1938 looked back over his preaching career:

> Throughout the 57 years of his ministry, Dr. Elderdice kept a faithful record of his preaching dates, places and subjects. The grand total is 3,153. The last recorded sermon was at Sandy Mount Church on the occasion of the 110th anniversary of the church. His sermon was *The Beautiful Gate,* preached for the 152nd time. . . . *The Invisible Christ* was the sermon most frequently preached. It was delivered 244 times in 16 states and the District of Columbia. *The Royalty of Service* is second on the frequency list. It was preached 214 times.

His lecturing record is similar, for in that age of Chautauqua and Lyceum circuits, his position as head of the one Methodist Protestant seminary and his pleasing platform skills put him much in demand.

Elderdice's best-known popular address was entitled "Old

Sweethearts," and it was given, according to his notation, 124 times over a period of forty-five years. In 1904, James H. Straughn, a Methodist Protestant pastor in Lynchburg, Virginia, invited Elderdice to give the "Old Sweethearts" lecture there. Elderdice agreed, but only on condition that it not be published, presumably because that would mean he could not continue repeating it in person. Newspapers, nevertheless, did report it, often in great detail. The Steubenville (Ohio) *Herald-Star* for Saturday, 27 February 1926, gave an account of the previous evening:

> The audience assembled at the First Methodist Protestant Church last evening enjoyed an unusual lecture replete with pathos, philosophy and laughter. It was given by Rev. Hugh Latimer Elderdice, D.D., L.L.D., of Westminster, Md. under the auspices of the Christian Endeavor Society.
>
> Dr. Elderdice proved to be a pleasing speaker and brought a wealth of experience gleaned out of his life as a minister and theological seminary president for 29 years. His subject was "Old Sweethearts." He stated that the lecture was delivered the first time 35 years ago.

The article proceeded to summarize the main points of the speech and concluded by noting that "Dr. Elderdice is remaining in the city and will preach in the Sunday morning service of the church upon "Looking Like Jesus."

The last time Elderdice gave the lecture was at a Valentine's Day party at the seminary in 1936. He shortened it considerably for the occasion but kept the introduction he most often used.

> Forty-five years ago on the 12th of next month, I delivered this lecture in the Mt. Tabor Church, Washington.
>
> The effect on my audience I do not know; but it so bewildered me that I lost my way home. Instead of taking the midnight train to Baltimore I entered another one which landed me next day near a cozy cottage. . .among the mountains of Pennsylvania. There I found my Dulcinea. Something happened. I asked no question; she gave no answer. But somehow, some way I know not why—within three months she was my Kitchen Cook, my Parlor Queen—and within a year the Angel of my Nursery.

Unaware of what a later age would call patriarchal sexism, he sincerely sought to convey his profound gratitude for a loving wife, a strong marriage, and a Christian home.

Another lecture Elderdice gave often was on Robert Burns. This one he usually reserved for women's literary societies, poetry clubs, college literary societies, and men's service clubs (Rotary and Kiwanis). When asked why Burns was his favorite poet, he responded in an editorial for *The Methodist Protestant* of 6 December 1927. There were three reasons: he loved the man, he admired his poetic style, and "his messages suit my moods." Elderdice particularly appreciated Burns's religious poems.

> Though dissipated and immoral he was never an unbeliever. He was "impatient of scoffers and skeptics." In *The Cotter's Saturday Night* he portrays the God-fearing home and the family altar in language that would have made him immortal even if he had never written any other poem. Nor is there found in any devotional Literature a prayer more fervent than the one he composed when he believed he was facing death: O Thou Unknown Almighty cause of all my hope and fear. . . .

Elderdice was reluctant to lecture in the church sanctuary, preferring rather a rented hall. The pulpit, he felt, should be reserved for the preaching of the gospel. Preaching was, in truth, his first love. As a "practical" preacher, he was neither theologian nor philosopher in the professional sense, but he made skillful use of the best scholarship he could find from those who were. The seminary's archives contain a vast collection of his sermons, carefully collated by Dorothy Elderdice; they are written in impeccable, somewhat florid penmanship, large and clean for easy pulpit reading. Sometimes quaint, often profound, and always interesting, his sermons reveal intense moral earnestness, expert knowledge of the Bible, and deep commitment to make Christian teaching the rule of all life. Reluctant to define "Christian teaching" narrowly, he drew upon the whole of the biblical record and the subsequent history of Christianity. He dwelt long on the life and death of Jesus and on the apostolic witness to Jesus as the Christ. Although he loved the Old Testament prophets and preached often from their books, his favorite texts came from the Sermon on the Mount.

On the first Sunday of every May it was the president's

solemn duty to preach a baccalaureate sermon to the graduates. There are thirty-five such sermons, the composing of which he described as "going through the swithers" because they had to be written in the turmoil of preparation for commencement and the Board of Governors meeting. His method of selecting subjects and texts was a bit "whimsical," as he confessed, but nonetheless effective. He called his plan "The Minister's Alphabet," and on the occasion of his twenty-sixth baccalaureate in 1923 he explained how it worked. The first year he had selected a subject beginning with the letter "A," the second year "B," and so on through the alphabet. "Little did I dream a fourth of a century ago," he confessed, "that I would preside long enough to preach on Z"; but with twenty-five years behind him, he could survey the whole list with satisfaction:

> A. Anointed—The Minister's Call (1898). "He hath anointed me to preach the Gospel" (Luke 4:18).
>
> B. Banners—The Minister as Denominationalist (1899). "In the name of our God we will set up our banners" (Prov. 20:5).
>
> C. Comfort—The Minister as Sympathizer (1900). "Comfort ye my people saith your God, Speak ye comfortably to Jerusalem" (Isa. 40:1). . . .

In 1921, confronted with the letter "X," he admitted that there was no word in the Bible beginning with that letter, so he resorted to the sound with the word "excellent" and preached on "Excelsior: The Minister's Heaviest Asset," based on I Corinthians 12:31, "Yet I show unto you a more excellent way." When with "Z" he ran out of letters, he had eight more baccalaureate sermons to preach. But by that time the "swithers" were long gone and he needed no "whimsical" mnemonics.

Elderdice was generous with his sermon outlines. He offered them freely to all and urged his students especially to use them. They did, Sunday after Sunday, borrowing texts and topics from his blackboard models. For the Methodist Protestant Young People's Day in 1933, he prepared a sermon outline which was mailed to pastors across the church "for all those electing to use it." The subject was "Serving Christ by Serving Man," based on the text, "Inasmuch as ye have done it unto one of the least of these my brethren, ye have done it

The Subject is: Looking Like Jesus.

"Does Jesus Look like any one WE Know?"

This was the question of a little girl, at her mother's knee, at the close of an Evening Prayer.

unto me" (Matt. 25:40). After setting forth the interpretation of the biblical passage, he listed some "practical lessons": there is a difference between worship and service, neither philanthropy nor "mere morality" by themselves can secure salvation, and serving Christ by serving people in need is the creed of all Christendom. His illustrations included references to Milton, Abou ben Adhem, Charles Dickens, Father Damien, Clara Barton, and Jane Addams, along with a "Russian legend" about a poor peasant who gave his coat to a freezing soldier and found, when he went to heaven, that Jesus, the King of Glory, was wearing it. This was the kind of material that almost any busy pastor could use with gratitude.

Students learned from their president's preaching that sermons must be more than moral platitudes and clever uses of texts and stories. All world events of the day were subjects for serious examination, and Elderdice applied to them his convictions about the Christian life. Wars, depressions, strikes, the Titanic, Prohibition, women's suffrage, the League of Nations, the Interchurch World Movement, criminal justice, the Scopes Trial, the World Conference on Faith and Order— all these and much more, his students learned, were themes for their pulpits as well as for his. If they followed his example, and most of them did, they became known as moderately conservative pastors, biblically grounded but not biblical literalists, orthodox adherents to the Apostles' Creed but avoiding the extremes of Fundamentalism, modernism, holiness sects, Unitarianism, and Roman Catholicism. They knew no solution for the problems of poverty except the traditional "Protestant ethic" and the benevolence of the rich; the Social

Gospel was still suspect. Most of them were content to heed Elderdice's admonition (quoting Alexander Pope): "Be not the first by whom the new are tried, / Nor yet the last to lay the old aside."

The moderate churchman

The strong currents of the Fundamentalist controversy swirled inescapably about every enterprise of theological education during the years of Elderdice's presidency. The crucial role of the seminary and the high visibility of its president made his office something of a lightning rod for critics and fault-finders from all quarters. With the ability to turn the seminary in any one of several directions with equal ease, Elderdice chose to mark out a moderate middle way of evangelical orthodoxy without surrendering to either rigid Fundamentalism or the naturalistic reductions that marked some of the modernist camp. As an educator in a confessedly conservative denomination, Elderdice was not afraid of any honest search for truth. Although he had little affinity with Fundamentalism's concepts of biblical literalism, verbal inerrancy, and a closed revelation, he could not alienate his church, nor did he wish to. He never doubted his own orthodoxy nor that of his faculty, and he always insisted that the seminary's teaching was truly scriptural, apostolic, and soundly Methodist. A regular contributor to the seminary, Hattie Bollinger, who often sent long letters from her world travels, wrote from Australia in 1904 that she was anxious about an archaeological expedition to Queensland and its possible damage to biblical truth. Elderdice reassured her: "I suspect that it will be many a day before it can be proven scientifically that Queensland was originally the Garden of Eden. . . . I want you to know that the Seminary is orthodox on all subjects."

But there were many who could not tolerate any openness toward new ideas about theology or the Bible, especially in the tensions of the 1920s. Letters of inquiry and sometimes of accusation came regularly to Elderdice's desk. "It is a sad fact indeed (but nevertheless true)," wrote John Seaman of Hollisterville, Pennsylvania, in 1921, "that our own Seminary is advancing a great many . . . [heretical] theories." Seaman said that preachers should preach the Word of God and the facts recorded in the Bible, "not the theories men may advance in regard to Scripture." Elderdice replied by return mail:

> You are mistaken. No teacher here teaches as a fact what he knows is only a theory. My classroom policy is to give all views of a subject and the arguments for and against, and end the discussion with the view that meets my judgment . . . and I urge [the students] to study for themselves and accept that interpretation into which they are led by their own study and prayer for the guidance of the Holy Spirit—the true test of a Christian is the possession of the Spirit of Christ.

The exchange with Seaman is typical of many exchanges in a time when "modernism" was a common topic in the churches. So many rumors and charges were noised around that in December 1921 the Eastern Conference demanded an investigation of the doctrines being taught at the seminary. Elderdice prepared a statement which he sent to the Board of Education of the Methodist Protestant Church, along with a request that the board transmit the statement to the General Conference for approval. He then wanted it published in all the denomination's papers. The statement set forth the seminary's approach to controversial views and added that if any faculty member were charged with heresy, the president would demand a trial; and if the accused professor were found guilty by the highest official authority of the church, Elderdice would demand his resignation—and offer his own at the same time. Needless to say, the thought of losing Elderdice was, in the minds of the board's leaders, more disconcerting than the suspicion of a few lurking heresies. When the Executive Committee met in Pittsburgh on 21 December 1921, it voted "its absolute confidence in the Seminary and in the members of the Faculty" but decided against publishing Elderdice's paper. George H. Miller, secretary of the board, recorded that "there was a fear among the brethren present in the meeting that the publishing of this paper in our church organs might arouse a discussion that would be harmful."

The Board of Education undoubtedly exercised a wise discretion in deciding not to spread Elderdice's statement through the "church organs." Besides, no official apologia for the seminary's theological stance would have quieted the rumblings of suspicion that spread through all denominations in the 1920s. Dr. S. S. Stanton, a venerable member of the Indiana Conference and a leader in that body's determination to uproot the teaching of evolutionary theories in the church's schools, wrote to Elderdice that he believed Adrian and Westminster were "tainted" with heresy. Elderdice promptly invited Stanton to the seminary to air his views, and Stanton gave three rousing lectures on "The Scientific Validity of Genesis." Elderdice thanked him gravely and said, "You've told us things we've never heard of before." Elderdice could always count on the support of his old friend, mentor, and predecessor, Thomas Hamilton Lewis, who had retired from the presidency of the college in 1920 and was now living in Washington, DC. In 1923, when criticisms of the seminary were mounting, Lewis wrote to Elderdice: "Let me advise you to go ahead as if all were praising. Don't lower your crest for nincompoops."

It is likely that conservative anxiety was increased by the presence of Montgomery J. Shroyer on the faculty after 1919. Coming from Yale and showing unmistakable signs of commitment to the Social Gospel, Shroyer always gave a light touch to the stuffy traditions of orthodoxy while discomfiting Fundamentalists with his deft humor. In the summer of 1921, while studying at Garrett Biblical Institute, he wrote to Elderdice about his courses—Judaism during the Intertestamental Period, Religious Leaders of the Hebrews, The Lord's Prayer, and The Country Church. He disclosed that he had made a pilgrimage to Zion, Illinois, "the city of [John Alexander] Dowie—beautiful, beautiful Zion with its ugly welcoming sign to unregenerate Gentiles." He added, "I will study the House of David in Benton Harbor [Michigan], then after taking a few lectures over at Moody [Bible Institute] I think I will be in shape to teach in good orthodox style next fall." In Shroyer's home state of Indiana, where arch-Fundamentalist J. C. McCaslin was demanding the removal of modernists from Methodist Protestant schools, Shroyer in particular was suspect. Walter Williams, a friend of both Shroyer and McCaslin, once asked Shroyer, "Did Joshua make the sun stand still?" When Shroyer answered with a simple negative, Williams said reassuringly,

"Well, I'll never mention it."

Elderdice affirmed the same biblical basis for the seminary's teaching that was used by his Fundamentalist inquisitors. When one asked, "Does your Seminary instruct in Dispensational Truth?" Elderdice replied, "Our instruction includes every truth taught in the Bible." When asked, "Does Westminster believe in the literal, actual, and imminent return of our Lord Jesus Christ?" he answered, "Westminster believes every Biblical revelation on this subject." The somewhat snide question, "Is a student at Westminster required to wade through the infidelic slush of modern criticism?" received the reply:

> We do not require a student to wade through any kind of "slush"—whether higher or lower criticism, or any other kind of criticism. But we do require all students to be able to quote the views of those who deny Biblical truth and to answer correctly their false arguments and state exactly the true teachings of the Bible.

The questioner persisted, "Do you believe in the unqualified verbal inspiration of the Bible?" and Elderdice responded, "I do not believe in 'unqualified verbal inspiration' in a passage like Psalm 114:4—'The mountains skipped like rams and the little hills like lambs.'" Sensing that his correspondent might be a prospective student, he added:

> If you have made up your mind what you will and will not believe concerning the Bible, I advise you not to come to the Seminary. The purpose of going to school is to learn what you do not know. He that knows all that is to be known and has all the grace that can be received, needs no more. . . . Our motto is that of Paul, "Prove all things; hold fast that which is good" (I Thess. V:21).[7]

When faced with the trends in mass evangelism, Elderdice seemed to hesitate. He had respected Dwight L. Moody, but "since Moody died [in 1899] there is no evangelist with whom I am acquainted that I would invite to my parish." In 1907, when invited to assist in a revival in North Carolina, he wrote: "Please understand that I am not an evangelist and have no special qualifications for revival work; so all that I can promise to do is preach the simple Gospel in my own way." The hundreds of his sermons in the seminary library exhibit many homiletical skills, but the evangelistic emphases and practices

90

of the early twentieth century are not evident among them. He was equally cool toward the doctrine of sanctification advocated by the holiness movement. When he was asked to recommend books on the subject and to state his view, he told his inquirer to read "Pope, Miley, and Field, *The Tongue of Fire* by William Arthur, and *The Spirit of God* by G. Campbell Morgan." He then added his own view: "In all my study I have found no foundation for the theory of sanctification by means of a second blessing."

In philosophy Elderdice felt and often expressed his own shortcomings. In an honest attempt to keep informed about contemporary thought, he turned to old Yale friends for help. Writing on 29 May 1925 to "My dear Patrick" (George Thomas White Patrick, professor of Philosophy in the University of Iowa), he expressed gratitude for Patrick's gift of his newly published *Introduction to Philosophy* and promised to "give it my best thought not only because I need its instruction and inspiration but also because of the sentimental considerations which arise from personal contact with the author—especially with his boxing gloves in old West Divinity Hall." But Elderdice's stronger reason for writing was to request Patrick's help on a paper that Elderdice was preparing on "Modern Philosophical Tendencies."

> I am to read it before a convocation of the theological presidents and professors of every denomination and of every shade of opinion from the most bilious fundamentalist to the most unbridled modernist. For the last twenty-nine years my work has been in the department of Practical Theology and I have given little thought to the coming and going of Philosophical thought. . . . My general view is that Science correctly demonstrated, Philosophy logically declared and Theology sanely taught must be harmonious— for truth is truth wherever found and He who is the Source and Revealer of Truth is not a God of confusion.

Apparently Elderdice had considerable confidence in the judgment of Boston's Edgar Sheffield Brightman, whose *Introduction to Philosophy* had been reviewed in *The Congregationalist*. He wrote to Brightman in 1925, confessing again his limitations in philosophy and asking Brightman to supply the titles of "two or three books recently written, by purely mechanistic, or distinctly anti-religious and anti-Christian, philosophers and specify to which philosophical school each belongs. I am especially eager to learn the arguments of any who either directly or indirectly attack any of the formulated faiths of the Church.''

Elderdice's diffidence disappeared when, in the familiar precincts of his own church, he was asked to recommend books for ministers. Thomas H. Lewis sought his help in revising the Conference Course of Study in 1920, and he responded with two terse paragraphs. First, negatively, he said that Wesley's theology is too antiquated, Drinkhouse's *History* (of Methodist Protestants) too prolix, Nicolas's *Helps to Bible Study* inadequate; *Mental Science* is an obsolete term, Barrows's *Sacred Geography* has outlived its day, and Miley's *Theology* is too philosophical for untrained minds absent from a teacher. Then, positively, he advised Lewis to select a modern and readable volume of systematic theology, a sane work on psychology, a comprehensive history of missions, a condensed work on social service, and ''last and best,'' a good book on rural church problems. The fact that he did not prescribe specific titles suggests that knowing precisely what he did not like, he remained open to broad-gauged works of contemporary appeal.

The Methodist Protestant Recorder for 1 January 1921, commenting on the recent dedication of the new seminary building, summarized as clearly as a short statement could the school's stance in the Elderdice era: ''The young man who goes to Westminster will find the citadels of his faith are not to be assailed there by the wavering opinions of the mere explorer, but guarded at every gateway by the established convictions of an evangelical Christianity.'' Again and again Elderdice repeated the seminary's position in terms his church could understand. In 1921 a worried mother in Pennsylvania addressed to him many pages on her suspicions about ''modernism'' at the seminary, adding her own views about the return of Christ, the Virgin Birth, biblical inspiration, and other Fundamentalist beliefs, including even her own unfavorable opinion of Seventh-Day Adventists. Patiently the president replied as he had so many times before:

Westminster Theological Seminary when it was organized in 1882 placed upon its seal the declaration of its doctrine as expressed in I Cor. 1:24, "Christ the power of God and the wisdom of God." . . . These words of Paul are sealed upon the diploma of every man who graduates and goes on to preach the Gospel. Moreover, in all our studies we adopt as our motto the motto of St. Paul in I Thess. 5:21, "Prove all things; hold fast to that which is good."

A measure of the respect which Elderdice earned for the integrity of his moderate stance may be seen in the fact that the Methodist Protestant Church chose him as its delegate to two successive world conferences on Faith and Order, the first at Lausanne in 1927 and the second at Edinburgh in 1937. On the way to Edinburgh he attended the Life and Work Conference on Church, Community, and State held at Oxford. He sent to Forlines some comments about the Oxford conference.

The seminary seal, shown here in its modern form, dates from the earliest years. Inscribed in Greek is a portion of 1 Corinthians 1:24, "Christ the power of God and the wisdom of God."

> On the whole it was a remarkable meeting. . . . I am inclined to believe that our work at Edinburgh will not have as smooth sailing. . . . Oxford (emphasizing life and work) dealt with the heart and hand, while Edinburgh (emphasizing creed) must tackle the head. You know the average man will fight harder for his creed than for his ethics.

Elderdice's full reports on these meetings appeared in several issues of *The Methodist Protestant* in 1927 and *The Methodist Protestant Recorder* in 1937. They show a keen understanding of the discussions and a sensitive interpretation of the variant points of view. Judiciously seasoned with his own brand of humor, the reports also demonstrate a remarkable consistency in his own theological perspective, the moderate convictions by which he guided the seminary for thirty-five years.

In 1932 the seminary ended its first half-century of existence. The *50th Annual Catalogue of the Westminster Theological Seminary of the Methodist Protestant Church: The Golden Jubilee*—forty-seven pages, with gold cover and many photographs—is a handsome record of the years of hard work that had brought forth a now solidly established "school of the prophets." The ministers on the Board of Governors were John M. Gill of Baltimore, who had been on the board since 1900 and its president for twenty years; Joseph W. Kirk of Denton; Dwight Custis of Toronto, Ohio; John Williams of Middletown, Ohio; L. E. Bee of Fairmont, West Virginia; and, of course, Elderdice, ex officio. The laymen were J. E.

Cunningham of Pennsboro, West Virginia; F. R. Harris, M.D., of Henderson, North Carolina; George K. Mather of Westminster; and Fred Herrigel of Newark, New Jersey. Pliny Fisher, on the board since 1901, had just died. Gill was still president, Mather treasurer, and Elderdice secretary—a distribution of duties that would continue another half-dozen years.

The Golden Jubilee catalog listed a full-time faculty of five: Elderdice in Hebrew and Practical Theology, Forlines in Systematic and Historical Theology, Shroyer in Biblical Theology and Christian Sociology, Holloway in New Testament Greek (with some work in Hebrew), and Dorothy Elderdice in Public Speech and Church Drama. Several special lectures were announced on missions, evangelism, ministerial etiquette and ethics, the rural church, and pastoral work. The curriculum still had its traditional eight fields of study (Old Testament, New Testament, Historical Theology, Systematic Theology, Practical Theology, Public Speech, Religious Education, and Christian Missions) and the same four programs of study (Degree, Diploma, Graduate, and Special). But there was a striking change in the school's statement of purpose. The old intention of "preparing men for the actual work of the ministry" was displaced by a new wording: "designed for both men and women and for both clerical and lay Christian workers." Units of study were now to be measured in credit-hours, with ninety-six credits required for graduation. Some courses were becoming elective, permitting students some choice of subjects along with those in the required "core." The seminary would admit "men and women of all evangelical faiths," and admission requirements still reflected Elderdice's standards. "Applicants must present certificates or letters certifying to their Christian character and approving their purpose in preparing for definite Christian service." They must also "furnish to the Faculty satisfactory evidence that they possess such education as will qualify them to accomplish the required work."

Student costs reflected conditions of the depression. Tuition was one hundred dollars, with room, heat, electricity, and "Janitor's attention" an additional fifty dollars. Some returning students were happy to read that they were no longer required to eat in the college dining hall but that board could be secured "in restaurants and in private homes in town at reasonable rates." Books still cost about fifteen dollars a year. The total of scholarship funds available for 1931-32 was $4,363 in contrast to $300 the year Elderdice became president. Sixty-four students were enrolled, a sharp contrast to the five uncertain youths Elderdice found on the day of his arrival in 1897.

The clearest evidence of what Elderdice had done was seen in the physical facilities. The new building in brick and stone crowned the seven-acre hill, and a spacious brick home for the president stood close by. Three faculty residences bordered the campus, and the whole setting with its ancient trees and old-world architecture presented a picture of stability and security unknown in the school's early years. It seemed hard to recall the anxieties, disappointments, sacrifices, and miracles behind the achievement.

And now, retirement. In 1932 the president was seventy-two, and he knew it was time to turn his post over to another. Twice he had asked the board to let him go; twice they had urged him to stay one more year. But now at last they released him and made him president emeritus, although he continued to teach some Hebrew and Practical Theology. He moved his family from the "parsonage" they had enjoyed for eight years to the home he had built on West Green Street. Teaching, preaching, lecturing, and traveling to represent his church in various assemblies, he seemed as busy as ever. But soon the walks with hat and cane down Main Street or to Seminary Hill became increasingly infrequent. His wife Annabel died in 1935, and three years later he was gone, quietly. His daughter Dorothy wrote down his last words. "Every man to his post," he said softly; "there is rest for the weary—there is rest for me." The Elderdice era had ended.

4

Depression, church union, and war

It was not necessary for the Board of Governors to look far or long for a successor to Hugh Latimer Elderdice. The retiring president simply told the professor of Greek and Hebrew that he was the one, and hurrying to the board meeting already in session, proposed his name. Before Professor Holloway could recover from surprise, he was informed that he had been elected unanimously as the fourth president of Westminster Theological Seminary.

Fred Garrigus Holloway

Fred Garrigus Holloway was born in 1898 in Newark, New Jersey. After earning the A.B. degree at Western Maryland College in 1918, he attended Westminster Seminary for one year and then transferred to Drew, where he received the B.D. degree in 1921. He served Methodist Protestant churches in Wilmington, Baltimore, and Arlington (Virginia) before coming to Westminster in 1928 to teach biblical languages. At the time of his election to the presidency, he was thirty-four years old. Elderdice had been thirty-seven when he became president, and the board could have expected that this was the beginning of another long term in that office. But Holloway stayed only three years. As the first seminary president, Thomas H. Lewis, had done in 1886, he left in 1935 to become president of Western Maryland College. In 1947 he became dean of Drew Theological Seminary, then president of Drew University, and in 1960 bishop of The Methodist Church for West Virginia.

Holloway's inauguration and the close of the seminary's Golden Jubilee were observed together on 30 September 1932. The academic procession, greetings from representatives of colleges and other seminaries, a speech by Professor William J. Thompson from Drew, Holloway's Inaugural Address, and a Golden Jubilee luncheon with President Emeritus Elderdice as toastmaster highlighted the festivities. It was a day of promise and high hopes. Holloway spoke on "Adequate Motivation for the Task of the Ministry," deftly joining the two themes that Methodists were beginning to emphasize: the necessity for individual goodness and the church's need to develop a social consciousness on such matters as world peace, racial equality, and economic justice. "We can not make a socially righteous nation out of personally unrighteous individuals," he said; nor can individual piety alone suffice to solve the pressing social problems of the time. Prominent in Holloway's address were contemporary phrases like "awakened conscience" and "internal motivation," which tended to update old ideas and give them appropriate academic standing.

The seminary's fourth president was Fred Garrigus Holloway (1898—), who had taught New Testament since 1928. Although he served only three years before assuming the presidency of Western Maryland College in 1935, he raised academic standards and strengthened the seminary's standing among American theological schools.

But no one could update the church's official vocabulary with one speech. That spring, reporting to the General Conference on Holloway's election, the denomination's Board of Education had expressed its hope for the newly chosen president in characteristically quaint style: "May he prove to be the worthy Timothy, treading in the pathway marked out by our noble Paul." Both Elderdice and Holloway may have been somewhat uncomfortable with this apostolic comparison, but one line of the board's 1932 report was acceptable in any style: "Westminster Seminary has just closed its 50th year and best year without debt." Although the next year's report of a small deficit was less encouraging, student enrollment reached seventy, "the largest yet." The deficit disappeared in 1934, although enrollment fell off slightly to sixty-four.

Fred Holloway brought to Westminster a unique combination of scholarly and literary gifts united with exceptional administrative skills. During his brief presidency the seminary moved toward palpably higher academic standards, and at the same time it embraced more contemporary modes of thought in theology and social analysis. Instruction began to incline

Winifred Jackson Holloway, wife of the president, played the role of Mary in the nativity pageants of the 1930s.

perceptibly away from the older interpretations of traditional orthodoxy. Holloway developed a noteworthy competence in the field of literature, and his lectures on American poets were in wide demand. Whereas Burns and Browning had given words to Elderdice's thoughts, Holloway was more at home with Emily Dickinson and W. H. Auden. His readings from Dickinson were always popular with college audiences, leading a seminary student of 1935 to observe, "Wherever two or more are gathered together, there is Holloway in the midst of them entertaining." Furthermore, it was commonly said that the new president possessed no gifts of his own greater than his good fortune in having Winifred Jackson Holloway as his wife. Her gracious presence added to both seminary and college parsonages in turn a charm seldom equalled, a blessing he was always quick to acknowledge.

Holloway, as all presidents before him had done, continued to teach. Very much at home in the classroom, he devoted considerable time and effort to raising the standards of scholarship in the seminary. Since the resources of the school were not really adequate to sustain a doctoral program with integrity, the S.T.D. degree was quietly dropped in 1934. At the same time the catalog announced that students would be admitted to the S.T.M. program only if their work for the S.T.B. had been "for the most part of an A grade." But the most striking change in 1934 was the replacing of the traditional senior thesis in both the Degree (S.T.B.) and Diploma programs with a required practicum in Field Work. The shift marked a determined effort by the seminary to maintain rigorous standards of classroom work and at the same time to educate its students for effective pastoral ministry. As the catalog described it, Field Work was intended to serve the purpose for seminarians that an internship served in the educating of physicians.

> Each graduating senior will be assigned to a church where he shall act in the capacity of assistant to the pastor for a period of three months and shall be responsible to the work of that church from Friday to Monday of each week. The work thus done shall be correlated to the work of the Seminary by the Professor of Practical Theology or another member of the Faculty to whom he may be assigned. At the

expiration of this period, each student will present a report analyzing the problems of the modern church as he now sees them, and setting up the methods by which he believes these may be overcome.

Although it was listed as a course for purposes of record-keeping, Field Work was a non-credit experience required of all seniors.

In 1935, Holloway's last year as president, prerequisites for admission to the Diploma Course were raised to include at least two years of college work. A statement recommending pre-theological studies of a "broad, cultural type" to "concur with the position of the [other] theological seminaries of this country" was to expand in succeeding years into a detailed description of the type of college program that would best prepare a student to enter the seminary. (The statement on pre-seminary studies recommended by the American Association of Theological Schools appeared first in the catalog of 1946.) By the close of the decade Holloway's efforts to raise academic standards had produced a requirement that S.T.B. candidates must "pass a comprehensive examination at the end of the Senior year covering the courses basic and elective in the major field over the full three years." The prospect of such an examination struck terror into the hearts of a good many seniors, but the faculty held on doggedly, describing the exam in the catalog of 1948 as designed to test

> a. The student's ability to integrate what he has learned within each of the seven fields of study;
> b. The correlation of his knowledge of these seven areas, taken as a whole;
> c. His ability to relate his fundamental theological training to the life of the Church and the function he must serve as a minister.

The seminary did not abandon comprehensive examinations until 1956, when the catalog announced simply that students would be required to demonstrate, "to the satisfaction of the faculty, the ability to relate the basic theological seminary training to the life of the church and the functions of a minister"—without specifying precisely how this might be accomplished.

Holloway made some adjustments in the teaching assignments of his small faculty. The Hebrew courses he taught

99

himself; these were no longer required but "to be arranged" for those who wanted them. Holloway's New Testament Greek for Beginners was required of Degree students without previous Greek, as was his exegesis course in the Gospel of Mark, but his course on the Gospel of John was elective. Shroyer offered the required courses on The Religion of Israel, The Apostolic Age, and New Testament Theology, along with electives on Bible Versions and Manuscripts, Old Testament Lands and Jewish History, and The Life of Jesus. Forlines taught the courses in Historical and Systematic Theology, including those required in Theism and general Church History. Elderdice, though retired, continued in Practical Theology, which included History of Preaching, Homiletics, and The Pastor and Kingdom Problems, all required; he also supervised, with the assistance of other members of the faculty, the field work experience described above. The Department of Religious Drama, Dorothy Elderdice's first love, was unique in the 1930s and offered more than was commonly found in other seminaries. She regularly taught courses in the writing and producing of plays, acting, and voice training. The Department of Religious Education offered Psychology of Religion (required) and Principles and Methods (elective), both taught by Forlines, Recreational Leadership and Story Telling by Dorothy Elderdice, a course in Christian Worship, and three courses in Christian Art.

The art courses were the creation of one of the rare souls of the Methodist Protestant Church, Dr. Richard Larkin Shipley (1879-1947). A 1903 graduate of the seminary, ordained in 1905, Shipley was the pastor successively of eight Methodist Protestant churches during his forty-two years of ministry. In the decade before the Methodist union of 1939 he was editor of *The Methodist Protestant Recorder.* Having developed early in life a love for religious art, he studied it extensively, collected a large library on the subject, and lectured on it at the seminary for fourteen years (1933-47). His first-semester course was described as "an outline of the history of Christian Art with special reference to Christ in Art. Religious and educational values in Christian Art . . . [are] illustrated by prints and stereopticon." Residents of the community often audited Shipley's courses, and he welcomed them. A lively and sparkling man, he was a close friend of Elderdice and had traveled with him in Europe and England, gleaning much of his own knowledge of Christian art from firsthand observation.

Traditionally the last and least field of the curriculum was Christian Missions. Not until the coming of Murray Thurston Titus in 1951 did this department achieve stature commensurate with its importance. Until then, offerings in Missions fell by default to Shroyer, who taught the required course in History of Religions and announced (but seldom taught) other courses in missionary history, problems, methods, and leaders. Most frequently studied were missions in Japan, which was the Methodist Protestants' principal missionary field.

In an attempt to make the seminary more useful to the church, several experimental ventures were launched in the 1930s. Correspondence courses appeared in 1933 as "a service to graduates of this Seminary and open only to those who are graduates of recognized schools of theology." Forlines offered three courses and Elderdice one, with no academic credit given. But there was so little demand for this kind of continuing education that correspondence courses were soon discontinued. In 1934 an extension summer school was tried briefly at High Point College in North Carolina, where Holloway taught Modern Preaching, Shroyer The Apostolic Church, and Forlines The Doctrine of God along with The Ministry and Psychology. The catalog for 1935 announced a summer school "for pastors and religious leaders who desire to keep abreast with modern theological study." Offered the last two weeks in August, the summer session also provided an "additional two hours of credit to students already enrolled in the Seminary." By 1942 the summer school had expanded into two terms of one month each, permitting regularly enrolled students to earn six credits per term; and in 1945 a further lengthening allowed eight credits per term, or a maximum of sixteen for the entire summer. The first summer courses were taught by President Holloway (Old Testament), Dr. John Patterson of Drew (New Testament), and Professor Forlines (Miracles in History and Recent Thought). In the fall of 1935 an extension school was begun at the Baltimore Y.M.C.A., meeting on Monday mornings for thirty weeks. The indefatigable Forlines, "lecturer for the year," offered Recent

Developments in the Idea of God in the fall and Recent Ethical Thinking in the spring. The fee for this course was five dollars for a semester of fifteen weeks.

In the depression decade seminary studies were not easily made "to serve the present age." A new vocabulary was emerging out of the sorrow, fear, and anger evoked by such things as the Lindbergh kidnapping, bank failures, the "Bonus Army" encamped in Washington, the dust bowl disasters in the Midwest, and the lamentable (to many) repeal of Prohibition. Westminster people talked of the New Deal, the Good Neighbor policy, emergency relief, Social Security, unemployment, and the "packing" of the Supreme Court. They adjusted to "government by alphabet" as PWA, WPA, TVA, RFC, and many other new federal agencies came into existence. Seminary teaching was somewhat more relevant to all the turmoil and confusion of social change than the course titles imply. Certainly Shroyer never missed a chance to apply the gospel to contemporary life, and Holloway was often "viewed with alarm" by conservatives who sought reassurance through the traditional platitudes. But constituent support for the seminary remained remarkably steady throughout the decade.

Charles Edward Forlines

Most Methodist Protestants were pleased to have a man of Holloway's stature at the head of their seminary, and therefore they were considerably dismayed when he resigned in 1935 to accept the presidency of Western Maryland College. Their dismay was no greater than their surprise over the identity of his successor. Charles Edward Forlines (1868-1944) had been quietly teaching Systematic and Historical Theology at Westminster for twenty-nine years, and probably he was as astounded as any when the Board of Governors asked him to assume the presidency. His innate modesty and gentle reticence had to be worn down, and rumor had it that Mary Scott Forlines was useful to that end. She knew her husband's real abilities.

There are accents of Dickens in the Forlines story. Many throughout the church were familiar with it, for he had occasionally shared with students and others recollections of his boyhood. He was born in Buffalo Springs, Virginia, on 2 August 1868. His father was John Wesley Forlines, a marginally successful miller and a less successful farmer. His mother, Lucy Green Yancy, died when Charles was six years old. The family moved in 1871 to North Carolina, where almost everybody went to work at an early age in the cotton mills. Charles Forlines was no exception. His first wages as a sweeper in the Belmont mill came to twenty-five cents for a twelve-hour day. For five years his regular hours were from 1:00 P.M. to 1:00 A.M. Extra duties sometimes extended his working day to eighteen hours.

Depression, Union, War

While very young, Forlines discovered in himself a love for books, but at the age of twelve he was still unable to read. After being converted during a revival, he joined a local Sunday School and began to struggle with the New Testament. At fourteen he was teaching a Sunday School class, and at sixteen he was superintendent of the Sunday School and class leader in charge of the midweek prayer meeting. A gift of ten dollars made it possible for him to attend school for two months. He read at every available moment, sometimes even at work, his hands doing the mechanical motions while his eyes followed the book. Friends said he retained all he read in an "encyclopedic mind." By the time he was sixteen he was earning $2.40 a week, while with his brother he trapped rabbits and caught fish for food and a little cash. Somehow he managed to save fifty dollars with which he entered Yadkin College, a "normal school" (or high school) operated by Methodist Protestants in North Carolina.

On borrowed money Forlines came to Western Maryland College. He graduated in 1897 with high honors but a thousand dollars in debt. Four years later he earned a degree from Westminster Seminary with yet more honors and had fifty dollars in his pockets. Returning to North Carolina, he was appointed to a rural circuit. A year later he wrote to President Elderdice: "You will find enclosed one dollar, my subscription to the Alumni Scholarship. I desire to do much more but circumstances will not now permit me." He could not have imagined then how much more he would do for the seminary and how large a part his life would have in the

103

school's history. Forlines's exceptional record in college and seminary studies had caused Methodist Protestant leaders to take note of the budding scholar in their midst. Before long he was teaching at Adrian College in Michigan. But Elderdice wanted him at Westminster, and Elderdice usually got what he wanted. Forlines came in 1906 at the age of thirty-eight and remained at the seminary for another thirty-eight years.

He loved all of God's creation. Many nights he walked with students, naming the stars and describing the various constellations. Daytime walks in fields and woods, in spring and fall and at Christmas time, evoked extempore lectures on soils, farming, animals, birds, and insects. Buster, a handsome collie, and later Laddie, added zest to the walks and routed squirrels and rabbits along the way.

Forlines was no conversationalist, but his silences were golden. Once Professor Holloway drove him to Harrisburg (about fifty miles away) and reported later that Forlines rode in silence until the return trip when, upon seeing a herd of cows in a field, he swept his arm in their direction and said cheerfully, "Cows!" This, said Holloway, was his only word on the whole journey. On the other hand, Forlines could be the life of a party. He knew all the Uncle Remus stories by heart and could recite them in the accent of his southern origins to the delight of all with whom he socialized. Children and youths loved him, and he entertained them patiently for hours with seemingly no end of stories, puzzles, tricks, and stunts. For years he held offices and directed summer camps and institutes for Christian Endeavor and the Youth Department of his church. Some of the seminary students referred to him affectionately as "Pappy," but they were careful never to let him hear it.

In the classroom Forlines's effectiveness rested on his unusually retentive memory, stored with information and ideas from continuous wide reading. His breadth of knowledge kept his peers in wonder and his students in awe. His lectures were organized in tight logical progression and presented in clear, succinct terms, with "firstly's," "secondly's," and "thirdly's" (sometimes the sequence was very long), and with no embellishments, allusions, or humor. He spoke slowly enough to permit note-taking but not boredom. His orthodoxy was matter-of-fact, never pedantic or provocative, and he always regarded his teaching as the scriptural view rather than his own. Although he would expect to be considered "conservative," he was so ingenuously open and receptive to inquiry as to preclude all bigotry.

Forlines preached and wrote as he lectured, in a simple and unadorned style. In the pulpit he exhibited not one single gift of what passed for oratory in his time—no "purple patches," no bravura, and seldom a discernible emotional climax. But his sermons were clear and logically developed; their straightforward quality reflected the integrity of the man himself. A few were published, such as "The Sovereignty of God," "God's Kingdom," "The Supreme Good," and "The Functions of the Christian Ministry." The best were collected for a volume entitled *Finding God Through Christ* (Abingdon, 1947), edited by Richard Larkin Shipley and published posthumously with a biographical introduction by Fred G. Holloway. The sermon on "The Sovereignty of God" illustrates something of Forlines's thought. Several paragraphs could have been (and probably were) taken directly from his classroom lectures on Theism. He described three "kingdoms"—the kingdom of nature, the kingdom of history, and the kingdom of grace—each governed by the almighty, eternal, omniscient, holy, and gracious God. All people are citizens of the first two kingdoms through natural birth, but it is only through spiritual birth that they become citizens of the kingdom of grace, the only kingdom that is eternal and growing.

Paraphrasing does some damage to the original material. A quoted paragraph will illustrate the short sentences and plain thoughts that were the hallmarks of Forlines's lectures and sermons. Here is the conclusion of his Baccalaureate Address on "God's Kingdom the Supreme Good," delivered to the graduating class of 1937:

Charles Edward Forlines (1868-1944) joined the faculty in 1906 as professor of Theology. In 1935 he became president and guided the seminary through the critical times of Methodist union and World War II. In 1943 he resigned the presidency and returned to full-time teaching, always his first love.

> Materially we are equipped for an Eden. We can produce and distribute all we need for creature comforts and physical protection. This we can do by a very few hours of work each week. We have gone a long way in the conquest of disease and the alleviation of pain. We have overcome the fears of superstition. We have come to understand the

nature of war, its barbarities and stupidities and the means of preventing it. We have enough expert knowledge for governing our public dealings with intelligence and efficiency. We have great schools for the instruction of our youth. We have the leisure and facilities for the highest and best culture. But there is one thing we lack—the moral and religious goodness necessary for the wise and beneficent use of these great achievements.

And he proceeded to describe the dimensions of that necessary goodness. The graduating seniors had heard this many times before; but they always listened patiently, for they remembered who was speaking to them and by what labors and difficulties he had become what he was.

Holloway's resignation became effective on 1 December 1935, and Forlines was acting president until the board met the following spring to elect him as the school's fifth president. He was not young when chosen, but nobody objected to that. The consensus seemed to be that this was an honor well deserved, an appropriate recognition of effective service, proven wisdom, and trustworthy character. It fell to Forlines to guide the seminary through the exciting years of Methodist union when the school ceased to be the only seminary of the Methodist Protestant Church and became one of ten in a mammoth new denomination.

President Forlines's first report, for the academic year 1935-36, was dismal. The faculty was "greatly weakened" by Holloway's departure, even though he continued to teach a class in Hebrew. Most of the "allotted scholastic work had been done and done well" by President Emeritus Elderdice, Professor Shroyer, Dorothy Elderdice, and (though he did not say so) Forlines himself. But the faculty was understaffed and consequently spread too thin. The resident student body was much smaller—only twenty-nine—although counting six special students and six graduates "doing in absentia work," Forlines brought the total enrollment up to forty-one. Twenty-nine of the students were Methodist Protestants, five Methodist Episcopalians, two United Brethren, two Reformed, and one each from the Church of God, the Lutherans, and the Primitive Methodists. The president explained that the small enrollment was due largely to efforts to raise academic standards by requiring students to present before admission "a more

President Forlines, like his predecessors, did most of his own secretarial work himself.

106

thorough academic training'' and ''better personal qualifications.'' This necessarily meant rejecting some applicants. The attempt to tighten admission requirements simply continued efforts initiated by Holloway in 1932.

This first report of the new president did have a few brighter paragraphs, however. The summer school was ''a great success,'' as were the extension courses at High Point College. Forlines's own extension courses in Baltimore had attracted twenty-one registrants, and he was planning another summer of extension courses at High Point. But the financial section of his report solemnly pointed to ''a real deficit'' that had required him to borrow from various funds what now would seem small amounts in order to try to keep ''the current fund'' balanced. Although this juggling had not erased all the red ink, the deficit was diminishing because students were paying up overdue accounts, and his own special appeal for contributions had brought in more than $1,400. A somewhat ambiguous consolation was that ''by the resignation of Dr. Holloway and the failure to secure another full-time member of the faculty almost $200 a month was saved in salaries.''

In reporting improvements made in his first year, Forlines made the most of some small items: a copy of *Webster's New International Dictionary* added to the library; a new typewriter and a Dalton adding machine in the office; a new pulpit Bible, new hymnals, and new chairs in the chapel; and a ''proscenium'' in the chapel given by students in the Department of Religious Drama in memory of Miss Dorothy McNurlan, ''a student of the Seminary who passed away last summer.'' Finally, the Pittsburgh Cottage (Shroyer's residence) had been repapered, a new boiler installed in the West Virginia Cottage (another faculty residence), and all the property connected to the city sewer system. A few sentences in the report dutifully noted ''spiritual life at the Seminary.'' The students had needed ''less play than usual,'' Forlines observed, because they had gotten plenty of exercise by excavating a basement with shovels and wheelbarrows to provide for a recreation room and a vault for the archives. Efforts were under way to deepen the students' devotional life through a ''greatly enriched daily worship service in chapel and weekly prayer meetings.''

Depression, Union, War

According to custom, the president's report to the board concluded with a section on "Our Pressing Needs." The first of these in 1936 concerned what Forlines had always regarded as the school's most serious weakness, the library. His own library was the core of the seminary's resources, and he himself had long been the librarian. Now he asked for "an annual income of not less than $250 for new books and periodicals [and] within the very near future a part-time librarian." He asked also for additional teaching help at once and for full-time faculty increases "in the near future." Finally, he concluded, the campus needed to be beautified. The board was well aware that the seminary needed all this and more, but resources were limited. One item, however, Forlines got without additional funds or delay. Dorothy Elderdice later reported with wry amusement that the president came to her and said, "Miss Dorothy, you will be the Librarian now." Dutifully but with little sense of pleasure or excitement, she made some hurried preparation at Enoch Pratt Library in Baltimore and added to her work in Speech and Religious Drama the duties of library cataloguing and circulation. For the next eleven years she conscientiously carried this added burden but without any real love for the assignment. She welcomed the opportunity to pass it over to Mrs. Emily Chandler in 1947.

New courses, new professors

Biblical languages, although no longer required, still enjoyed the approval of tradition and the prestige of scholarship. Herbert E. Hudgins, class of 1927, illustrates again how useful the more scholarly of the school's graduates could be. In the spring of 1936 he came to teach a course in beginning Greek at a salary of $100 a semester. After three years he returned to his pastoral assignment in the Virginia Conference. Again the college supplied a part-time Greek teacher in William R. Ridington, but for one year only. President Forlines then found another alumnus who could take on both Greek and Hebrew. Paul F. Warner was a 1921 graduate who served as a missionary in Japan, first of the Methodist Protestant Church and, after 1939, of The Methodist Church. With his keen mind, bouncing energy, and contagious humor, he was much loved at home and abroad. His wife, Dorothy Linthicum Warner, accompanied him to Westminster, and their presence on campus brought new information about Japan and a quickened interest in overseas missions. Warner came and went several times from 1931 to 1944, in between his service in a Maryland parish and further missionary work in Japan, and the seminary always considered itself fortunate to engage him for another year of teaching.

Assistant, part-time, and temporary professors multiplied as Forlines tried to "cover" the curriculum adequately. Richard Shipley was always available for another semester in Christian Art at a cost of seventy-five dollars for one day a week. From the college came Lawrence Little to teach Religious Education for three years and James Earp to teach Christian Sociology for two. Instruction in Church Music had to be improvised. Richard Weagley, the choir director at Brown Memorial Church (Presbyterian) in Baltimore, "gave one day a week to training the students in the appreciation of hymns and hymn music" at a salary of fifty dollars a semester. After one year he left to work with organist Virgil Fox at Riverside Church in New York City.

In 1936 Forlines found a "music man" among the theology students. James A. Richards had graduated from Western Maryland College with a major in music, and now he was enrolled in the Peabody Conservatory in Baltimore. He was also studying for the ministry at Westminster Seminary, so President Forlines enlisted him to teach Church Music and direct the Seminary Singers. Douglas R. Chandler, who came as professor of Church History in 1939, served as accompanist. Weekly rehearsals, chapel anthems, and concerts in nearby churches gave the Singers many memorable experiences. Forlines often traveled with the Singers to give a short talk on music or about the seminary just before the offering. Richards had a rich baritone voice, and his solos were dramatic additions to the hymns and chorales of the evening program. His "Shortnin' Bread" and "Ole Man River" were special favorites. There was universal agreement that the Singers were as good a public relations department as the seminary could want. Richards could not continue this part-time relationship indefinitely, however, and since the seminary could not afford more of his services, he left after six years. The college again came to the rescue, releasing Alfred de Long one day a week for three years to give instruction in Church Music.

Before 1938 the courses in pastoralia commonly regarded as "practical" were taught by the professors of Bible and Theology, with frequent help from visiting ministers who had achieved some success in their own churches. The seminary's first full-time professor of Pastoral Theology was John Nicholas Link (1893-1979), who came in 1938 from the First Methodist Protestant Church of Newark, New Jersey. Link's energy and ambition were evident at an early age. An article in *The Baltimore Sun,* 30 December 1910, describes him as a serious seventeen-year-old City College student who arose at three in the morning to deliver newspapers before six o'clock on his East Baltimore route. Finishing classes at 2:30 P.M., he "prepares lessons" for the next day and "studies theological books" until nearly midnight, driven by one ambition: to become a minister in the Methodist Protestant Church. "At City College," the *Sun* reporter added, "he is considered one of the best debaters and orators in the school." Link transferred to Western Maryland and graduated from both the college and seminary in 1925. After advanced study at Columbia University and Union Theological Seminary in New York, he served several churches before coming to Westminster Seminary to teach.

John Nicholas Link (1893-1973) came in 1938 as the first full-time professor of Pastoral Theology. He taught many "techniques" and furnished abundant "helps" to the students.

Link renamed his department Pastoral Theology. It always seemed clear to him that the seminary's sole function was the training of persons for the pastoral ministry, and that for this purpose his department had the major responsibility. He said once that he could see how the other disciplines—biblical, historical, and theological—naturally flowed into and supported the aims of the practical courses. His assumption sometimes nettled his colleagues, but he was so genial, helpful, and, above all, tireless that nobody wanted to engage him in controversy. By nature an intense person, he walked with quick, eager steps, always seeming to be in a hurry, and this intensity carried over into everything he did as a professor. The mimeograph machine had come into its own, and Link

110

believed sincerely in its usefulness for ministers. Students, particularly student pastors, carried reams of "helps" from his classes: sermon outlines, class notes on how to prepare sermons, illustrations, pastoral prayers, programs for every season or day in the church calendar (not excepting Mother's Day, Children's Day, Rally Day, and Harvest Home), instructions on how to conduct an official board meeting, lists of books for further reading—all these and much more he distributed in abundance to grateful students. Former students confessed that they found Link's helps useful for years after graduation. They remembered, too, his familiarity with the poems of Edgar A. Guest, for he often entertained them and other audiences with recitations of the homespun rhymes.

Depression, Union, War

Convinced as he was of his department's primary importance in the seminary's curriculum, Link worked to update it. The changes he made were not revolutionary, but he did introduce some new terms. He liked the word "techniques," and gave his courses names like Pastoral Techniques, Evangelistic Techniques, and Counseling Techniques. Counseling was a new word in seminary vocabulary, and the last-named course proposed to examine "normal and abnormal types of Christian personality . . . difficulties," emphasizing "symptoms, principles of diagnosis and counseling procedures." Link introduced another course, Sermonic Clinic, two semesters of which were required for seniors. The students, he announced, would "preach sermons of various types in the Seminary Chapel to members of the class." Evaluation and constructive criticism by professor and fellow students followed in the classroom.

After seven years, Link resigned in 1945 to return to pastoral work in the Peninsula Conference. Here his own sermons reflected the same meticulous care that he had tried to impress on students at the seminary, although they were sometimes described by friendly critics as "linkthy." He gave his church twenty more years of devoted service, was a district superintendent, and, at the last, directed and taught courses in continuing education at the Methodist retirement home in Seaford, Delaware. He died there on 2 March 1979.

Until 1939 courses in Church History were subsumed under Historical Theology, and Forlines had taught them for more than thirty years. But in that year he was able to pass this duty to another. Douglas Robson Chandler (1901—) was reared in Methodist Episcopal fundamentalism in northern New York State. After graduating from Asbury College in Kentucky, he taught English and Latin in the New York State Regents System, where he discovered the attractions of a teaching career. He returned to Asbury Seminary, however, with the pastoral ministry in mind. After one semester he departed for Westminster and a student pastorate in rural Maryland, accompanied by his new bride, Emily Morrison (daughter of Asbury's president), whom he had married in 1926. After graduating from Westminster and being ordained in 1929, he made his way to Yale, as two admired professors, Elderdice and Shroyer, had done. While in Connecticut he served the Congregational church in Trumbull, then returned to a pastoral appointment to the Methodist church in Solomons, Maryland. Chandler's election to the seminary faculty came in 1939, the year of Methodist union. This marked the first time a non-Methodist Protestant joined the seminary's full-time faculty, and it seemed a fitting symbol of union. Chandler was thirty-eight years old, as Forlines had been when he began to teach at Westminster.

The manner of Chandler's coming was "old style." After two interviews there came a brief letter from the president announcing that the board had elected him to the faculty. On an August day preceding the beginning of classes in September, Forlines gave the new professor a brief preview of the courses he would be expected to teach: Church History, of course, with a few special studies—perhaps a history of missions, a history of preaching, and most certainly Methodist History. Then in his soft southern accent Forlines added a startling demand: "There is another course we would expect you to teach, the History of Religions." In dismay but without the courage to protest, Chandler gave silent thanks for that tedious course in World Religions under John Clark Archer at Yale and agreed to do it. Later he learned that last-minute cramming to teach was not uncommon among professors, especially those without experience.

Chandler's love for Church History made him often slow to notice students' lack of enthusiasm for the subject. Yale

Douglas Robson Chandler, the first full-time professor of Church History, was also the first non-Methodist Protestant to join the faculty. His appointment in 1939, the year of Methodist union, was a fitting symbol of the broadening horizons of Westminster Seminary.

models were his inspiration, and he naively assumed that Williston Walker (the author of a durable textbook) would be enjoyed by all. Luther Weigle's course in American Church History and Roland Bainton's History of Christian Social Teachings he reproduced at Westminster as faithfully as his student notes from Yale permitted. Bainton graciously sent a lifesaving bundle of outlines, enough to guide a seminar for a whole year. Chandler's perennial offerings came to be (in addition to the required introductory survey) Reformation, Early Church, History of Christian Social Teachings, and Christian Biography. The last-named course was a long-lasting result not only of personal interest but of episcopal command, for at Chandler's appointment Bishop Edwin Holt Hughes (who after the union of 1939 included the seminary in his jurisdiction) charged him: "Young man, in your teaching make much of Christian biography." Methodist History, of course, had to be a permanent fixture, since it was required by *The Book of Discipline*. A popular adjunct to this course was the annual "Evening with John Wesley's Journal" in the Chandler home. Known as the "Pie and Journal Society"—Mrs. Chandler always served refreshments after Professor Chandler read extracts from Wesley's Journal—it became an established tradition affording sentimental pleasure along with historical appreciation for many generations of students and their spouses.

Union, war, and a change of presidents

Forlines was well into his presidency when the main divisions of American Methodism began to coalesce. Methodist Protestants had maintained a separate existence since 1830, when Episcopal Methodists spurned their cherished reforms; and their one seminary, while not exactly standing in "splendid isolation" from the rest of American Christianity, had nevertheless fought through many lonely struggles to keep alive the enterprise of theological education in the small denomination. The Methodist Episcopal Church itself divided when the internal dispute over slavery became irreconcilable, and since 1845 southern Methodists had pursued their own course as a separate church. Although the Methodist Episcopal

Church, South, suffered huge losses in the Civil War and its painful aftermath, by the twentieth century it had developed several strong institutions, including theological schools at Duke in North Carolina, Emory in Georgia, and Southern Methodist University in Texas. Meanwhile, the Methodist Episcopal Church (northern) had also expanded its institutions, as well as the means to support them; and its established theological schools in Massachusetts, New Jersey, Illinois, Colorado, and California were flourishing.

The merger of these three Methodist denominations in 1939 created a huge new organization, The Methodist Church, with more than seven million members and—what is more significant for our story—ten seminaries. For no other Methodist seminary were the conditions of existence changed so drastically as they were for little Westminster with its forty-five students and four full-time professors. Now Westminster had not only to become accustomed to bishops and all the accouterments of episcopal jurisdiction, but also to learn how to manage its affairs in the context of a large ecclesiocracy with many diverse interests. Some of the other Methodist theological schools remained accountable mainly to regional judicatories, but from the time of union Westminster was an institution of the general church. The new situation brought heightened status and a much broader base of funding, but it also brought a nexus of new and unfamiliar relationships, some of which could be (and sometimes were) competitive as well as supportive. It was President Forlines's task to pilot the seminary into these far-reaching changes, and to his credit it can be said that he met his responsibilities with wisdom, insight, and respect for the seminary's primary reason for existence.

No startling shifts in the seminary's administration or internal life occurred immediately after the union of 1939, but there were some interesting activities "in the wings." The new Board of Governors elected by the first General Conference of The Methodist Church in 1940 included several members who had not been Methodist Protestants. New names were Benjamin W. Meeks, Thomas Holt, and Lester Allen Welliver, ministers; and George W. Culberson, layman. Another new member, F. Murray Benson, was a Methodist Protestant layman, while the Methodist Protestant faithfuls who continued were Reuben Y. Nicholson and L. E. Bee, ministers; and William C. Scott and George K. Mather, laymen. At its first meeting the board acted to change the charter as required by the terms of union. When President Forlines "explained that the only change really necessary was to drop the word *Protestant* wherever it occurred," the board authorized him to have the change made and then voted that henceforth the school's new name would be "The Westminster Theological Seminary of The Methodist Church." The next question was how to defer properly to episcopal dignity, since the stiff Methodist Protestant rejection of bishops was now an anachronism. The board therefore voted "to amend the Charter so as to make the Bishop of the area an ex-officio member of the Board," and the bishop came speedily from the wings to center stage. Bishop Hughes had retired in 1940, but Bishop Adna Wright Leonard was present at the next meeting of the board in 1941 and took an active part in the deliberations (though he was not formally listed as a member until 1943).

At the 1941 meeting Forlines gave a straightforward summary of the six years he had served as president. Landscaping, new roadways, improvements to buildings, growth of the library in both books and furnishings, and an enlarged faculty were all good news. The most exciting announcements were that the seminary was now accredited by the American Association of Theological Schools and that the total endowment had increased to $151,310. A sobering report from auditors Wooden and Benson, however, called attention to an operating deficit of $3,384, which evoked "considerable discussion." But in time this small cloud dissolved and nobody seemed unduly alarmed. In high spirits the board adjourned for dinner at Westminster's Charles Carroll Hotel, guests of President and Mrs. Forlines.

At the meeting of the board's Executive Committee in February 1942, Forlines offered his resignation. He was seventy-four years old, and he noted that this was two years beyond the compulsory retirement age specified in the *Discipline*. Bishop Leonard commented that "while no one could be appointed by the Conference to any position, who had passed this age limit, [the rule] did not prevent any corporation from electing to any office such a person should they see fit to do so.'' The board did nothing until May, when, following the recommendation of its Executive Committee, it accepted Forlines's resignation with regret and elected him acting president until his successor should be installed. Gratifying announcements at this meeting were that all salaries and bills had been paid to date, student enrollment was up to seventy, salary increases of one to two hundred dollars were being provided for the faculty, and the library had received as a gift the Charles Eggleston collection of more than seven hundred volumes of valuable Methodistica.

For Forlines's successor the board turned to its own secretary, significantly one of the new members from Methodist Episcopalianism. He was Lester Allen Welliver (1896-1973), new pastor of the Pine Street Methodist Church in Williamsport, Pennsylvania. Welliver was elected at a special meeting of the board called for that purpose in March 1943. Although the procedure was straightforward enough—report of the Nominating Committee, supporting speeches by Benjamin Meeks and Bishop Leonard—there was also a letter from Welliver about some little details. How much teaching, if any, would he be expected to do? Will there be a summer session requiring his presence? Can he receive a salary of $3,600 per year with furnished house? Can the salary begin on 15 April? And will moving expenses be paid by the seminary in accordance with Methodist custom? So far as the record goes, no former president had exercised such caution and expressed it with such candor, but the board surrendered its expectations for a teaching president—a historic first—and agreed to all of Welliver's requests. Then it elected Forlines vicepresident and left details to be worked out by the two administrators.

It was the spring of 1943. Although the churches long ago had ''outlawed'' war, World War II was in its fourth wearying year. Westminster was far from Guadalcanal, El Alamein, the Maginot Line, and Stalingrad, but not so far as to escape the sound and meaning of new words like blitzkrieg, kamikaze, saturation bombing, and blackout. Common talk now dwelt on gasoline rationing, food coupons, and withholding taxes, but on Seminary Hill these topics created less anxiety than the moral dilemmas posed by the war. Of the eight professors on the faculty, six were pacifists, members of the Fellowship of Reconciliation and active in the anti-war protests of the 1940s. On 7 December 1941 several faculty families had been at the Patapsco camp for conscientious objectors and heard there in that anti-war atmosphere the stunning news of Pearl Harbor. The campus reflected strong sympathy for the Baltimore Quakers, and for many years representatives from the American Friends Service Committee visited the seminary annually, distributing its literature and answering students' questions. The Women's International League for Peace and Freedom, through its Carroll County Branch in Westminster, drew into its active circle several women of the seminary and the college.

Seminary devotional life reflected concern for the state of the world. "Cell groups" were popular, and certain hours were set apart almost daily for such groups to gather for prayer, Bible reading, silent meditation, or expressions of social concern. An all-day retreat, held annually at some nearby country church or camp, focused on Christian responsibility in a broken world. On such days students and faculty listened to well-known figures like Frank Laubach, Rufus Jones, Howard Thurman, John Oliver Nelson, and E. Stanley Jones. World events found their way into classrooms and chapel, and there were few days when "causes" and social concerns were forgotten. The general rural and "pastoral" location of Westminster could well have fostered detachment from the world and an introspection that grows in isolation, but the seminary deliberately refused to withdraw from wider concerns. Its openness to world events was reinforced by the local Methodist church, where pastor Orris G. Robinson and his wife kept social consciousness alive. There were also the Westminster Church of the Brethren, with its historic peace testimony, and the activities of Church World Service in nearby New Windsor.

On the other hand, much of the seminary's wider community had little tolerance for suggestions of social radicalism. Consequently, peace advocacy during the war years was both conspicuous and suspect. A group of conservatives visited the seminary and, in a meeting permitted by President Forlines, accused the faculty of unbiblical teachings and "red" leanings. Professor Shroyer took the occasion as an opportunity to enlarge upon the Sermon on the Mount and similar New Testament passages enjoining love for enemies and the return of good for evil. As war tensions increased, rumors spread of subversive activities at both the college and the seminary, and a local Lutheran pastor advertised that he would preach on "Carroll County Fifth Columnists." He did, but popular reaction was minimal. Student pastors reported that some of their country charges believed that Western Maryland's President Holloway had in his basement (or was it his attic?) a direct "hot line" to Hitler or to some other overseas enemy; no one seemed clear on the details, but these rumors usually aroused more chuckles than real trouble. Postwar suspicions produced another spasm of excitement in 1948 when Whittaker Chambers produced from a pumpkin on his nearby farm a microfilm of alleged State Department documents to support his accusations against Alger Hiss. College and seminary people were not involved in this except to warn occasionally against hysteria, and the commotion subsided with no permanent damage to the traditional friendship between town and gown.

At the board meeting in October 1943 retiring President Forlines made his farewell report, a summary of his eight years in office. It was a plain collection of facts in simple declarative sentences, as usual bereft of adverbs and adjectives. But the facts would show the incoming president what the seminary had become and assure him that the administration would no longer be expected to "make bricks without straw." Heading his summary "Then and Now," Forlines began:

> In 1935 I was made President of the Seminary. The Methodist Protestant Church was suffering the evil consequences of a great national financial depression. Methodist union was in the air. It seemed that the Methodist Protestant Church might let the Seminary go before the new Methodist Church could take hold of it.

That, he was happy to say, had not happened. There were many achievements to list: accreditation by the American Association of Theological Schools and approval by the University Senate of The Methodist Church; an increase in student enrollment from forty-one to seventy; paving of seminary roads and campus landscaping; construction of a basement recreation room and fireproof vault; faculty salaries raised; total receipts for operations increased by $15,000, the scholarship fund by $48,000, and the general endowment fund by $14,000; and an increase of $84,000 in the total assets of the seminary, so that they now stood at $317,000. Forlines's conclusion was completely in character.

> I salute the new President of the Westminster Theological Seminary, Dr. Lester A. Welliver, a lovable Christian gentleman, a wise and capable administrator. To him I pledge my loyal support and offer my humble services.
>
> I bid farewell to the President's Office with a profound gratitude to the Board of Governors, the Faculty and the Student Body, who have so loyally supported me, and with very deep regret that I have been unable to do more in that office for the beloved institution that has done so much for me.
>
> I welcome the opportunity to go unencumbered to my classroom to teach. For the great work of an educational institution is not done in the President's office, but in the teacher's classroom.

Forlines enjoyed his classroom only one more year. Many noticed the slowing down. There were no more long walks in fields and woods, no more Uncle Remus stories or romps with children. In 1944 President Welliver recommended that Forlines be relieved of summer school duties and sent him to Berkeley Springs for two weeks of rest. Dr. James B. Pritchard, professor of Old Testament at Crozer Theological Seminary, filled the gap in the summer school faculty. Shroyer drove Forlines to the train station and later recorded his last experiences with the weary man:

> He was quiet, as usual, and I, too, was quiet for I had long since learned that a great deal does not need to be said. We sat out on a bench at the station platform. Dr. Forlines was interested in something moving on the brick walk. . . . It looked like a leaf being blown by the wind . . . but [it was] a dried up butterfly wing [carried by] an ant trying to take it somewhere . . . working hard to move what seemed to be far beyond his strength. And watching the ant was a man who had just about used up his strength in working at hard tasks.

119

A week later Mrs. Forlines called Shroyer with an urgent request that he meet her husband, who was returning home ahead of schedule. As soon as Forlines stepped off the train, Shroyer knew that he was a very sick man. That night the stroke came, a cerebral hemorrhage, and death two weeks later. As Shroyer put it, "the man had come to the end of his pleasant tramp through God's woods." And the seminary had come to the end of another era.

5

A search for
new directions

The presidency of Lester A. Welliver was marked by significant growth in several areas: increase of student enrollment, expansion of the curriculum, addition of new faculty, rising budgets, and ever more pressing needs. Although he came to Westminster in the midst of war and had to deal with the problems which that tragedy created for the seminary, he soon made it plain that he envisioned for the school a much larger future than its present status might augur. But there were other leaders of The Methodist Church thinking about the future of Westminster too, and the clash of conflicting visions engendered a struggle over the shape and direction of the seminary's postwar development.

Welliver and
the Forward Movement Program

Lester Allen Welliver was born in Stockton, Pennsylvania, in 1896, one of a large family. His early years he described laconically: "I was a coal-town boy." He was also a Phi Beta Kappa graduate of Dickinson College and a Drew Seminary alumnus of the highest scholastic rank. Because of his outstanding record as pastor of several churches in the Central Pennsylvania Conference, he enjoyed the respect of his colleagues and the confidence of his bishop, Adna Wright Leonard. He was married to the former Eleanor Frieda Yeaworth, whose gifts and graces were the admiration of every parish they served, and Westminster received her with appreciation. As

Lester Allen Welliver (1896-1973) became president in 1943, the first non-Methodist Protestant to hold the office. During his twelve-year tenure he added to the faculty many new people from diverse backgrounds, a clear sign that union had brought Westminster into the mainstream of American Methodism.

soon as Welliver finished the conference year in April and was free to leave his church in Williamsport, Pennsylvania, he moved with his family to Westminster. The president's house was not quite ready, an unavoidable circumstance which Forlines lamented, but welcoming receptions and inaugural plans were already in the making and a feeling of happy anticipation prevailed. Especially exciting to daughters in faculty families was the discovery that the Wellivers had five handsome sons.

Inauguration Day was 29 October 1943, and October's bright blue weather seemed to portend good times ahead. For the first time it was necessary to give out "Information for Delegates": directions about registration, robing, the order of the procession, the reception at the president's home, the luncheon for official guests in the college dining hall, transportation to bus and train, and the location of the lavatories. There was some fear that little Baker Chapel might be too small for the expected crowd, but those in the overflow managed to hear and see a little from the entrances. James Henry Straughn, formerly a Methodist Protestant and now a bishop in the united church, led the Litany of Thanksgiving and Consecration; Nolan B. Harmon (soon to be elected bishop) offered the Inaugural Prayer, and Bishop Edwin Holt Hughes gave the Charge to the President—clear signs that episcopacy had prevailed over at least one Methodist Protestant tradition. Investiture was by Reuben Y. Nicholson, president of the Board of Governors, and the benediction was by the venerable Charles E. Forlines. Bishop Leonard's absence was noted with sorrow; he had been killed the preceding summer in a plane crash in Iceland while on a mission for President Roosevelt to the armed forces. He would have wanted to be present to honor one of "his men."

Welliver's Inaugural Address was an optimistic, energetic proclamation entitled "Westminster Faces Her Task." He noted that occasions such as this usually called for an address on contemporary theology or on some aspect of theological education, but he wanted to talk about the seminary as standing now "on the threshold of a new era of her life." This, of course, was the topic uppermost in the minds of his auditors as it was in his. He used two events of worldwide significance to dramatize the importance of the hour: Methodist union and the world at war, "the drawing together of religious forces on one hand, of which Methodist Union, the World Council of Churches and similar movements are examples, and the tragic breaking apart of the nations of the world in global conflict." Recognizing the seminary's "rich heritage," he pointed to its awareness of the world's sin and despair, the desperate need for spiritual leadership, and the church's right "to look to its seminaries to produce a leadership which is warm hearted, zealous and spiritually dynamic." He made his hearers feel that it was a time of great promise, and for the moment war campaigns in North Africa, Italy, and the Pacific could not dim the hopes for a new day for the seminary.

In assuming his official duties, President Welliver made no immediate announcement of plans for change. His naturally cautious disposition and general sense of propriety led him to move slowly during his first few months in office. On his recommendation, the board at its meeting in October 1943 authorized a *Seminary Bulletin,* to be issued quarterly beginning in March 1944. The following April he reported a good year coming to its close with the largest enrollment of students the seminary had ever had. He predicted, however, that

Baker Memorial Chapel, the scene of Welliver's inauguration, belonged to Western Maryland College. The seminary, having outgrown its own chapel in the seminary building, used Baker regularly during its later years in Westminster.

> if the directive issued by the Selective Service authorities last week providing for the cancellation of the deferments of all pre-theological students who are unable to enter Seminary by July 1, 1944, is not modified we will face a very

123

serious situation with respect to enrollment in a year or two.
We . . . are doing everything possible to care for the interests
of prospective students and the Seminary.

Some other items in Welliver's first annual report were more
pleasant to hear. Ralph W. Sockman, the popular pastor of
Christ Methodist Church in New York City, would be the commencement speaker on 15 May. Every one of the twenty-four
graduates (the largest class yet) would receive a degree, "the
first class in thirty-five years of which this can be said."
Receipts from the denomination were "a little in excess of
last year," and there were modest increases in the recently
authorized Living Endowment Fund and the endowment for
the Elderdice Chair of Theology. In his recommendations to
the board Welliver urged that the president be given authority to make necessary adjustments for part-time teachers, that
semesters be lengthened from fifteen to sixteen weeks, that
insurance on the seminary building be increased to $57,000,
and that Shroyer's salary be increased by $100 "in view of
his [new] duties of Registrar in addition to his work as a full
time Professor."

At the end of his report, with a "Finally, brethren," Welliver
unveiled his ambitious plan for the future. He began with a
brief description of the position in which the seminary found
itself in a new church competing with other Methodist
theological schools: Boston, Drew, Duke, Candler, Garrett,
and Perkins, all with millions in endowments and strong
university connections. He spoke of Westminster's underpaid
faculty, inadequate resources, and limited financial support.
Then he said: "Westminster in my judgment is now in a position which is best described by the well-known interpretation of the Chinese word for crisis—namely, dangerous opportunity. . . . Unless we launch out and strengthen our position
at once our glorious opportunity may pass." His recommendation for "launching out" was simple—and somewhat startling. He asked the Board of Governors to approve at once
a Westminster Forward Movement Program to raise $200,000
for a new building to house the expanding library, a chapel,
and offices for administration. At the same time he urged an
increase of the general endowment fund, with the unprecedented implication that this was the board's job and that they

should get busy on it at once. The board's response was something less than ecstatic. They accepted the plan "if and when such a move becomes possible," and they voted with similar caution "a $100 raise for each faculty member if possible." Welliver strove mightily to convince them that his recommendations were both imperative and possible. By the sheer force of his own vigor and optimism the Forward Movement Program was launched, and as the months passed, all life at the seminary revolved increasingly around it. Welliver's plan became his dreamship into the future, and the scuttling of it a decade later was to be for him a shattering disappointment.

Curriculum development and faculty expansion

The next ten years were strikingly different from all of the earlier decades. Appropriations from the now united Methodist Church increased—not enough to fulfill all needs, of course, but enough to increase total receipts by a significant amount. Veteran's Administration contracts also helped on tuition income. Student enrollments shot upward, creating serious overcrowding. The library overflowed, spreading into the classrooms and around the basement recreation room. And that incontrovertible evidence of growth and prosperity, inadequate parking, brought daily complaints.

Admission standards were upgraded again in 1945 as two years of college work became prerequisite to the Special Course for all except student spouses, who were allowed to enroll for four hours per semester. Special students could become candidates for the S.T.B. degree only if they completed their college work before beginning the senior year at the seminary, while those who did not qualify for the S.T.B. could receive a diploma for ninety-six hours of such seminary courses "as in the judgment of the faculty they are qualified to enter." The Diploma Course was phased out entirely in 1950, though Special students could still take any course for which they met the prerequisites. The ninety-six hours of the S.T.B. program, heretofore specified as the same for all degree students, now required seventy hours of "core" courses in designated fields of study; the other hours were distributed among electives, twelve of which had to be in one field as a major. In 1948 the S.T.B. curriculum was reduced to ninety hours total, with a core of sixty-three hours (which became fifty-seven in 1955). S.T.M. standards were raised so as to admit only those who had earned a "B" average in S.T.B. studies, and no credit toward the advanced degree was allowed for any course in which the grade was less than "B." The S.T.M. program was shortened to thirty hours beginning in 1948, and this now included a six-hour allowance for the thesis. By 1959 S.T.M. requirements called for a "reading knowledge of a foreign language . . . if research in the field of study presupposes it."

Most significant in the Welliver years, however, was the increase in the faculty from five to fifteen, with seemingly a new face or two almost every year. In addition, sixteen people were needed to teach part time, two or three each semester, with most staying only one or two years. Some of the new appointees taught in the traditional fields, but others

At the beginning of Welliver's presidency the full-time faculty was still comparatively small. Left to right: Douglas R. Chandler, John N. Link, Charles E. Forlines, Dorothy Elderdice, President Welliver, Paul F. Warner, and Montgomery J. Shroyer.

brought expansion and enrichment to the curriculum.

Systematic Theology

The first vacancy for Welliver to fill came at once with Forlines's death in 1944. For one year John R. Van Pelt was visiting professor of Systematic Theology while a search was launched for a permanent full-time successor. The Executive Committee and "some invited members of the Board of Governors" met in Baltimore at 516 North Charles Street, location of the former Methodist Protestant Book Concern, now the headquarters of the Baltimore Conference. First, they voted that the new building planned by the Forward campaign be named the Forlines Memorial Library. They then took up the matter of the vacancy in Systematic Theology. Welliver said it would be impossible to find a suitable replacement for Forlines at the proposed salary of $3,000, so they agreed to offer $3,250 and a house. The committee adjourned after acting on a few minor items, and John Baker (a local lay member of the board) took them to lunch at the Belvedere. At the full meeting of the board after lunch Welliver introduced Bishop Charles W. Flint and welcomed him as a new member. The president then proposed the name of S. Paul Schilling for the chair of Systematic Theology. Bishop Flint spoke in praise of Schilling. He expected that Schilling's teaching would arouse in students a lively interest in evangelism, since the prospect's previous service at the Brookland Methodist Church in Washington, DC, had produced each year a considerable number of new members received on profession of faith. At one time, the bishop explained, he had been worried about Schilling's pacifist tendencies; but after interviewing him and examining his attitude on war and peace, Flint concluded that the candidate was "safe." Benjamin Meeks and John Baker also spoke in support of Schilling, and the board elected him to succeed Forlines beginning 1 June 1945.

Before Schilling came, Systematic Theology had been a subdivision in the Department of Theology. Now the whole field was renamed Systematic Theology and Philosophy of Religion. Forlines could never have been unsystematic in anything, but his theology was really more encyclopedic than systematic and tended usually to be expressed in nineteenth-century terms. Schilling brought the department into the twentieth century. Born in 1904 in Cumberland, Maryland, he came to Westminster by way of St. John's College in Annapolis, Boston University, Harvard University, and the University of Berlin. He was thus well grounded in both American and European theology. To his scholarship he had added twelve years of pastoral experience.

Schilling had by nature those qualities and disciplines of mind which mark a philosophical theologian. He expected his students to think clearly and independently. They were not to memorize the doctrines of the Christian church so much as to discover them, and there was no hard rule that they must

S. Paul Schilling (left) taught Systematic Theology and Philosophy of Religion at Westminster from 1945 to 1953, and his wife, Mary, taught Christian Art and Remedial English. After a tour of duty at Boston University School of Theology, they returned to Wesley in Washington and he again taught Theology from 1970 to 1973. Their children were Paula and Robert, the latter a musician who composed the music to the seminary hymn, for which his father had written the words (see Appendix 4).

tailor their thinking to his. They were to "work out a theology they could state lucidly, defend intelligently, preach and teach effectively, and live convincingly." (The adverbs, while precise enough, mark a sharp contrast with Forlines's Spartan style.) Theology, according to Schilling, ought to be systematic but not rigidly so; there needed to be room for growth and new ideas. Students were unaccustomed to this. Awed by their professor's erudition, they were sometimes dismayed by his insistence that they think for themselves—or maybe it was just his demanding assignments and meticulous grading. Some could not grasp the fact that he sought a holistic understanding of the Christian faith, by which he meant an integration of worship, thought, and life. One way he worked at living his own

128

theology was to gather small groups of concerned students and faculty members for prayer, reading, and discussion. One such group, called "The Fellowship of the Covenant," endured for several years, stimulated by retreats at Kirkridge in eastern Pennsylvania.

Convinced that in theology there can be no detours or short-cuts, Schilling argued that the evidence for truth is cumulative; abbreviation, therefore, is self-defeating. He was nothing if not thorough, and his devotion to detail extended from the lecture room to the pulpit. One Sunday morning, preaching in the Westminster Methodist Church, he seemed to be at the point of concluding an already long sermon when he added that there were still three important aspects of his subject requiring consideration. An impatient professor from the college groaned audibly, "This is outrageous!" But Schilling's humor would surface easily too, and his spontaneous laughter often punctuated his most serious reasonings. He fully shared the class's amusement at discovering in his early morning classroom a bed, put there as a prank by anonymous students claiming that they had had to study all night for an examination in his course.

Mary Schilling also contributed much to the seminary's life. Her Christian Art, a one-hour course that she taught for two years (1951-53), focused on interpretations of the life of Christ as depicted by famous artists. For five years, beginning in 1948, she taught Remedial English to first-year students whose Orientation Week tests showed that their English proficiency was not up to graduate school standards; and for the Homiletics courses she hunted out grammatical errors and mispronunciations in the students' recorded sermons. The Schillings were at Westminster for eight years. In 1953 they left for Boston University, where he was to teach Systematic Theology in the School of Theology. They would be back in 1970 for a three-year post-retirement stint at Wesley in Washington.

There was general dismay in the spring of 1953 when Paul Schilling announced that he would be leaving at the end of the academic year to join the faculty of Boston University School of Theology, his alma mater. President Welliver regretfully reported the news to the Board of Governors at their April meeting, reminding them that the school was losing "a scholar, a sincere Christian, a cooperative worker and a rare spirit, one who has made an incalculable contribution in his seven years at the Seminary." Welliver spoke also of Mrs. Schilling's helpful work. Obviously, it would not be easy to find replacements. But the search for Schilling's successor had already met with unexpected good fortune, and Welliver had a nomination to make: Reuben Eugene Gilmore, a prospect supported by many strong recommendations. Albert C. Knudson of the Boston faculty had written: "He has a winsome personality, has had considerable experience both as preacher and teacher, is an enthusiastic student both of philosophy and religion, writes very well and has scholastic ambitions. I would feel about as certain of his making good with you in a large way as I would with reference to any man." Harold DeWolf, also of Boston, and Earl Furgeson of the Westminster faculty both knew Gilmore, and they concurred with Knudson.

At the time, Gilmore was pastor of the Hyde Park Congregational Church, a ministry he rendered while pursuing graduate studies at Boston University. But although he joined that church for the time of his pastorate, he was no Congregationalist. He grew up in the Church of the Nazarene in Arkansas, where he was born in 1902, and was rooted firmly in the tradition of the Wesleys with most of the features and much of the vocabulary of evangelical pietism. He had taught philosophy in Nazarene colleges and had been president of Northwest Nazarene College in Nampa, Idaho. He pursued graduate studies for a time at the University of Chicago, but the decisive period in his theological formation came under Knudson at Boston. Struggling to grow beyond the traditional orthodoxies of his upbringing, Gilmore found Chicago's scientific modernism unsatisfying. The philosophy of personalism taught at Boston, however, literally possessed him and he it. His devotion to Knudson and other theistic personalists knew no bounds. He became a missionary for their views in classroom and pulpit, expounding them with all the evangelistic fervor of one who had come after stormy seas into a safe harbor and who longed to bring others to the same anchorage.

Following Knudson, Gilmore held that the human capacity to respond to God is a gift granted to all rational creatures and that religious experience, resulting from God's action on

130

each person, carries its own autonomous validity. Gilmore encouraged every student to undertake a personal quest to discover the self-verifying character of religious faith. His enthusiasm and confidence, acquired in his own theological pilgrimage and strengthened by several bouts with severe illness, served to convince many. More than one traditionalist student, caught in the pain of a mental expansion, has testified, "Gilmore saved my faith." In 1968, after teaching fifteen years, Gilmore retired with his wife, Era, to what was always "holy land" to them, the hills of Arkansas. Later they moved to Des Moines, Iowa, to be near their only child, the wife of an Episcopal priest.

Reuben Eugene Gilmore, professor of Systematic Theology 1953-68, always had time to stop and talk with a student

Music and Speech

In 1945 Church Music was again without a professor, since Western Maryland's Alfred de Long was unavailable for another year. There were some weeks of anxious searching until Welliver found the right person. Preaching as a guest one Sunday at the Mount Vernon Place Methodist Church in Baltimore, he was impressed with the music there. He invited the church's minister of music, J. Edward Moyer, to come to Westminster one day a week to teach a one-credit course in Church Music, and Moyer accepted. It was a tentative beginning of a relationship which subsequently enlarged and extended over thirty-two years.

Moyer was born in Silverdale, Pennsylvania—a place easily found, he liked to say, because "it was just two miles east of Perkasie, where Frances Apple [his wife] was born and reared." He was of Mennonite stock and she of Lutheran, and after their marriage in 1937 they became a musical team in the Sellersville (Pa.) Reformed Church (now United Church of Christ). A graduate of Wilson College in Chambersburg, Mrs. Moyer was a gifted musician: teacher, singer, pianist, and from 1937 onward her husband's accompanist and colleague. Edward Moyer graduated from Temple University, earned a Master of Church Music degree at Westminster Choir College in Princeton, and in 1939 went to Mount Vernon Place Methodist Church, where his pietist background harmonized

By the mid-1950s the Seminary Singers had established a solid reputation as a choral group. Tours took them into many churches, both in the Westminster area and in other states nearby. Director J. Edward Moyer is at the right end of the front row.

comfortably with Dr. Harold Bosley's celebrated preaching of the Social Gospel. When the Moyers came to Westminster, they brought not only their talent and training in music but also the peace testimony of his Mennonite forebears.

Moyer's first-year duty, as the catalog described it, was "to develop appreciation of hymns and anthems of the church, and to train the Seminary Chorus for singing in public." As his schedule became established, his course offerings were Church Music (required of first-year students), Advanced Church Music (elective), and Seminary Singers (selected by audition). His aim was to impart to ministerial students a working knowledge of the hymnal, an understanding of the music most appropriate for public worship, and a sense of collegiality in working with musicians and music committees in the local church. Not all students met his expectations; some thought his courses were only for the musically inclined, and there were always a few who, to his distress, continued to prefer "In the Garden" and "Beulah Land" over more stately hymns.

132

At first Moyer defined the Singers as "an organization of Seminary men devoted to the study of choral music." They had been offering occasional concerts on Wednesday evenings in nearby churches, but under Moyer's leadership they soon ventured on overnight trips and within a few years were making two-day and week-long tours. In January 1956 came their most ambitious tour yet, a ten-day trip presenting sixteen concerts in Pennsylvania, Ohio, Indiana, Illinois, and Michigan. The values of the organization went far beyond "the study of choral music," for the concerts combined Christian witnessing, ministerial recruitment, and public relations in one memorable experience. After the mid-fifties the Singers included black students and women, which added to both the music and the witness.

Moyer had no way of knowing when he came to Westminster in 1945 that five years later he would become the seminary's professor of Speech, but if he had been present at the Board of Governors meeting in November 1947, he might have had some intimation of it. President Welliver said then that Dorothy Elderdice had asked to be relieved of her duties as librarian but would continue to teach her courses in Speech and Drama. This "provoked some discussion." According to the minutes,

J. Edward Moyer wore several hats: professor of Church Music, director of the Seminary Singers, chapel organist, professor of Speech for Ministers, registrar, and director of admissions. Students who mastered in song and speech the precise enunciation which he taught were then said to be "Moyerized."

> Bishop Straughn suggested that (leaving out all personalities) since the student body is usually made up of those of the masculine persuasion, this department should have as professor a man. He felt that a man could better understand the needs of men and could meet them more effectively than could a woman. It was voted that the Executive Committee make a careful study of this matter and bring their findings to the next meeting of the Board.

There were no subsequent reports of any "findings," but Welliver knew what the board wanted. In June 1950 he reported that Miss Elderdice had resigned as teacher of Speech (but not Religious Drama) and that Professor Moyer would move into the vacancy. Moyer's teaching duties now expanded to include Speech for Ministers (required of first-year students) and Radio Speech for Ministers (elective). He spent many hours training students in the proper use of the materials of public worship—Bible readings, prayers, litanies, and sermons—and

133

seemed never to weary of the countless sessions of "personalized diagnosis and correction" or of the endless taping and evaluation of student assignments. Under his tutelage, most of those who came to the seminary speaking the accent and dialect of their regional culture learned to round their vowels and reclaim their dropped consonants.

Moyer was still not quite full time, but Welliver found a way to increase his usefulness to the seminary by offering him in 1954 a "third hat" as director of admissions. Now the Moyers could move to Westminster, which meant a welcome end to commuting from Baltimore. But the new assignment also required office space in the already overcrowded building, a problem neatly solved by putting Moyer together with John Howes (the director of Field Work) in a renovated storage room in the basement beyond the ping-pong room. The indignity was eased somewhat by providing them a secretary, a luxury that none of the other faculty yet enjoyed. Shroyer was still registrar—without a secretary—in his little office at the top of the stairs.

A New Librarian

For several years Dorothy Elderdice had hoped that someone could be found to replace her in the library. She was an efficient librarian but had not come to love the work as her father had hoped. Perhaps in order to speed the search for a replacement, she resigned; and upon her suggestion and encouragement, Emily Morrison Chandler became librarian in 1947. Mrs. Chandler prepared herself for her new duties by taking courses in Library Science at Western Maryland College and at the University of North Carolina. She loved the work. In addition to developing a proficiency in handling the books and periodicals of the various seminary disciplines, she participated in countless student discussions at her desk—enough, some said, to justify credit for a course entitled "The Library Seminar." The personal problems of individual students, along with current issues in church and world, supplied the agenda for these ad hoc sessions.

From 1951 to 1955 Mrs. Marjorie Cowles Crain served as assistant librarian. The wife of Dr. Charles Crain, a professor in the Department of Religion at Western Maryland College, she was well informed about theological subjects. Her knowledge of the literature of the field and her firmness with students increased the effectiveness of the library, while her unfailing good humor helped to ease the strains caused by rapid growth and overcrowding. Robert Beach, librarian of Union Theological Seminary in New York, came to study the library situation; and upon his recommendation, the stacks expanded further into classrooms and basement, the card catalog took over some central hall space, and various ingenious space-savers facilitated ongoing operations. But the seminary badly needed a new library.

Mrs. Emily Morrison Chandler became librarian in 1947. Here she and Professor Chandler are examining a volume in the vault, which served as the Rare Book Room.

Mrs. Marjorie Knowles Crain, wife of a Western Maryland College professor, was assistant librarian 1951-55. During the last few years in Westminster the library was seriously overcrowded.

The seminary's location in an agricultural county-seat town seemed to be a natural situation for training students in rural church work. President Welliver was sensitive to this, and when the Department of Town and Country Work of the Board of Missions and Church Extension of The Methodist Church promised funds to supplement a professor's salary, he was able in 1947 to appoint John Baxter Howes as professor of Rural Church. Howes was a graduate of Union College in Kentucky and of Boston University School of Theology. He came to Westminster directly from the Central Pennsylvania Conference, where he had been president of the Pennsylvania Christian Rural Fellowship, editor of the *Methodist Rural Fellowship Bulletin,* chaplain of the Pennsylvania State Grange, and chairman of the Policy Committee of the National Methodist Rural Life Conference. His assignment at the seminary was to include supervising the placement and parish work of student pastors as well as encouraging the work of Town and Country Commissions in neighboring annual conferences.

Howes brought unique gifts to the life of the seminary. With homespun wit and an endless store of anecdotes, he gave the impression of being a combination of Henry Thoreau and Will Rogers. His colleagues sometimes envied the popularity of his courses, but all knew the value of his work and the quality of life he modeled for the students. Because two-thirds of all Methodist churches were rural and the first appointments for almost all beginning ministers would be in country churches, it seemed important that students be prepared to serve such churches with integrity and skill. Howes scorned the bureaucratic habit of speaking of big city churches as if they were more important; small churches, wherever located, were equally significant in the eyes of God. His visits to students' churches and his supervision of their work in parishes added a strong new dimension to the school's curriculum.

Under Howes's direction Westminster's summer program was enhanced by two special schools that were immediately popular. The School for Town and Country Ministers began in 1946 as a venture in continuing education. It was staffed largely by visiting professors from other seminaries, from the Board of Missions and the Board of Education of The Methodist Church, and sometimes from the United States Department of Agriculture. Money for salaries and scholarships came from several general agencies of the denomination, as well as from the Sears Roebuck Foundation. The second school originated in the summer of 1949, when Howes planned and directed a three-week school for "supply pastors," i.e., provisional ministers who lacked formal seminary (and usually college) training and were expected to seek their education through the Conference Course of Study. Providing an institutional structure for the Course of Study was a venture that became one of the most rewarding experiences in the seminary's history. The students were mostly older men serving in rural parishes, but they were mature, receptive, and deeply grateful for an opportunity to qualify for appointment as local preachers by a seminary experience that was far more satisfying than their solitary struggle with the Course of Study. Though the name designating this class of ministers changed several times, the seminary continued to offer a Course of Study School every summer, even after its move to Washington. In the 1960s this summer student group included a growing number of women. A summer seminar for city ministers was attempted in 1950, but that was of short duration.

Howes also began the transformation of Field Work into Field Education, a curriculum enhancement that grew with the seminary. This meant establishing supervision over the students' remunerated church work so that they could be learning on the job. After 1958, when the seminary relocated in a large metropolitan area, the number of student pastors and assistants multiplied rapidly; and by 1976 Howes was supervising some 150 students in various forms of parish responsibilities. At that point he turned the responsibility for Field Education over to another, taught three more years, and retired to serve a rural parish in western Maryland. Thus after an interlude of thirty-two years in the classroom, he was back where his heart had been all along.

PILGRIMAGE *of* FAITH

John Nicholas Link joined the faculty in 1938 and for seven years taught a wide variety of courses in the practical field. His list of offerings included Pastoral Care, Parish Administration, Counseling, Evangelism, Rural and Urban Church Program, Church Architecture and Symbolism, Homiletics, History of Preaching, Sermonic Clinic, Public Worship, and Church Finance. Even allowing for some window dressing in the catalog, such an agenda seems incredible for one person, and Link's resignation in 1945 left a large vacancy that took three years to fill adequately. From time to time two esteemed Baltimore pastors—Harris Elliott Kirk of Franklin Street Presbyterian Church and William A. Keese of Grace Methodist Church—came to deliver special lectures in Homiletics. The practical department also housed a course in Christianity and the Social Order taught by Frank Smith Depro on a part-time basis for five years. Depro was a 1940 graduate of the seminary, now a progressive pastor in the Baltimore Conference. His explicit applications of the gospel to contemporary social issues stimulated lively discussions in his classrooms and some uneasiness among the school's more conservative supporters. But the most urgent need seemed to be for instruction in pulpit ministry, and after a long search President Welliver finally announced in the summer of 1948 that the new professor of Preaching, Pastoral Theology, and Worship would be Earl H. Furgeson.

Like Shroyer, Furgeson was born (in 1906) in Indiana, but there the similarity ended. After graduation from DePauw University with Phi Beta Kappa honors, Furgeson went to Boston University for doctoral study. That completed, he remained in the area for ten years more as minister of the Harvard Epworth Church in Cambridge, director of the Wesley Foundation at Harvard, and lecturer in Homiletics at Boston University School of Theology. In New England he met Edith Boothby and married her in 1935, the year of his ordination; her own skills in teaching and administration complemented his.

Furgeson brought a new look to the practical department as he replaced Link's mimeographed outlines and promotional ideas with more sophisticated issues and theories. He was at home with the ideas of Erich Fromm and Paul Tillich, and he was fascinated by the application of psychoanalytic theory to the practice of ministry. The old courses in Preaching and Worship now had much new content, and they were augmented by a seminar on Interpretations of Religion in Psychology and Theology. Furgeson's intention, as he put it, was "to expose the developing minds of young ministers to the thinking of two of the seminal minds of the twentieth century, and perhaps to scatter some cross-field fertilization in the traditional disciplines of the theological curriculum." He wanted these disciplines to focus on the encounter of the church with the contemporary culture which "impinges on its method and message." It was impossible, he thought, to separate the work of the ministry from the person of the minister; and he visualized these in one comprehensive quadrilateral framed by the Bible, the church, the minister, and the world in dynamic tension, "inseparable and ideally in harmony, servants of one another and all in a common cause: the salvation of the individual and the world."

Earl H. Furgeson brought a new look to the practical department. As professor of Preaching, Pastoral Theology, and Worship from 1948 to 1973, he sought to develop in prospective ministers both scholarship and discipleship.

As he began his teaching in the fall of 1948, Furgeson delivered the Matriculation Day sermon; and there was general rejoicing that the old practical department, now named Preaching, Pastoral Theology, and Worship, was to become his responsibility. Always stimulating in the classroom, he also excelled as a preacher. His sermons were models of clarity and organization, exposition and application. Students longed to be like him. But there was a price to pay, and he did his best to see that they paid it. His Sermonic Clinic became, in their argot, "Furgatory," as they winced under his critique of their sermons, pastoral prayers, and orders of worship. But his stern discipline was frequently lightened with memorable anecdotes, as when he required them to write out their public prayers so as to avoid slips like that of the student pastor who prayed one Sunday morning, "Lord, forgive our many mistakes and our falling shorts." Furgeson's hours per week on the job were unmeasured. As other professors sometimes sought to limit their weekly hours, his mounted to a staggering total—

partly because he was a good technician, and all the new equipment for sermon recording, playback, listening booths, and taped evaluations became his constant care. His wife did not always share his enjoyment in these never-ending labors, but she tolerated them in good spirit.

A perennial task of any seminary is "pastoral formation," i.e., helping students to clarify their concepts of ministerial identity and vocational purpose. Furgeson took special interest in this question. He could accept the traditional notion of a divine "call" to ministry, but he also insisted that one must validate that call. Such a call may begin to take shape in a dream or some mystical experience, but it should end with a demonstration. "It must be shown that He has chosen us, and His favorite way of judging trees is by their fruits." He told students that they should begin producing the fruits of sound scholarship or else, as Wesley advised, "return to your trade." He drove the point home in a chapel sermon of 1966. "The idea of a Seminary as an academic cafeteria with drive-in facilities and service at the curb is completely incompatible with the idea of the minister as a scholar. . . . Our first calling is to make ourselves at home in the realm of ideas."[1] But Furgeson also saw study as fulfilled only in the obedience of active faith; to the life of scholarship must be added the life of discipleship. One who would be a minister, he concluded, must

> confront his own estrangement and alienation, open every inner barrier and wall of separation to searching inspections as a part of his obligation to validate his call. . . . For the minister to discover who he truly is and to whom he truly belongs would be to free himself for the work he is truly called to do.

One of Furgeson's favorite quotations came from an elderly rabbi who testified, "When I was young I sought to change the world. As I grew older, I limited it to my community. Now that I am older and wiser, I see that I should have begun with myself."

Furgeson did more than introduce into the classroom modern theories of the psychology of religious experience. His emphasis on the person of the minister led the seminary to pay more attention to the emotional health of the students.

In 1949 psychological tests became a regular part of the activities of Orientation Week, and this expanded into a program of testing and counseling that attempted to identify psychological problems and to arrange affordable therapy for those who needed it. Furgeson supervised the program, and from 1954 to 1973 he had the able help of Dr. Michael Finn, a clinical psychologist with unusual competence in dealing with the emotional problems of religious workers. After Finn resigned to devote full time to his established counseling practice in Baltimore, the seminary enlisted various other professionals in the Washington area for the needed services in psychological testing and counseling.

Ernest E. Bruder (left), professor of Clinical Pastoral Education and Protestant chaplain at St. Elizabeths Hospital, worked intensively with small groups of students learning pastoral care.

The department moved a step further toward Clinical Pastoral Education in 1949 with the appointment of Ernest E. Bruder as special lecturer in Pastoral Counseling. Bruder was a Canadian and an ordained priest in the Protestant Episcopal Church, two credentials he always referred to with evident satisfaction. Born in 1910 in Winnipeg, Manitoba, he graduated from the University of Manitoba and from McMaster University in Hamilton, Ontario. Following three and a half years as a parish clergyman in Manitoba, he undertook clinical pastoral training in Michigan and New Jersey hospitals. After a few years of clinical teaching and chaplain supervising in hospitals in New York and Pennsylvania, he came in 1944 to Saint Elizabeths Hospital, a public mental health institution in Washington, DC, as its first full-time Protestant chaplain. There he developed an accredited program in Clinical Pastoral Education and chaplaincy training that became nationally recognized. Bruder lectured and wrote extensively, and he also edited *The Journal of Pastoral Care.* His best known work is a small volume entitled *Ministering to Deeply Troubled People,* published in 1963.

It was Chaplain Bruder's goal to join religion and psychiatry in a clinical setting designed to develop effective pastors. Always concerned about emotionally disturbed people, he believed that pastoral care should include them and that ministry even to "normal" people could be enhanced by pastors clinically trained in a mental hospital. Although he did not wish to make the parish pastor a practitioner of psychotherapy, he did offer in his program at Saint Elizabeths "an opportunity to gain first-hand experience in visiting [under careful supervision] people in a major crisis situation." Following the seminary's move to Washington, Bruder's teaching role expanded; and in 1962 he became a full professor as occupant of the Howard Chandler Robbins Chair of Clinical Pastoral Care, the endowment of which he was instrumental in securing. Clinical Pastoral Education expanded further as the seminary established relationships with other teaching hospitals of the Washington area. Ten courses eventually appeared in the catalog, offering to students a wide variety of learning experiences in Pastoral Theology, Psychology of Religion, and several forms of clinical training.

Old Testament

Dividing the Bible department into Old and New Testament sections had never been easy. Shroyer had "covered the waterfront" for many years, and various part-time lecturers and assistants had come, especially for Old Testament subjects. In 1946 Eugene Ashton, an assistant professor at Goucher College, taught some Hebrew and Old Testament, but he left after one year to accept an invitation from Tufts College. Robert Emil Hansen followed Ashton, coming in 1948 from doctoral studies under William F. Albright at The Johns Hopkins University. A scholarly Presbyterian, he liked teaching but loved the pastorate; he left after three years. In 1951 Welliver's search for a durable Old Testament professor came to a happy end when he found Lowell B. Hazzard (1898-1978), and for the first time all the Old Testament courses became the responsibility of one teacher.

Hazzard was a native of Illinois, a churchman, and a Methodist through and through. Educated at Ohio Wesleyan, Garrett Biblical Institute, and the University of Edinburgh, he had been assistant professor of English Bible at Ohio Wesleyan and professor of Religion at Illinois Wesleyan University. Widely known as a writer of Methodist church school literature and as a popular Bible lecturer, he was in much demand to speak to a wide variety of audiences on many subjects pertaining to the Christian faith and life. His wife, Stella Tombaugh Hazzard, taught and lectured too, as they both

Lowell B. Hazzard (1898-1978) taught Old Testament from 1951 to 1970. He and Mrs. Hazzard (Stella) were in great demand for religious retreats, leadership training schools, and Bible study classes in local churches.

143

made the rounds of church groups, leadership schools, and religious retreats. It seemed at times that the Hazzards knew more Methodists than there really were. Their "open door" policy made their home a crossroads of the world as students and their families from many nations found welcome there, many lodging for extended periods.

Hazzard took over Hebrew and the traditional courses in Old Testament Introduction, History, Theology, and Geography; and he added as occasional seminars Poetry and Wisdom Literature, Historical and Legal Books, and Biblical Customs. In class lectures Hazzard frequently thundered and roared. He was dramatic and intense, impersonating Jeremiah and Isaiah with flashing eye, shaking head, and trembling jaw. He fascinated most students; but when one of them "couldn't take it" and told him so, Hazzard simply instructed the student not to come to class but to read the books, write the papers, and take the exams, and he would receive whatever grade his work merited. Some students thought that Hazzard was unnecessarily reluctant to give a grade of "A" or even "B." One complained that his term paper had been evaluated "Good work—C + ." Since the student could read the comment, one may surmise that it could not have been in the professor's appallingly illegible scrawl but in the clear printing he used on rare occasions.

Dramatic in his impersonations of the Old Testament prophets, Hazzard remained a diligent student all his life.

God's concern for righteousness in the social order was Hazzard's meat and drink. He extracted from the Old Testament all the Social Gospel of the New. In his interpretation, the prophets were preachers of world peace, racial equality, and economic justice. They denounced militarism, conscienceless wealth, political dishonesty, and idolatrous nationalism. Hazzard's published commentaries on the church school lessons infuriated many a conservative church member. One Sunday in the Wesley Class at the Westminster Methodist Church, a nettled member who had just read the *Quarterly*'s notes for the day stormed in anger, "Whoever wrote this stuff had his head in a bag!" When told that the writer was his friend and neighbor, Dr. Hazzard, he lapsed into scowling silence.

Hazzard never disparaged disciplined scholarship, yet as a teacher he leaned towards the needs of the average church member. For the laity he wrote *A Pocket Book of Methodist*

Beliefs (1962), which enjoyed wide popularity. Although he never talked down to students, he planned his courses for their pastoral needs rather than their intellectual titillation. When he served on the Library Committee of the faculty and was asked by the president for an opinion about the proposed purchase of some European theology volumes in German, he acknowledged the importance of the works but thought the money might be invested more profitably in books in English, which more students could read. Hazzard remained vigorous until his retirement in 1970, at which time he and Stella returned to Illinois and resided in Pontiac until they died, she in 1977 and he in 1978.

Christian Education

In November 1950 President Welliver told the Board of Governors that the Department of Christian Education was "the one important place on our faculty remaining to be filled." (The old term, "Religious Education," had been discarded in 1948 in favor of the more specific adjective, "Christian.") He was in correspondence with a prospect, he said, and was looking forward to filling the position the next fall. He was successful. In September 1951 Robert R. Powell (1909—) came to be professor of Psychology of Religion and Christian Education. These two fields had long been bracketed together; but in 1956 a curriculum revision put Psychology of Religion with Pastoral Theology, and Powell's title was shortened to professor of Christian Education. The regrouping of fields, however, in no way took Psychology out of his portfolio, as his teaching regularly demonstrated.

Powell was from New Jersey, a graduate of Drew (B.D.) and of the University of Pittsburgh (Ph.D.), with post-doctoral study at Teachers College of Columbia University. He served several pastorates in New Jersey and was for five years (1940-45) executive secretary of the New Jersey Conference Board of Education. He taught Religion and Sociology at Mount Union College in Alliance, Ohio, and came from there to Westminster. He moved with the seminary to Washington, and after teaching twenty-one more years retired in 1979.

It would be inaccurate to say that Powell reconstructed the seminary's Department of Christian Education; he practically created it. He inaugurated a broad sweep of courses newly designed in both content and teaching method. While other professors continued their traditional lecturing, Powell broke the pattern of graduate school instruction by resorting to the techniques of group dynamics. Curious colleagues wondered at the groups huddled in his classroom; some saw only chaos, some envied the students' obvious enjoyment of "buzz sessions," and a few sought to improve their own teaching method by imitating his. Powell's theories were not confined to the classroom. He wrote *Managing Church Business Through Group Procedures* (1964) and was weekly, it seemed, guiding church leadership schools and workshops up and down the East Coast and even in some western areas. He also developed a specialty in youth ministry and regularly offered courses on that subject. His published counsel to young people included such books as *Choose Life* (1959) and *Enjoy Your Parents* (1962).

For years the seminary's class chedule was Powell's responsibility, a task tedious and intricate enough to be the despair of several committees. In the details of arranging hours and days for the courses, he developed a consummate skill in spreading classes so as to require each student's presence on campus nearly every day in the week, or at least from Monday noon to Friday noon. Unlike Elderdice in an earlier era, Powell doubted the need for students to take off both Mondays and Fridays for parish duties. This also had a bearing on maintaining accreditation, since the American Association of Theological Schools frowned on "part-time" curricula.

In 1935 Powell had married Gertrude Woolverton, who was an accomplished Christian educator in her own right. Working sometimes with her husband, sometimes independently, she led retreats, offered leadership training classes, and guided youth groups. Like so many other professors' spouses, she was actively involved in the life of the seminary. After the school moved to Washington and began to enjoy rapid expansion, she helped in the Development Office; and at the president's request, from 1965 to 1972 she served as a part-time assistant to Professor Moyer in the Admissions Office. In the latter function she planned visits to the seminary for college and high school students, and visits by seminary professors to colleges and universities for recruitment. As the enrollment of women in the seminary increased, she defended their discovery of new roles in the church and encouraged their full entry into the ordained ministry.

In time Professor Powell persuaded the seminary to offer a program leading to the Master of Religious Education degree. This required additional faculty. In 1957 Mary Alice Douty came to teach one course in the department, an arrangement that continued for two years. In March 1959 President Trott advanced her to full-time teaching, announcing that the M.R.E. program would begin that fall. Douty was born in 1913 in Rochester, New York, but always thought of Baltimore as her "home town." She was a graduate of Goucher College and held graduate degrees from Union Theological Seminary and Columbia University. She had had more than twenty years of experience in public school education and with the Baltimore Conference Board of Education, and she was executive secretary of this board when she was invited to become a member of the seminary faculty. A year after her coming the campus buzzed happily with the announcement that Dr. Douty had married Dr. Philip C. Edwards, scion of a prominent Baltimore Conference family of ministers and himself a leader not only in this conference but also in the general church's Board of Missions.

Mary Alice D. Edwards's first book, *How to Work with Church Groups* (1957), confirmed her sympathy with the methods and goals that Powell had already established in the department. Her central focus was on the relation of the ministry to human development—how and what to teach children, youth, adults, and the elderly—in sum, the organizing of an effective educational ministry for the whole congregation. That concern prompted her to design such courses as Life Span Ministry, Children and Religion, Ministry to the Aging, and The Family and Christian Education. She also offered courses in Religious Drama, Worship in Christian Education, and Camping as occasional electives. There were laboratories for group dynamics, group teaching, and a two-semester supervised field project (required for M.R.E. candidates). Edwards complained that "too many churches are pouring money down the drain by employing people inept at working with people." The preface to her book, *Leadership Development and the Workers' Conference* (1967), summarizes her basic goal: "Leadership and leadership education must be rooted in love or we deny the very thing we aim to teach. 'See how these Christians love one another!' As we grow in skill and grow in love, our Father's work does indeed become our highest joy."

The Department of Christian Education continued for many years with two full-time professors, but the offerings were enhanced from time to time by several part-time teachers. Jean Harnish, Bryn Mawr graduate and psychiatric social case worker, began coming in 1955 to assist in the group dynamics laboratories. In the 1960s new courses in Campus Ministry appeared. Teachers of this subject have included William E. Smith, Jr., vice-president of the seminary 1961-64; Ira Zepp, dean of the chapel and professor of Religion at Western Maryland College; and Bruce Poynter, chaplain at The American University.

Missions and World Religions

Until 1949 courses in Missions were given by visiting lecturers or by one or another of the seminary professors from another field. Usually the visitors were Methodist Protestant missionaries home on furlough or retired, or executives from the church's Board of Missions. In April 1918 President Elderdice had thought he might have found the money for a full-time professor of Missions when he received a letter from J. Norman Wills, one of his board members. Wills, the secretary-treasurer of a hardware company in Greensboro, North Carolina, wrote to say that he ought to resign from the seminary's Board of Governors. He was never able to attend their meetings because he was also a member of the denomination's Board of Missions, and the meeting dates often conflicted. Being forced to choose, and feeling that missions was "the one supreme need of our church," he had decided to give to that cause all the support his resources permitted. Elderdice replied immediately:

> We all agree as to the value of missions. . . . Is not a thoroughly trained minister—trained in theology, church history, modern methods of church work and especially in missionary work—the best agent for advancing the interest so dear to your heart? What will be the value of all the money you invest in machinery if your engineer is not competent?

The letter ended with an appeal to Wills's family pride as well as to his professed interest in missions: "Is it not worth your while," wrote Elderdice, "to consider the wisdom of founding a chair [here] to be known as the Reverend Richard Wills Memorial Missionary Chair?" However, such a memorial to his father seems to have been more than Wills had in mind, for no such chair of Missions was founded. Instead, Forlines, Shroyer, and Chandler in turn taught World Religions and History of Missions, giving some curricular recognition to the field, and in 1948 Howes inaugurated a course called The Christian Mission to Rural People.

Visiting lecturers continued to carry most of the responsibility for the subject. Fred C. Klein and Paul Warner from Japan, Paul Cassan from India, Samuel Lin Sheng Lee from China, and a half-dozen others came in the 1940s under the auspices of the Board of Missions and Church Extension. Then in succession came Orville L. Davis, Corliss P. Hargraves, and Charles F. Johannaber, each for one year, as "assistants" in Missions, sometimes adding instruction in Christian Education as well. At last in November 1950 the Board of Governors voted Welliver the power "to engage Dr. Murray Titus of India as Professor of Missions and World Religions beginning with the next fiscal year."

Murray Thurston Titus came the next year (1951) as the seminary's first resident professor of Missions and World Religions. A graduate of Ohio Wesleyan University and of Hartford Seminary, he had been in India for forty years as a Methodist missionary serving as professor of Philosophy and (later) as principal at Lucknow Christian College and also as superintendent of the North India Conference of The Methodist Church. He was thoroughly conversant with India and its religions and a recognized authority on Islam, especially in India. He had written widely acclaimed interpretations of that faith, and his long familiarity with missionary life and his firsthand acquaintance with other religions of the world made him a valuable addition to the Westminster faculty. No faculty family was more loved than Titus and his wife. People had a casual habit of referring to them as "dear Murray and Olive," and the warm hospitality of their home, with Indian food and graces, endeared them to all the town. He taught for four years before retiring in 1955.

Titus's replacement came immediately. In the fall of 1955 James Howell Pyke assumed teaching duties as professor of Missions and World Religions, bringing to an end the long accumulation of brief and part-time incumbents in that field. Pyke was born in 1915 in China, where his parents and grandparents were missionaries. After early schooling in north China, he came to Willamette University in Salem, Oregon, and from there went on for the M.A. degree at Boston University and the S.T.B. at Harvard Divinity School. In 1940 he returned to China as a missionary with the Methodist Board

The faculty almost doubled during the first decade of Welliver's presidency. In 1954 there were, front row, left to right: Earl H. Furgeson, J. Edward Moyer, President Welliver, Montgomery J. Shroyer, Douglas R. Chandler, and Murray T. Titus; back row: Robert R. Powell, R. Eugene Gilmore, Edith B. Furgeson, Emily M. Chandler, Lowell B. Hazzard, and John B. Howes.

of Missions and was assigned to the mission-sponsored Yenching University as instructor in English Language and Literature and as secretary to the Student Christian Fellowship. During World War II he was interned by the Japanese in a concentration camp, and after his release he continued his service at the university. While on furlough in 1947-48 he studied at Columbia University and Union Theological Seminary in New York, where he met Margaret Felton. They married in 1949. Returning to China with his wife, Pyke again taught at Yenching until Communist armies overran the country in 1951. Since conditions no longer permitted missionary work, the Pykes went to the island of Sumatra, where he was assigned to be principal of a Methodist high school. After two years there they returned to the United States, and he completed a Ph.D. degree at Drew University.

Throughout all this coming and going, study and teaching, Pyke was also on a spiritual and theological pilgrimage. He later recalled the various stages: a loving Christian home where morning prayers were conducted in Chinese with the servants present; a "surrender" of his life to Jesus at the age of twelve; boyhood hero-worship of E. Stanley Jones; rebellion and independence in the midst of intellectualism at Harvard; a brief fascination with Brightman's "limited God" at Boston; a discovery of Moral Rearmament, which emphasized repentance and commitment to Christ ("this was a crucial point in the recovery of my faith"); a new conversion experience while studying Reinhold Niebuhr's *Nature and Destiny of Man* in China; an introduction to neo-orthodoxy and its stress on the importance of biblical revelation; and an Anglican bishop, the Eucharist, and the Elizabethan liturgy sustaining him through the years in the concentration camp. All of this and more went into making Pyke more conservative and evangelical than any other member of the faculty.

Pyke's gentle speech and pleasant manner belied his granite-like orthodoxy. He saw in recent missionary thinking a revival of the old debate between William Ernest Hocking's modernistic approach to "rethinking missions" and Hendrik Kraemer's "radical biblical realism," and he sided unequivocally with Kraemer. He lamented the growing tendency to agree with Arend Theodoor van Leeuwen, *Christianity in World History*

(1964), that "as western culture has and presumably will continue to spread world-wide, missionary work will be no longer necessary. The job all unbeknownst to us is being carried forward in secular vessels." Pyke rejected this view as theologically unsound and naively optimistic, though he feared that "the majority of the professors of missions in American Methodist seminaries hold to this position, believing in effect that the era of foreign missions is at an end." Every course he taught was a sustained, insistent protest against such thinking. His conviction regarding the absolute uniqueness of Christ made it impossible for him to view Christianity "in terms of Hocking's horizontal conception of One among Many." Pyke wanted to simplify what he regarded as unnecessarily complex. He was convinced that "all the complexities of Christian theology can be reduced to a basic relationship, as between One who loves and those who are in need of love, as between Him who saves and those who need salvation." Such language, echoing the themes of traditional evangelicalism, was gratefully received by many students who were having difficulty adjusting to the critical stance of contemporary theology. They saw their professor of Missions as a conservator of the faith of their forebears, and they preferred that tradition to what they understood of more modern options.

Questions about the future

It might appear that the rapid expansion of the faculty and the enriching of the curriculum during Welliver's presidency were propelling the seminary into a bright new future. There is a more somber side to the story, however. The Board of Governors, it will be recalled, had accepted Welliver's proposal for the Forward Movement Program with little enthusiasm. He set about promoting it as vigorously as he could, but to his dismay the seminary soon found itself unexpectedly the subject of a sweeping evaluation that threatened its very existence. In 1947 the Association of Methodist Theological Schools requested the denomination's Board of Education to make a thorough study of all the seminaries of The Methodist Church. The stated purpose was to inquire fully into the situation of each seminary—the advantages and disadvantages of its geographical location, curricular offerings, specialized fields, finances, physical facilities, student personnel, and "doubtless other pertinent questions . . . to point out the weaknesses and short-comings of the institutions and give recommendations for their improvement and enrichment." It was entirely possible that as a result of this study one or more of the smaller schools might be closed.

Examiners were chosen for each school, and those delegated to visit Westminster were John Seaton, president of the University Senate of The Methodist Church, and John K. Benton, dean of the School of Religion at Vanderbilt University. Their inspection was meticulous and their findings no surprise: the library was inadequate, the building unfit, endowment and scholarship funds insufficient, the general financial situation precarious. The published report was critical of all the seminaries, as it was meant to be, and it exposed with devastating clarity Westminster's many weaknesses. The examiners' conclusion was ominous:

> In the judgment of the surveyors the Seminary faces obstacles which cannot be easily surmounted and which raise grave questions concerning its future. The church plainly does not need on the Atlantic seaboard six theological seminaries, five primarily for white students and one for Negro students. Moreover, geography and the pressure of far better seminaries to the North and South are against it. Westminster being relatively weak and . . . off the main lines of travel has various disadvantages. Among them and more serious than has been recognized is the lack of really practical university connections and of other educational values related to a university or a city.

Other problems of Westminster Seminary, they continued, were "the limited campus . . . and the one crowded educational building which serves a variety of purposes not normally congenial with one another and quite incompatible in a building so small." The surveyors estimated that "large sums of money will be required to make the school really standard as a theological seminary of graduate rank," and even then it would need to confine itself "of necessity to a relatively restricted program." In all these dismal judgments, there was no mention of the remarkable advances the seminary had made since the union of 1939. The examiners were not interested in past history; they were evaluating the present and calculating the future. The situation was, in fact, so serious that the published report concluded by noting that "certain important matters have been omitted from this report and referred directly to the Board of Governors for primary consideration." This private communication has not been found, but its substance may be inferred from subsequent revelations of growing dissatisfaction in some quarters with the seminary's leadership.

There was little use in protesting the report. At Welliver's urging, the Board of Governors proposed "A Minimum Program for Westminster Theological Seminary," which they hoped would satisfy those who had sponsored the survey, and this was duly forwarded to the Board of Education. The "Minimum Program" sought to salvage the main features of the Forward Movement, but it was also a strategy for survival. It made several proposals: a full-time faculty of eight, a full-time professionally trained librarian, an annual library appropriation of "at least $3,000 a year for several years to bring up the collection to something like standard," a reasonable increase in faculty salaries to an average of $5,000, and an increase in enrollment to seventy or eighty students adequately housed with their own dining room. To demonstrate their flexibility, the governors conceded that the dining room was not essential. But nobody ventured to suggest where the money to do these things might be found.

The denomination took no immediate action on the report of the survey team, nor did it reply to the Board of Governors' response, and the seminary struggled on. Some people said that Welliver fought "with his back to the wall." Frank Shaffer, who became a member of the Board of Governors in 1947 and served as vice-president from 1951 to 1953, gave in later years a thoughtful interpretation of what he thought may have been the most trying years of the school's history. Of the president he said:

> Here was a man of deep and personal dedication to a task which at times seemed impossible. Had he been less dedicated we could have lost the Seminary. . . . Immediately following Methodist union [some] assumed that the

> Seminary would be closed. Lester Welliver, with a stubborn will, opposed all such moves [when] a man of less conviction might have capitulated and given up.[2]

Back to the wall or not, Welliver proceeded doggedly to address the school's most urgent problem, the need for additional space.

Physical facilities had been inadequate for some time, and Welliver wanted badly to get on with constructing a new building. One troublesome problem was that Western Maryland College also needed to expand. When college officials asked to buy a small piece of seminary land for a new men's dormitory, Welliver's zeal to protect every inch of the seminary's seven acres made negotiations fruitless. Committees appointed to adjudicate the competing claims extended their debate over several years. Complicating the question was the hope some had of exchanging the seminary's acreage for a comparable tract of college land, perhaps at the back of the golf course, so that neither institution would be in the way of the other's expansion. Some suggested that since the college had given the seminary its land in the first place (in 1882), some flexibility on the seminary's part would be an appropriate sign of gratitude; but just what this might be no one could say. There was no real desire on either campus to make any concessions.

In 1949 Welliver reported to the board that a planning committee had been working steadily for a year and a half on a "long and thorough exploration" of the college's request that the seminary make "some adjustment in [its] location," but that it "finally appeared impossible to work out a feasible plan." Brushing aside the potential for conflict with the college, Welliver concluded with evident satisfaction: "The Committee has therefore proceeded to make plans for the development of our present campus site." He gave some "now-is-the-time" reasons: "We have the largest enrollment in our history [ninety-four], we have the largest faculty we have ever had [six full-time, five part-time] and we are far stronger financially than we have ever been." The financial improvement he attributed to increases in tuition, new contracts with the Veterans Administration, and increased appropriations from The Methodist Church. "The audit of our accounts for the last

could find a hearing. In 1950, when Welliver was leaving for Europe, he had written to each faculty member: "Kindly keep your weekends as free as possible in order to help us in presenting the cause to various churches throughout the Conference." So, sometimes singly or by twos, professors went Sunday after Sunday to churches not only in Maryland but in the neighboring states preaching and "presenting the cause."

To lead the Building Committee were the president, vice-president, and Bishops Flint and Straughn. The faculty was represented by Shroyer, Schilling, and Furgeson; and from the Board of Governors came John J. Porter, Benjamin W. Meeks, E. Ralph Lewis, and Reginald G. Mowbray. The committee engaged as architect John B. Hamme of York, Pennsylvania. His plans for the new building were extremely attractive, and putting them on display increased enthusiasm all around. The most desirable location was at the very top of Seminary Hill, but this would require purchasing from the college a small triangular parcel of land adjoining Welliver's home. The college agreed to transfer the tract on condition that it be allowed to "approve the location, type of architecture, roads, walks, etc." The college further specified that the transfer not take place until it was "satisfied that the Seminary is financially able to complete the needed building," but it magnanimously agreed to postpone its own financial campaign in order to "give the Seminary the right of way until the first of the year." President Lowell Ensor of the college supported Welliver's appeal to the Baltimore Conference's Committee on World Service and Finance, which had to approve any campaign to raise funds. Both presidents appeared personally before the committee, and as a result the conference voted to include in its campaign for church extension $200,000 designated for the seminary's building program "on condition that it be used for building within the bounds of the Baltimore Conference." The restriction would squelch further talk about moving to Ohio, and it was exactly what Welliver wanted.

By 1952, four years after the damaging survey report was published, Westminster was enjoying unprecedented prosperity and Welliver's September report to the Board of Governors was jubilant. The seminary had just opened with the admission of 55 new students out of 121 applicants, "making an entering class almost as large as the entire student body five years ago." This brought the total enrollment to 150, the largest in the school's history. Most hopeful of all was a promise of increased support from the denomination. The 1952 General Conference had made ministerial education an integral part of the Division of Educational Institutions of the General Board of Education, and it had provided for a full-time director for theological schools. The seminaries, Welliver reported, were to receive "two and one-half times as much as was previously appropriated for their work. . . . This could not come at a more opportune time." Westminster's increase in enrollment had created problems, of course, but these were being managed. Dormitory rooms intended for single occupancy were now double rooms. The seminary was renting the Cassell Home (formerly a Methodist Episcopal home for the aged) for additional dormitory space, and married students were finding housing elsewhere in the town. The college was furnishing chapel and classroom space for a modest fee, and seminary students were still eating in the college dining hall. Welliver's report rang with the conviction that the seminary surely had a future, and as he envisioned it, that future was on top of Seminary Hill in Westminster.

There were other signs of permanence and progress. The summer schools were thriving, and graduate seminars in Baltimore were enrolling a gratifying number of students. Clinical training at Springfield State Hospital was supplementing the work in Pastoral Counseling. Powell was expanding his work in group dynamics by offering laboratory sessions. Alumni interest was rising, as witnessed by their recent request to elect two of their number as advisory members, without vote, of the Board of Governors. Such new signs of growth, stability, and prosperity were regarded by most of the seminary's constituency as clear evidence that the school was now securely fixed in the life of the church with a future full of promise. Hopes were rising for a ground-breaking in Westminster soon.

There were some, however, who envisioned for the seminary a new era strikingly different from its rural Maryland past. The swift-moving events that dramatically changed the direction of the school's development began when Bishop G.

Bromley Oxnam was transferred from Boston to Washington in 1952. He soon revived Emory Bucke's call to transfer the seminary to the nation's capital, and much of what happened to bring this about was due to the energy and ambition of this brilliant, hard-driving, controversial churchman.

6

'We are on our way
to Washington'

The astonishing alteration in the seminary's course was
engineered by a triumvirate of Methodist leaders: G. Bromley
Oxnam, Norman L. Trott, and Hurst Anderson. Bishop Oxnam
took a lively interest as well as a direct hand in the seminary's
affairs immediately upon coming to Washington in 1952.
Trott, already secretary of the Board of Governors, served as
acting president of the seminary during a six-month furlough
granted Welliver in 1953, when some of the crucial decisions
respecting the seminary's future were made; and in 1955 he
was elected president with the understanding that he would
plan and direct the move to Washington. Anderson became
president of The American University in 1952, and his active
cooperation made it possible to locate the seminary's beautiful
new campus adjacent to his own. The story now unfolds
around these three men.

G. Bromley Oxnam, 1891-1963

Bishop Oxnam's life cannot be summarized easily, but he
almost succeeded in doing so in a paragraph he wrote in 1955
for one of his chatty letters to the ministers in his area.

> Next year marks my fortieth as a Methodist minister and
> my twentieth as a bishop. Surely it was only yesterday that
> I attended conference for the first time in Santa Ana, Califor-
> nia, and was appointed to a little rural charge in Poplar—
> salary $600, no parsonage—well, there was a shack without
> running water, no sanitary facilities and a rental of $8 a

161

month which the minister was to pay. But it was a grand year among wonderful people. They built a new church and a parsonage that year—one of the happiest years of our lives. Ten years followed at the Church of All Nations, with its four buildings built and what is much more important, a decade of fellowship with people, real people. A year of teaching at the Boston University School of Theology followed, then eight years at DePauw University as President, and now twenty in the episcopacy! Where have they gone?

This is sketchy, for Oxnam was writing in haste, as usual. Speed and decisiveness marked his every action; he had no patience with hesitancy nor tolerance for incompetence. He thought clearly, reached conclusions quickly, and defended his judgments vigorously. Some of his progressive social views provoked the House Committee on Un-American Activities to label him as a communist sympathizer, and soon after he came to Washington he had an open confrontation with that committee. The public hearing which he demanded was held on 21 July 1953; it lasted for ten hours, and his spirited refutation of the committee's charges did much to expose the slipshod methods of its "investigation" of him. Oxnam published a full account in a book of 186 pages, *I Protest* (New York, 1954), and the affair stands as something of a milestone in the development of religious liberty in America.[1]

Oxnam's assignment as bishop of the Washington Area made him a member ex officio of the seminary's Board of Governors, and he was elected chairman at once. This was irregular, to say the least, since the charter stated that board members were to be elected by the General Conference. But it was a simple matter to change the charter later and retroactively to legalize the board's action. Some idea of what Oxnam's presence was going to mean to both the board and the seminary's future may be seen in his own recital of a year's schedule at that time. In a breezy letter to "my dear Colleagues" the bishop described his pace—it could be called his "life style"—at that time. The year was 1955, but all his years seemed to race at the same speed. He reported that he and Mrs. Oxnam were closing their camp at Lake Winnepesaukee, New Hampshire. It was the day after Labor Day, so his summer "vacation" was just ending. He had planned much reading

162

and a great deal of rest, but there was "no achievement here." Mail had been forwarded from Washington daily, and a secretary had phoned from the office each day at 11:45 A.M. The illness of Mrs. Oxnam's mother summoned them to the Pacific Coast for several days, but

> trips back to the [Washington] area were necessary to keep promises at the Lay Retreat in Newton, . . . and for the Board of Trustees of Sibley Hospital and conferences with the architect, the Centennial address at Michigan State University, conferences with the Commission on Theological Education and the Board of Education at Nashville and the Methodist Radio and Film Commission . . . and the National Convocation of Methodist Youth at Purdue University. All this to say I am returning to work dead tired.

After reporting on the summer just past, Oxnam wanted his readers to know about the year ahead. Included in "the regular work" would be the administration of his episcopal area, along with many responsibilities on the Council of Bishops, the Commission on World Service and Finance, the commission planning the new quadrennial program for General Conference, the National Council of Churches, and the World Council of Churches. "And because the invitations come, I shall speak at Howard, Yale, Vassar, Bowdoin, Carnegie Tech, Wisconsin, Dickinson, Bryn Mawr, Cornell, Duke, Tuskegee, Monmouth, Kansas, Berea, Rutgers, and Randolph-Macon as well as a few important secondary schools such as Andover and Choate." He and Mrs. Oxnam would soon fly to Berchtesgaden in Germany for a retreat with Methodist chaplains and their wives serving in Europe, then to Budapest for an honorary degree from the Reformed Theological Seminary where "Karl Barth, John Baillie, Martin Niemoeller and others are to be similarly honored." Following the Washington Area retreat at Buck Hill Falls, Pennsylvania, he and Mrs. Oxnam expected to fly to Australia for a meeting of the Executive Committee of the World Council of Churches, with a lecture on the way in the Fiji Islands. Then he would visit chaplains in the Far East—Manila, Hong Kong, Formosa, Okinawa, Korea, Japan— and return by way of Honolulu and Alaska. A scheduled visit to India had to be cancelled, he said, "because as every minister knows . . . you can't do everything."

"On Our Way"

A new direction set

Oxnam was once described by a fellow bishop as "an implacable foe of injustice, a kind of moral bulldozer that could bite into and level out all barriers of opposition."[2] When he arrived in Washington, he found almost immediately three institutions that needed some bulldozing. Sibley Hospital needed to find a new location, The American University needed to establish a School of International Service, and Westminster Seminary needed to move to Washington. For these institutions he dreamed great dreams and then acted decisively to bring the dreams to fulfillment. A key figure in Oxnam's grand scheme was Hurst Anderson, the new president of The American University. Anderson had come in 1952 from the presidency of Hamline University, and he began immediately to furnish the kind of energetic leadership needed to make the university a school of national and international importance. Oxnam saw in Anderson qualities matching his own, and their teamwork was mutually gratifying.

Oxnam's impatience with long discussions, his ability to make decisions quickly, and his deft exercise of episcopal authority gave his ideas a compelling momentum. Once the crucial decision was made to move the seminary, it took only six months to bring the key pieces into place and get legal approval. More than that, in this same brief interval of time, Oxnam found the money needed to guarantee success. Early in 1953 he approached the Kresge Foundation, recording the contact in his diary for 28 January of that year:

> I had planned to remain at the General Board meeting [in New York] until noon but the opportunity to see Mr. Howard C. Baldwin, one of the Trustees of the Kresge Foundation, could not be missed, so I caught an early plane from Newark for Detroit and . . . was able to meet Mr. Baldwin at his suggestion at three o'clock. I outlined to him the needs of the American University with particular reference to the School of International affairs and of the Westminster Theological Seminary. . . . Funds, he thought, might be available. I think he really felt that if we make a strong case there was reasonable hope of substantial help.

After the talk with Baldwin, despite a feeling that "the flu had got ahold of" him, Oxnam lectured that night at Henry Hitt Crane's church before catching a plane back to Washington. The next day he met with the Executive Committee of The American University, had lunch with President Anderson, and "recounted what had been done in the case of the Kresge Foundation." A few days later he was at Westminster with Lowell Ensor, president of Western Maryland College, whom he found to be "a man of unusual ability." They had "a long talk . . . concerning educational policy," and Oxnam concluded with evident satisfaction, "I think the educational line-up is beginning to emerge with clarity." Events the following week were to show how clear that "line-up" was. On 12 February he met with the seminary's Board of Governors, which promptly elected him its chairman. Then, according to his diary, he "apologized for precipitating immediate consideration of a fundamental matter of policy but discussed the possibility of the School moving to Washington. They were more than cordial; a committee of seven was authorized and we shall be on the way."

The minutes of the board for this first formal meeting with Oxnam on 12 February 1953 provide further information regarding the proposed move. Norman L. Trott, secretary, recorded Oxnam's presentation.

> . . . He began by expressing interest in the educational program of the [episcopal] Area, then proceeded to list the great possibilities latent in our American University, and expressed the hope that careful consideration would be given to bringing the Westminster Theological Seminary to the campus of the American University. The Bishop also spoke of the high regard in which the Seminary was held by both ministers and laymen in the Area. Upon Oxnam's suggestion that a committee be appointed [and] charged with immediate and thorough study of his proposal Mr. [George] Culberson moved, and Mr. [Lynde] Ryman seconded, and it was passed that a Committee of Seven be authorized for this purpose. It was unofficially suggested that Drs. [John W.] Hawley and [Frank] Shaffer be included in such a Committee. The others were: Bishop Oxnam, Bishop Straughn, Norman L. Trott, B. W. Meeks, and President Welliver, ex-officio.

Subsequent discussion became somewhat complicated as the board considered a letter from Western Maryland College, written in November 1952, requesting a joint committee to consider the proposal of transferring to the seminary the small triangle of land on which Welliver wanted to erect the new building that was the centerpiece of his plans for the Diamond Jubilee at Westminster. Secretary Trott noted tersely, "Oxnam suggested a delay in the appointment of such a committee until the Committee of Seven on the move [to Washington] had reported." And it was done.

The Committee of Seven, "charged with immediate and thorough study" of Oxnam's plan, did not meet until 30 March. In the meantime, on 24 February Hurst Anderson was inaugurated president of The American University. In his Inaugural Address, while describing his intentions for the future of his school, he said: "We desire to move to Washington one of the established Schools of Theology, for it is our belief that the opportunities of this city ought to be made available to those studying theology." Many in the audience were startled by what seemed to be a public announcement of a tentative proposal still under study. President Welliver, who was present, was shaken. He disapproved of the idea but saw no way to stop it. The speeding events over which he had no control began in him a sad erosion of will and spirit that were to enervate the next several months of his presidency.

On Monday, 30 March, the Committee of Seven gathered to "study" the move announced by Anderson five weeks earlier. Only Meeks was absent, being ill. Oxnam's diary for the day records his perception of what happened.

> I recounted in brief outline the careful thought I had been giving to the whole question of the educational policy of the Area. I had made reference to the Theological Survey conducted by our own University Senate and The Board of Education back in 1946 or '47, [and] noted the conclusion concerning Westminster. This survey raised serious questions as to its future and pointed out particularly that in all of its years since 1882 it had never received a substantial gift. I gave some fundamental reasons for a change. . . . Then we entered full discussion. . . . Dr. Shaffer strongly supported the move, so did Dr. Hawley, Bishop Straughn and Dr. Trott also. Therefore, all the regular members of the

166

Committee [present] were favorable to the move. Welliver, however, dragged his feet. He could think of nothing but objections.

At the close of the meeting the committee went to the campus of the university, where President Anderson led them to "a magnificent site," some nine acres bounded by Massachusetts and University avenues. Oxnam was delighted: "I have never seen a finer location. It is easily worth half a million dollars."

If Oxnam was pleased with Anderson, he was visibly irritated with Welliver. In the bishop's diary is no sign of sympathy for the seminary president's distress over a plan which would summarily abandon nine years of work on the development of the Westminster campus. The Oxnam bulldozer was without subtleties, as his barely veiled threat shows:

> I finally had to say, "Now Dr. Welliver let us get something straight. I happen to be the Bishop here and you are the President of the institution. It is your duty to lead this institution, to raise these funds, and to see it out. It is the duty of a Bishop to drop in occasionally and offer prayer upon some event. I personally am perfectly willing to forget this school and turn my attention to more rewarding educational opportunities."

Welliver at last professed support, and the committee drafted a recommendation to the board that, subject to certain conditions, the seminary should be moved. The bishop exulted in his diary, "We are on the way, at last."

The "certain conditions" were clear: the transfer of the seminary's property in Westminster to Western Maryland College "after a satisfactory settlement," the continued corporate existence of the seminary (though not necessarily under the same name), and an "immediate approach to foundations and other resources for funds for the expanding Seminary on the new site." The property exchanges were authorized within three weeks. On 10 April representatives of both schools met to negotiate the sale of the seminary's Westminster properties to the college. Oxnam's diary describes the bargain that was struck:

> I finally said, "What is the point of a long discussion? Ordinarily, a man never reveals the line to which he will retreat in negotiation but it seems to me since we are all Methodists

167

and we all desire the same thing it would be better for me to state what I believe to be the value of the Seminary properties.'' I then stated the value of the land, the buildings and faculty residences. They reached a total slightly in excess of $200,000. General Gill, a former military leader and a real estate man of great wealth said to the chairman [Murray Benson], ''Would you mind if I whispered something to Bishop Oxnam?'' He came to me and said, ''Bishop, what do you say we settle this at $175,000?'' I said, ''I think that is excellent.'' . . . It was done as quickly as that and happily and, with the exception of Welliver's statement (for $200,000) it was unanimous. He then changed his opinion so we could have an unanimous vote.

April was a busy month. On the sixteenth Oxnam made a hurried trip to Detroit, accompanied by Hurst Anderson. After meeting with Marshall Reed, bishop of that area, to enlist his approval and support, they proceeded to the Kresge Foundation. Stanley Kresge himself received them, with the attorney and secretary of the foundation. Oxnam recorded in his diary:

I made the presentation, asked for two million dollars. We had a very happy conference of an hour and fifteen minutes. They requested us to file a formal application which we will do. . . . It may mark the turn in the history of the American University. If we can secure such a grant, move the Westminster Theological Seminary and put religion at the heart of this school, we will really be on the way.

The formal application to the Kresge Foundation was duly submitted a week later.

Meanwhile Oxnam invited the Westminster faculty to come to his office in Washington. They previously had sent a long communication to the Committee of Seven that Oxnam thought naive and even improper, but he was willing to forgive. ''We must overlook the faculty's disregard for proprieties,'' he told the committee on 30 March; they ''had not been invited to participate in this matter'' and at the present stage it really was not their privilege to enter the discussion. Nevertheless, he recognized that ''the teachers love the school and their lives are given to its service,'' so he consented to hear them out. When they arrived at his office, the bishop made it clear that there was a distinction between administrative and faculty responsibilities. Then he recounted all that had been done, openly discussed the plans, and answered their questions. To him "it appeared that the members of the faculty were ready to give the plan full support."[3]

There remained yet the formal decision by the seminary's Board of Governors. Their 1953 spring meeting fell on 25 April at the usual place, 516 North Charles Street in Baltimore. Bishop Oxnam, of course, presided. Albert E. Day offered prayer. Bishop Paul N. Garber, Thomas Colley, George Culberson, and John Porter sent regrets. E. R. Lewis and W. C. Scott sent letters of resignation. Then came the president's report. Welliver was sober, cautious, and without the high expectations of other years. He noted Schilling's departure and recommended Gilmore's appointment. Other matters in his report were routine: summer schools, student activities, the Seminary Singers, property repairs, the approaching commencement on 26 May, and the monthly meetings lately begun of student wives with faculty wives. Finally Welliver spoke of the great issue that would be decided that day. With heroic control over his own apprehension and disappointment, he anticipated the report of the Committee of Seven on the proposed move to Washington. "Our meeting today will probably be epochal in the history of the Seminary. For seventy-one years this institution has served the church in the preparation of its ministry. . . . I am confident that any action taken by this Board will be such as to make certain that the Institution will be able to continue its work without serious interruption." That was all.

It is not likely that Welliver was hoping that his own development plan for Westminster might yet be salvaged by the board. In a few minutes it would be officially decided, but not until after an embarrassing interlude occasioned by the president's financial report. "For the first time in ten years," he said, "we shall probably have an actual deficit in our operating fund." The deficit was not large, and the reasons for it seemed obvious: a budget miscalculation the previous fall, rising costs, unexpected expenses, and so many more married students with families who "are finding it extremely difficult to finance their seminary training." But Oxnam was displeased and said so. He thought that Welliver had not given a true picture of the school's finances and that even the

169

auditor's report was inadequate. The board referred the matter to its Executive Committee for investigation.

Oxnam then presented the report of the Committee of Seven, of which he was chairman. He gave an initial statement of interpretation and asked for comments. Vice-President Shaffer spoke first. He talked of his debt to and affection for the Methodist Protestant Church, of the limitations of the seminary in its Westminster location, and of his hope that the school would seize the opportunity to move to a more advantageous site. Also supporting the move were John W. Hawley, Frank E. Masland, Bishop Straughn, and Bishop Fred P. Corson. Messages of approval came from Culberson and Bishop Garber. Not from Porter, however; and Scott and Lewis had already resigned to avoid the issue. Welliver declined to speak, pleading that "he had been so closely involved in the matter that he would prefer having the Board make the proper decision." The vote was taken, and the secretary recorded: "There were fifteen members of the Board present and all fifteen votes were cast in favor of the adoption of the report and the subsequent relocation on the campus of American University." Oxnam then led the group in prayer, asking God's blessing on the new venture, and the board authorized the Committee of Seven "to handle matters relating to the transfer of the Seminary and the sale of its properties." Reflecting on the meeting later, Oxnam wrote jubilantly in his diary:

> I am happy to say that the Board unanimously voted to move from Westminster to the American University campus. Thus all of this is now behind us by way of record. We have a little job of finding two million dollars. That's all.

That was on 25 April 1953. Three weeks later Oxnam was returning by train from Wilmington, Delaware, to Washington. According to his diary, Norman Trott and Earl Furgeson boarded the train at Baltimore "to recount the present situation at Westminster. I am fearful that Dr. Welliver is having a crack-up perhaps mental in nature and that we shall have to make a change. In any case we shall have to release him completely for a time and put someone [else] in charge." On 2 June the bishop summoned the Executive Committee of the Board of Governors to his temporary office at the annual meeting of the Baltimore Conference then gathered at Western

170

Maryland College. Albert Day, John Porter, and Norman Trott came; so did three faculty members (Shroyer, Schilling, and Furgeson) whom the bishop had invited. Nobody was smiling, for all felt the sadness of the event: President Welliver had collapsed. According to the minutes, Shroyer prayed; then

> Bishop Oxnam read a communication which had been addressed to the Board by the three faculty members listed above. The letter dealt with the gravity of Dr. Welliver's illness, his present inability to carry on the work of his office and the need for an adjustment that would provide an acting head for the Seminary in this difficult period.

After some discussion, Day "moved that Dr. Welliver be granted a six months leave of absence, at full salary, in order that he might have opportunity for rest and treatment." Seconded by Porter, the motion passed unanimously.

Who would carry on the work? The committee turned instinctively to Trott, asking if he would be willing to assume this responsibility in addition to his duties as a district superintendent. Trott agreed, his minutes note, on condition that "a) he be permitted to serve without compensation; b) the faculty work with him as a team sharing administrative labors as circumstances might require; and c) some provision be made for secretarial help to lighten the load." The committee accepted the conditions, unanimously elected Trott as acting president, and delegated him the necessary authority to sign checks and legal papers on all accounts and to have access to the safe deposit boxes held in the seminary's name.[4] Oxnam noted tersely in his diary:

> On Wednesday, June 2, I spent the day with the Cabinet except for an Executive Committee meeting of the Board of Governors of Westminster Seminary where we took up the case of President Welliver, took the action I recommended and elected Dr. Norman Trott as Acting President. He will not give up his work on the District. He is superbly qualified to lead here.

Welliver withdrew from the scene of his labors, his frustrated hopes, and his humiliations to the quiet healing of the Canadian woods, far from Oxnam's overpowering presence. In his absence, Trott began exercising the full powers of the presidency. In the acting president's November report to the board, just before Welliver's return, Trott said he had

171

given half of his August vacation to preparing for the new school year and was continuing to devote two days a week to the seminary. He had found many problems in jamming 150 students into facilities designed for 50, with only four classrooms, no office space for faculty and almost none for the president (circumstances which Welliver had long endured). The cramped situation in the library, Trott noted, was "impossible." Some small relief had been obtained by renting the Cassell Home, a former residence for the aged in the town. The financial picture was somewhat brighter, with a balance of $23,000 in the operating fund and denominational contributions increasing. The Baltimore Conference Church Extension Crusade, about to "reach its climax," promised an additional $100,000 for the seminary. This meant the possibility of immediate improvements in the library and at least one addition to the faculty. Trott urged that Professor Moyer be brought from part-time to full-time service.

In a paragraph on "The Shift to Washington" Trott's style and action were evident:

> First, you will be pleased to know that Bishop Oxnam, President Hurst Anderson of American University, Dr. Gerald McCulloh of the Department of Theological Schools [of The Methodist Church], and I met at the American University on Sept. 29 to stake off the tentative boundaries of the Seminary site preliminary to a survey and determination of the metes and bounds. This was an historical event.

Using a ten-pound maul, Oxnam drove one of the stakes "with the same dispatch he does everything else." Then, reported Trott, "all four men autographed the handle of the maul and it will be preserved for posterity." Trott had executed the proper legal documents for transferring the seminary's Westminster properties to the college, as authorized by the board in April, and Oxnam announced his intention to appoint a committee to select an architect and proceed with plans for the new campus in Washington. Everyone was pleased with the pace of progress toward the move.

The acting president's report concluded with several recommendations: 1) that faculty salaries be increased to be "in line with the general pattern"; 2) that $3,000 be set aside annually to provide sabbatical leaves for faculty members; 3) that an

172

With plans well under way for moving the seminary to a new location in Washington, DC, a site adjacent to The American University was staked on 29 September 1953. Bishop Oxnam drove the first stake. On the left are Hurst Anderson, president of The American University, and Gerald O. McCulloh of the denomination's Department of Theological Schools; on the right is Norman L. Trott, acting president of the seminary.

outstanding librarian, or librarians, be employed to survey the library and make recommendations for improvement; 4) that all students "settle for tuition and room at the beginning of each semester or make satisfactory arrangements with the office for time payments"; 5) that the seminary purchase liability insurance in the amount of $50,000 for each person and $100,000 for each accident, "a coverage that has not been provided before"; and 6) that since the seminary's buildings would soon belong to the college, they be tied now to the college electrical system, with the seminary making a monthly contribution based on the average monthly bill less 10 percent. Trott's genius for clean management was further exhibited in one final recommendation already approved by the Executive Committee, namely a plan to provide out of general scholarship funds matching payments on delinquent student accounts "to get these off the books of the Seminary and the consciences of the men involved."

Trott's report showed competence and confidence. The board was pleased and promptly passed a motion by Bishop Straughn "to give Mr. Trott a thousand dollars in appreciation for his services as Acting President." Then Oxnam raised "the question of Welliver and whether or not he could carry on the work." After several expressions of sympathy and concern for President Welliver's health, the board voted to appoint a committee "to study Dr. Welliver's future relationship to the Seminary."

Welliver's fading presidency

His leave spent, Welliver returned in December 1953 seemingly "restored in health and vigor." He appeared confident that he could resume his presidential duties. The situation was uncomfortable at best, however, and an omen of how quickly it would become intolerable came in a confrontation with Oxnam on his first day back in the office. The bishop questioned bluntly "whether the new load would break" Welliver, and before the president could answer, Oxnam went on:

> I told him I thought he ought to understand fully that there were serious situations that confronted him. I told him I thought the faculty felt there should be a change in leadership, that there might be a rebellion in the student body and that the Board, I thought the majority, was of the same opinion. I told him that while he was there for the rest of the [academic] year . . . no man had a position in perpetuity and that I thought he ought to give serious consideration to the whole question [of resigning]. I think he got the idea.

It was hardly a reassuring welcome home.

Welliver endured eighteen more months of strain and tension before submitting his resignation. During those months, although the pace of activity on campus never slackened, problems mounted. Vice-President Shaffer's enthusiasm for the proposed move to Washington had been so at odds with the president's reluctance that Shaffer felt compelled to resign. Returning to the West Virginia Conference, Shaffer became pastor of the Bluefield Church.

Welliver was left alone to deal with a Board of Governors that had deserted his program, a faculty torn between the excitement of the move and anxiety about their president, and the displeasure of a bishop notoriously intolerant of dissent. Physical facilities were increasingly overcrowded, resources strained. An emergency occurred in late December, when R. E. Gilmore, who was well started in his first year as professor of Systematic Theology, became seriously ill and had to be away from his classes for three and a half months. The college, as it had done so often, supplied a part-time substitute in Reuben Holthouse, also from Boston, who added part of Gilmore's work to his own load.

Despite these burdens, Welliver achieved some modest successes. For the library study recommended by Trott and authorized by the board he secured the services of Robert Beach, librarian at Union Theological Seminary in New York. Beach's report contained many fruitful recommendations for immediate as well as long-range improvement. A most pressing need was a fully trained librarian, and Welliver recommended one; but the Executive Committee deferred action to a later time. The library did gain a doubling of funds for books and periodicals, which was gratifying, along with some new shelving and a microfilm reader. A curriculum revision resulted in more elective possibilities for the students. Senior Sermon, a full-scale worship service in the chapel, became a requirement for graduation. The summer schools for supply pastors and for town and country ministers completed their ninth year with enrollments larger than ever and tuition receipts sufficient to make them self-supporting. For the first time in the seminary's history there was some small progress in "uniform and adequate pensions" for the faculty. Ministers became eligible for Social Security coverage, and at the same time many annual conferences began to upgrade their own pension programs. Welliver watched these developments closely and tried to keep the faculty advised of changes that might affect their personal planning.

The Diamond Jubilee Campaign was no longer big news, but gifts continued to trickle in and were gratefully received. There was promise now of more from the Church Extension Crusade of the Baltimore Conference and from General Conference appropriations, raising expectations that misled some churches and individuals to cancel their pledges to the earlier campaign. Welliver tried to encourage them to continue their gifts, at least until their pledges were paid, but was only moderately successful.

Both faculty and administration gave much attention to cultivating and deepening religious and intellectual life on campus. Welliver spoke of it in almost every faculty meeting. The school scheduled annual retreats for spiritual renewal. To these as well as to regular chapel services came a variety of speakers such as Rufus Jones, Frank Laubach, E. Stanley Jones, Howard Thurman, Milton Mayer, Albert Day, John Oliver Nelson, Rabbi Abraham Shusterman, Kiyoshi Tanimoto (from Hiroshima), Henry Hitt Crane, Thomas Kepler, Emory Bucke, and Harry Denman. Harold DeWolf came from Boston for a series of lectures on theology, and W. F. Albright came from The Johns Hopkins University to speak on archaeology. There were many more, as Westminster now moved in a much larger orbit of church life and thought.

The prospect of moving to Washington was a favorite topic of conversation with everybody but President Welliver. By nature cautious and by experience aware that it was unwise and probably futile to express his distaste for the plan, he tried to conduct a holding operation until other forces should move the scheme along. When necessary, he gave the project dutiful notice, as in his report to the board on 23 April 1954. The seminary was making as much preparation as possible for the move, he declared; faculty committees were studying plans for classrooms, offices, dormitories, library, and chapel. But, he warned, "some basic decisions about planned enrollment and overall plans of construction" should come first. There had been a proposal for "a study of the religious, social, and educational agencies in the Washington Metropolitan area . . . for laboratory, clinical and field-work training of ministers." Welliver agreed that such a study would have certain values, but he was "not altogether convinced that this is the time to make [the study] or that the person who offered to conduct it is fully qualified to do so." The Executive Committee of the board, moreover, would have to authorize the expenditure of funds for such a purpose. He added that "pending some word from the Foundation which has been appealed to for financial help we have made no direct contacts with other foundations." This was scarcely the language of enthusiasm.

Welliver made only four recommendations to the board in April 1954. He asked that a new faculty member be appointed either in Psychology and Pastoral Care or in Preaching and Worship; that a fully trained librarian be employed, as Beach had urged; and that "the usual faculty rank of Full Professor, Associate Professor, Assistant Professor and Instructor be observed in the employment of members of the faculty in the

176

future." But more than anything else he wanted an "assistant to the President." Shaffer had resigned after only two years, and Welliver renewed the plea that he had carried to the board so many times before for someone "to share in the administrative work of the Seminary and carry on a program of financial promotion in cooperation with the President." The board referred his request to a committee, and nothing came of it.

At the 1954 commencement and during the months following there was much talk anticipating the move to Washington. Welliver did not share the excitement over this prospect. Signs of his distress increased alarmingly, and so many unpleasant tensions developed that some faculty members ventured to ask for a conference with Bishop Oxnam to discuss the deteriorating situation on campus. He invited the entire faculty to his office for a "confidential session" on Thursday evening, 14 October, and later wrote—in addition to the brief account in his diary—a full memorandum on the meeting.[5] Invited with the faculty were the three board members who constituted the committee appointed to consider President Welliver's future relationship to the seminary: Norman L. Trott, Benjamin W. Meeks, and Bishop James H. Straughn.

According to Oxnam's account, he tried to put them all at ease by stating that he knew it would be difficult for them to speak frankly about their president in Welliver's absence. But he also reminded them that he had a responsibility as president of the board and so did the committee members present. "One of the professors broke in immediately and stated that he understood that they had been invited to come here and certainly they had not asked to come because such an asking would be disloyal." After some hesitation, several began to voice their concerns. While repeatedly professing their respect for Welliver and high regard for his personal integrity, they spoke of his lapse in leadership, indecisiveness, and withdrawal to himself. He seemed short-tempered with his secretary and with the janitor, contentious with the students, and too absorbed with minute details. He had no long-range vision of the future of the school. He failed to follow through on courses of action approved by the faculty and himself, and what actions he did take seemed arbitrary, almost capricious. Oxnam noted each complaint carefully, and when the meeting came to a close, he was convinced that the faculty supported him in the decision he felt he had to make: "the future of the school required new leadership." He concluded his memorandum with the hope that "we can work it out happily [and] proceed in the most brotherly fashion."

Two weeks later, on Wednesday, 27 October 1954, Oxnam drove to Westminster. In a "difficult conversation," he "conferred with Dr. Welliver at 2 o'clock relative to the possibility of securing his resignation as president of Westminster Theological Seminary." The encounter was long and at moments stormy. Oxnam's diary does not conceal the bishop's "bulldozer" style, nor does it make clear that Welliver thought he was proceeding "in the most brotherly fashion." The bishop delivered the *coup de grâce* when he told Welliver that "the Kresge Foundation at this moment is conducting a study and is about to make [a] decision as to what it will do in the field of theological education. Westminster will receive nothing under your leadership." Welliver had no further ground to stand on, and the two men reached an agreement. The president would submit a letter of resignation, but Oxnam would not announce it to the board until the following spring. The bishop in return promised to appoint Welliver as superintendent of the Williamsport (Pennsylvania) District, effective 1 June 1955.

At the next meeting of the board, on 5 November 1954, Welliver continued to insist on the thing he wanted most, an "addition of help in administration," now "long overdue." Over the years, he reminded them, both he and his predecessor had carried "altogether too heavy a load." To impress the board with the extent of his tasks, he enumerated the responsibilities of the president's office.

> They include the duties of Dean of the educational program of the Seminary; the management of all of its business including supervision of the details of its bookkeeping; the care of its investments; the handling of publicity and all aspects of public relations including the representation of the Seminary at annual conferences and other church meetings; the cultivation of the alumni; the care, maintenance and repair of all property including the Seminary building, five faculty residences and a seven acre

campus; the purchase of all equipment and supplies; the selection and employment of faculty and staff members; the visitation of colleges to recruit students; the directing and carrying on [of] voluminous correspondence regarding admissions; the soliciting of funds from annual conferences, the general church and individuals for operating expenses, scholarship and general endowment and new buildings; the entertaining of official visitors to the Seminary; and the rendering of endless reports to various bodies concerning the work of the Seminary. The above does not include the day-to-day administration of the ongoing program, counseling and interviewing students and public appearances in local churches such as are expected of one in such a position.

He listed these things, Welliver asserted, "not to complain of the amount of work which we have tried to do . . . [but] to state that any evaluation of the work that has been done through the years which does not take into consideration this almost impossible load which has been carried is neither just, fair, nor honest."

It was a long and heavy apologia, embarrassingly true— and futile, as before. The board again declined to act on Welliver's request for an assistant, referring it instead to the special committee appointed the previous year "to consider the future relationship of Dr. Welliver to the Westminster Theological Seminary." Oxnam prodded the committee to "proceed at once to complete its task, and report either at a special meeting of the Board or at its next regular meeting."[6] The bishop knew full well, of course, that the committee would have no need to report, or even to meet, for at the next meeting of the board, on 2 May 1955, Welliver resigned as he had promised.

His one-sentence letter of resignation gave no reason—nor was one needed—but his report to the board again reviewed in even fuller detail his twelve years at Westminster and the transformation those years had wrought in the seminary. The number of students in 1943 had been 67, of whom 14 were not college graduates; now there were 161, all with degrees from accredited colleges. There had been five full-time and nine part-time faculty members; there were now ten full-time and nine part-time professors, and their average salary had increased by 117 percent. The entire annual budget in 1943

179

was a little over $18,000; for the 1955-56 fiscal year it would top $132,000, an increase of 633 percent. Welliver pointed to the higher academic standards for admission as well as the "C" average required for graduation. He described the testing program and other features of Orientation Week for entering students, the counseling and guidance provided by an intensified system of faculty advisors, and the staff psychologist for students needing professional therapy. He told of the curriculum revisions, the greater flexibility afforded by a smaller core and more electives, the success of the summer schools, the alumni organization with chapters in eight annual conferences, the appearance of the *Seminary Bulletin* as a quarterly publication, the library expansion from one to three rooms, additional dormitory space rented and furnished in town, the new office in the basement, new audio-visual equipment, and even a television set. There was more, much more. This was Welliver's last report; he made it long, and it was all true. His concluding comment was a sober, restrained affirmation of faith.

> Through these years we have given to our task all the ability, devotion and strength we have possessed. We have done our best. The satisfaction in what we have accomplished is sufficient reward. We humbly and respectfully present the fruits of our labors to the Board to whom we are responsible. But more important, we lay them at the feet of Him, Whose we are and Whom we serve.

The board listened in some discomfort, for they all knew that Welliver was laying down the burdens of his office, and they knew why. Only two of them had supported his plan to expand and build in Westminster. Now they were listening to one who could not forget his dream even though he had been forced to abandon it. Only one solitary sentence near the middle of his report betrayed his disappointment. Noting that the building fund now stood at over $300,000, Welliver declared: "We are confident that had the decision not been made to move to Washington, we could have raised a sufficient amount to erect the building [in Westminster] authorized by the Board and for which preliminary plans had been drawn in accordance with the schedule of the Diamond Jubilee Program, namely in 1956."

In 1956? The Spring 1956 issue of the *Seminary Bulletin* would picture President-elect Norman L. Trott and Bishop G. Bromley Oxnam examining, with broad smiles, a topographical survey and aerial map. The caption would announce that the trustees of The American University had voted to deed to Westminster Theological Seminary a nine-acre site on the northwest corner of its campus "as the University's contribution toward the relocation of the Seminary in Washington." This was hardly what President Welliver had envisioned through the Diamond Jubilee Campaign over the last twelve years. But in resigning he wanted to describe his shattered dream one last time, and he put it all faithfully into his final report. It is only fair to add that without the achievements of his twelve years as president there might not have been much of a seminary to move to Washington.

His service at the seminary terminated, Welliver returned to the Central Pennsylvania Conference and became (as Oxnam had promised) district superintendent at Williamsport. He did not fade into obscurity. He was vice-president of the Judicial Council (the "Supreme Court") of The Methodist Church from 1956 to 1960 and its president from 1960 to 1964. He was a delegate to three General Conferences, to four Jurisdictional Conferences, and to two World Methodist Conferences; and he was one of the research editors for *The Journal and Letters of Francis Asbury* (3 vols., 1958). In addition to his clear understanding of the church and the ministry, his knowledge of church law, and his deep religious faith, he had a forgiving spirit and an ability to ignore past hurts. Bishop Oxnam later acknowledged Welliver's legal abilities and administrative wisdom in coming to depend on him for the solution of many problems in his annual conference.

After Hurricane Agnes destroyed their Harrisburg retirement home in June 1972, Dr. and Mrs. Welliver moved to the Asbury Village apartments in Gaithersburg, Maryland. A year later, while he was walking one morning to his nearby dentist, cheerfully greeting friends and neighbors along the way, his heart failed. He fell and died instantly. Five sons—Allyn in the pastoral ministry, Daniel as a physician, and Kenneth, Paul, and Glenn as university professors—carry on the Welliver tradition of devotion to the best in scholarship, character, and service. One who knew Welliver intimately wrote of him:

> His love for the church was a full-time vocation, never an avocation. He believed in and loved the church with all his heart and soul and mind and strength. For him, slipshod work and intellectual laziness were inexcusable. It was difficult for him to tolerate these qualities in others of his profession. He had very strong convictions concerning the church, her mission and ministry and his religious faith rested on similar deep convictions.[7]

One needs only to add that Welliver's recovery from the frustration of his own plans for the seminary in Westminster and the forgiveness he subsequently extended to those who had shredded those plans were also marks of his greatness.

Norman Liebman Trott

President Welliver's resignation on 2 May 1955 was to become effective on 31 May. The Board of Governors had exactly one month to find a successor. But this was ample time, for the board and many others had long known Bishop Oxnam's choice for president, and on this matter they were all in agreement. A committee composed of Bishop James H. Straughn, Albert E. Day, and F. Murray Benson carried out the formality of a search; and on 1 June, Day presented to the board their report recommending Norman Liebman Trott (1901-75) for "immediate election to this holy office." Day's nominating remarks were characteristically florid and sermonic, but they described the nominee accurately as a man with scholarly interests and a keen mind aware of contemporary issues, a good administrator with the confidence of his colleagues, and a sensitive leader "who has already wrought some real miracles in the spirit of the School." Trott's election was pro forma. Oxnam wrote to John O. Gross of the General Board of Education: "We have just elected a man to head the Westminster Theological Seminary who will surprise the church, I am convinced, within two or three years. He has unusual skill."[8]

There was good reason for Oxnam's elation. Norman Trott truly did bring to the seminary presidency phenomenal gifts, high endowments of mind and spirit, unique training, and experience exactly right for his new task. Baltimore born, he was also Baltimore bred except for a short while at Wesley Collegiate Institute in Dover, Delaware, when he was in his early twenties. His school days began in the utter boredom of Public School No. 86, where his teachers seemed to be unaware of what was needed to interest a small boy with a quick mind. After a good bit of truancy he left school at the age of fifteen to go to work. He joined the army at sixteen. Discharged at nineteen, he became the purchasing agent for a chain of shoe stores. At twenty-two, when he decided to enter the ministry, he resumed his high school education at Wesley in Dover, where for the first time he found teachers and schooling to his liking. "This late start," he said afterward, "was the beginning of an educational plan which was unorthodox, but satisfactory."[9] He graduated from The Johns Hopkins University in 1931 with a Bachelor of Science degree and did some graduate work in Hopkins's Department of Psychology. For three years he held the Rauschenbusch

Norman Liebman Trott (1901-75) was elected president of the seminary in 1955 with an explicit charge to move the seminary to Washington. By the time he retired in 1967, five buildings had been constructed, the new campus fully developed, and the school, renamed Wesley Theological Seminary, was becoming a major center of theological education in the nation's capital.

183

Fellowship from Union Theological Seminary while studying in the Oriental Seminary at Johns Hopkins. In 1935 he collaborated with Randolph Mengers, an Episcopal clergyman, to establish the visiting clergy service at The Johns Hopkins University Hospital. This also provided opportunity for study in psychiatry with Dr. Esther Richards at the Phipps Clinic in Baltimore.

Trott was pastor successively of four churches, all in Maryland: Arbutus, Milton Avenue in Baltimore, First Methodist in Brunswick, and St. Paul's in Hagerstown. Then in 1950 Bishop Charles W. Flint appointed him superintendent of the Baltimore South District, where for five years in a difficult area of declining inner-city churches he demonstrated creative and imaginative leadership. He came to the seminary from that position. By then, in addition to various pastoral distinctions, he had been dean of the Westminster Pastors' School, president of the Conference Board of Child Care, chairman of the Youth Study Commission, and president of the Board of Trustees of the Asbury Home for the Aged. He was three times a delegate to General Conference, delegate to the World Council of Churches and to the World Methodist Conference, Methodist representative to the Consultation on Church Union, and on more boards and commissions than can be named here. In 1930, while he was a student pastor at Arbutus, he and Lillian Durfee were married. She, too, was Baltimore born and bred, but she adapted graciously to the varying circumstances of the itinerant ministry. For forty-five years, until his death in 1975, she provided steady support and quiet strength in the serenity of their several parsonages. Together they transplanted easily to Westminster's rural campus.

The first years of Trott's presidency coincided comfortably with those Eisenhower years often described as a time of national peace and prosperity. It is true that the bus boycott by blacks in Montgomery, Alabama, and the Supreme Court's decision against racial segregation in public schools portended deep trouble for the nation, but the "race problem" did not yet disturb campus life in Westminster. Some of the seminary community felt gratified to have Bishop Alexander P. Shaw, who was black, preach in chapel; and it was good to see black

184

students in the Seminary Singers. Several of the faculty, both college and seminary, promoted the Westminster Interracial Fellowship, holding some of its meetings in their own homes.

Since most of the students were pastors, whatever urge for social action they felt usually found immediate outlet in their churches. One inspiring union of classroom and parish was the "Heifer Project" begun by Professor Howes in 1955 when he learned about a similar work undertaken by the Church of the Brethren in nearby New Windsor. Reverend Ellis Plyler, a Methodist minister in Puerto Rico, had sent out a call for heifers to be raised by young farmers in his area. When Howes presented the appeal in one of his classes, the response was immediate. The student pastors told their churches, and dairy farmers gave calves from their herds while others bought heifers. The animals were brought to the campus and kept in Professor Chandler's garage until, after a litany of dedication shared by students, faculty, and farmers, they were prayed over by President Trott and shipped to Puerto Rico. Herbert Bowers of Oakton, Virginia, a seminarian with a degree in animal husbandry, went along as caretaker. A second shipment was ready a month later.

"On Our Way"

The "Heifer Project" of 1955 was an effort to supply milk cows to depressed areas in other parts of the world, and the seminary collected a number of calves from nearby rural churches. The animals were kept in Professor Chandler's garage prior to their shipment to Puerto Rico. In the foreground are Professor John B. Howes (left) and President Trott; in the background is John Brown from the Church of the Brethren, who was helping to care for the calves.

Such doings delighted Trott. They advertised the seminary's readiness to undertake one aspect of ministry which he thought important and which had been prominent in his own pastoral work. But by necessity his first months after coming to office in July 1955 had to be devoted to more strictly academic duties and to preparations for the move to Washington. In all matters, whether working with the faculty on curriculum and student regulations or with the board in shaping the design for the new campus, Trott's skills were little less than astonishing. The faculty knew that he was not a seminary graduate, that his baccalaureate degree was in science, and that his whole preparation for ministry was (as he himself confessed) "unorthodox." They also remembered the interim months of 1953, when as acting president Trott had tended to chair faculty meetings with a minimum of direction regarding questions of curriculum. They therefore had reason to expect from him something of a hands-off attitude toward academic matters, perhaps even deference to their superior wisdom. They were soon surprised. Trott speedily demonstrated a competence equal to theirs, directing even the most tedious sessions on degree requirements, curriculum structure, course planning, evaluation procedures, extensions of time, faculty advising, counseling recommendations, inter-seminary relations, and all the minutiae of faculty business as skillfully as an experienced academic dean. Although debates sometimes waxed warm, president and professors confined themselves to the issue in question and their personal relationships were never disrupted. Once Trott emerged from a lively skirmish and observed with a grin that sometimes he had to deal with a few "prima donnas" on the faculty. A professor shot back good-naturedly, "It takes one to know one."

Faculty committees multiplied, unmistakable evidence of the Trott style of administration. The president clearly enjoyed his work and gave to it time and energy without measure. His complete self-assurance was evident in a friendly informality with students and faculty alike. To be sure, there were occasional expressions of benevolent paternalism, and there were times when a problem was settled summarily by fiat ("from Mount Olympus," some said).

Trott loved puns, even the corniest. He chuckled over his

own and shook with laughter over those of others. He seemed to enjoy most those that drew groans from the faculty. He also wrote lovely poetry, lines that showed sensitivity to human need, a delicate awareness of nature's beauty, and openness to the love of God. But his poetry was reserved for private uses or intimate sharing; it was not for public display.

Art was another matter. Here his interests and discernment were visible everywhere. He had discriminating taste, though not everybody shared it. When he hung Salvador Dali's *The Christ of St. John* conspicuously in the main hall and spoke about the artist in a board meeting, one of his most valued (and affluent) board members, Frank Masland of Carlisle, Pennsylvania, wrote to ask: "Were you serious or facetious when you referred to using Dali as the artist in conjunction with the new school? . . . He isn't by chance a Methodist, is he?" Trott replied with a vigorous defense of the artist, enclosed a small copy of Dali's *Last Supper,* and took the occasion to add: "I would like to see Mr. Dali do a painting for the Seminary on Christ's call to Discipleship, if I could find a donor." Masland seems to have ignored the hint, choosing rather to contribute to the new campus in Washington the carpeting for the president's office, the board room, and (together with James Law of the Magee Carpet Company) the new president's home.

Mutual respect and congeniality reinforced the general euphoria of campus life as all members of the community shared the excitement of entering a new era. Psychological tests and decisions about counseling now required many hours of faculty planning. The assignment of students to faculty advisors, an experiment begun in the 1940s, gained increased emphasis, and the fall orientation program expanded far beyond its initial purpose of acquainting new students with "the tradition, ideals, standards and opportunities of the Seminary." A more inclusive testing program was designed "to furnish a foundation for counseling with the faculty advisor." The tests attempted to assess "vocational interests, values, personality inventory, mental maturity, study habits and English achievement." This last, which had long been the despair of many graduate study programs, now became for seminarians an occasion for anger, chagrin, and even terror

187

because of the possibility of having to take Remedial English. The explanation given to entering students was crisp and uncompromising.

> Students whose scores in the English test fall below the median for college freshmen are required to enroll in a non-credit course in English at the Seminary. Those whose scores fall below the lower 25% of college freshmen are required to enroll in a three-hour course in English at Western Maryland College and to continue the course throughout the two semesters of the Junior [first] year, the cost of the course to be borne by the student. Students who are required to take the three-hour remedial English course in the College must reduce their Seminary load to 12 hours. Those taking the non-credit refresher course in English in the Seminary may be required to take a reduced load of regular Seminary work at the direction of the faculty.

This formidable paragraph caused some entering students to quake as if they were being threatened with John Calvin's "horrible decree" or a papal anathema. But the test remained an inescapable requirement of Orientation Week.

The Senior Sermon requirement occupied many hours of faculty discussion. The long-standing expectation that every student should lead chapel and preach once during the senior year became utterly impossible as the number of seniors far outgrew the number of available chapel services. Furgeson solved the problem by providing an alternative of preaching in a classroom situation and posting a schedule of dates (one per week throughout the academic year) for those who wished to preach in chapel. There was great surprise when seniors regarded preaching in chapel as an honor and rushed to sign for the available times. Senior Chapel became a gala day. Families and friends came to share the occasion, while parishioners often drove miles to support their young pastors. The academic requirements were set in May 1955 when Senior Chapel became a course in advanced preaching; it provided professorial critique and peer evaluation in a class period following the chapel service. The course carried only one credit hour, but successfully completing it became for students a climactic achievement.

At the end of his first summer in office, Trott sent the faculty a long list of regulations governing student life and asked if they had any changes or corrections to make. None was necessary; his codification of the old rules was complete. Whenever possible, he presented his regulations for seminary life as pleasant announcements or the amenities of mutual respect. The student newsletter begun in his 1953 interim now came from his office as an attractively decorated sheet, captioned in colors and asking on the masthead, "How shall they hear without a preacher? Romans 10:14." In the spring of 1956 an important issue announced that students would be excused from classes on 11 April to attend the inauguration of President-elect Trott at Washington, invited them to make reservations by 15 March for the alumni-student luncheon, and listed the visiting speakers as Dr. Henry P. Van Dusen, president of Union Theological Seminary in New York; Dr. Gerald O. McCulloh, director of the Department of Theological Schools of The Methodist Church; Bishop Shot K. Mondol, Dr. Sherwood Hall, and A. V. Klaus, all of India; Bishop Lloyd Wicke from Pittsburgh; and Dr. Sam Shoemaker from Christ Episcopal Church in Pittsburgh. Other items in this issue of the newsletter announced that there would be no classes during Holy Week and identified the Dali reproduction hanging in the hall. There was also a plea for parking courtesy and an explanation of the joint agreement with the college on interchangeable parking privileges. In another issue Trott emphasized the priority of the chapel services, springing one of his notorious puns.

> . . . there are often good reasons why students do not attend particular chapel services, [but] we do not think that ping-pong should be among these reasons. If you differ with us, we will respect your judgment, though we will not agree with it. We trust that such difference will arise out of conscience and concern and not out of a greater love for ping-pong. So the question is: Is ping-pong cricket during chapel hour?

Chapel attendance became a more controversial issue when Albert E. Day arrived in 1957 as the school's first chaplain. Day had just retired from the pastorate of the Mount Vernon Place Methodist Church in Baltimore. A poll conducted by *The Christian Century* identified him as one of the six leading preachers in America, while a *Christian Advocate* survey proclaimed him one of the ten most influential living Methodists.

He had delivered the Lyman Beecher Lectures at Yale, the Earl Lectures at the Pacific School of Religion, and the Sam Jones Lectures at Emory University. He was the author of several widely read books on prayer and divine healing, a founder of the Disciplined Order of Christ, a member of the seminary's Board of Governors, and a longtime friend of the president. Trott wanted him as chaplain and director of spiritual life, and Day agreed to come. From the outset Day assumed that the Tuesday "Chaplain's Chapel" was his opportunity to preach to the whole seminary community and that students, faculty, administration, and staff should all be present. Trott supported this concept and during the chapel hour closed all offices except those that provided essential services. For a while all went well; little Baker Chapel was filled and the chaplain was gratified. But as one might have expected, absences began to increase, especially as midterm exams drew near. The new chapel in Washington, occupied in 1958, was much larger, and the empty pews distressed the chaplain. In 1959, to the dismay of many, he asked that chapel attendance be made compulsory. When Trott presented the proposal to the faculty, it was so hotly rejected as "a medieval anachronism" that it was not mentioned again. The issue was of no great consequence in itself, though it did reflect the difficulties of trying to regiment spirituality and religious devotion. Perhaps also it presaged the stormy decade of the 1960s, when students everywhere despised all things compulsory. Day relinquished his chapel duties soon after the controversy and formally resigned in 1960, leaving the Board of Governors at the same time.

Five months after his election Trott presented his first report to his Board of Governors. By then it truly was "his" board. Oxnam was elated, as his account of the meeting shows.

> It was a new Board, a new world. Dr. Trott had every item in hand. His report which outlined the plans for the future was clear and convincing. It was quite apparent that his every recommendation would be carried and unanimously. He had gone so far as to fill out all the places on the Board that were vacant—I mean by that the nominating committee in cooperation with him had recommendations. He himself had called upon distinguished individuals [such] as

Governor McKeldin [of Maryland], Secretary Wilkins [Assistant Secretary of the U.S. Department of Labor] and others, strong men in business in Baltimore as well as the Church. This means we will have a Board of thirty members after the General Conference and it will be a Board of strength. I have never faced a new situation with greater satisfaction. . . . The future seems to be secure under the leadership of Trott.

In that meeting of 5 November 1955 the feelings of optimism and expectancy must have been extraordinary as the president reported what was happening. He began, in typical fashion, with students: there had been 138 in the two summer schools just past, and there were 142 enrolled in the current regular session. They represented twenty-two states, thirty conferences, and seventy colleges. Their morale was high, even in the face of what Trott had presented to them as "our financial situation." After he had apologized to them for poor equipment and deteriorating accommodations, asking for their patience and understanding, they "decided to raise the price of a new mimeograph and present it to the school as an evidence of their concern and appreciation of our difficulties." Already they had contributed $275 towards the needed $350. Faculty cooperation was excellent, Trott reported next, with all professors entertaining "high hopes for the Washington venture." Western Maryland College was demonstrating its customary generosity, allowing the seminary to use "three College classrooms, the College chapel and other emergency facilities to relieve our congested situation." But something would have to be done about Cassell Hall, the former home for the aged that the seminary had been using as an extension dormitory. It was now "greatly in need of repairs and shabbily furnished. . . . Some emergency measures should be taken to put at least our room furnishings in more reasonable shape." Trott, a skilled amateur photographer, had taken "a few pictures to document this problem," and he proceeded to show them to the board.

After seeing evidence of Westminster's limitations, the board listened to Trott's projections for "the shift to Washington." His timetable, he said, had been developed at the request of Bishop Oxnam and in consultation with a number of other persons. He referred to the projections modestly as a tentative proposal, but they had his own stamp of clarity, competence, and decisiveness. The architect was to be selected at once. Initial sketches of the overall campus and plans for a first unit were to be ready in a month, "refinements" in six months, detailed plans in a year. The first unit was to be released for bids no later than 15 December 1956, contracts placed and work begun by 1 March 1957, the building completed by May 1958, and the fall session to begin in September 1958 on the Washington campus. Although Trott presented these as "suggested steps," they became almost the actual schedule for the move.

No turning back

The process of choosing the architect had begun in the summer of 1953 during Welliver's temporary absence. When Welliver returned, he asked Trott how the selection was to be made. Trott's reply, dated 28 December 1953, disclosed that he had written to "all the principal colleges and universities of this Area" requesting information on architects engaged in institutional building projects and had "composed a list of the architects who had skill in campus design." He had written to these asking if they were interested in the seminary's plans and had received several replies, which he had forwarded to Bishop Oxnam. Trott added that the Board of Governors had appointed a committee on the selection of an architect, and he ended his letter to Welliver with the suggestion that "the next step would be to contact Bishop Oxnam and arrange for a meeting of the Committee to follow through on the choice of an Architect." But Welliver did not "follow through." It now became one of Trott's first duties as president to select an architect, and he turned to A. Hensel Fink of Philadelphia. He had been corresponding with Fink for at least two years and had listed him along with eight others for consideration. He was impressed by sketches of Fink's work at West Virginia Wesleyan and Lycoming College, and especially by his design of the Metropolitan Memorial Methodist Church in Washington. Furthermore, he liked Fink himself, finding him energetic, prompt, and congenial. The two teamed well together.

192

Along with the details of disposing of an old campus and designing a new one, there was the always pressing burden of finding the needed money. Negotiations with the Kresge Foundation were proceeding encouragingly, but Trott was not one to "carry all his eggs in one basket." One of his favorite maxims, the faculty could recall, was "have a plan; but have, always, an alternative." His own logical application of this precept was to cultivate every conceivable source of support while still working and hoping for the Kresge grant. "The Church, the churches and church people," he declared, "are the sole sources of [our] support and in turn the only recipients of our training. Our strength and effectiveness will increase, in large measure only in relation to this interest and support." So on 23 November 1955, following the board's approval of his timetable, he wrote to each graduate of the seminary:

> 1. We are on our way to Washington. Everywhere there is excitement over this significant venture. I hope we can be there in three years.

> 2. The architect for the Washington campus has been chosen. . . . We felt that, in the creation of a Seminary campus, we must have not only good institutional designing, but a campus design that has a sense of the Divine about it, so that it will bear outward witness to its inward purpose.

> 3. You will be pleased to know that the Board has voted to grant the Alumni Association the privilege of nominating two of the fifteen clergy . . . of the Board . . . a decision which the Board was happy to make and which I was pleased to recommend.

> Now! This imposes a high responsibility on the alumni of the school. Many of you have been desiring such an arrangement for years. . . . I will meet with the officers and key persons of your Association to devise a mechanism for these nominations.[10]

Trott's letter to the graduates also announced that the inauguration of "your new president" would take place on 11 April 1956 in Washington, "thus dramatizing our intent to move the Seminary there." After outlining the inaugural program, he asked the graduates directly for help.

> We have no wealthy graduates (if I am mistaken, please let me know) but we are a tithing fraternity and many of

us have access to persons of means in our congregations. Will you, therefore, please think seriously about some personal contribution to help enlarge our working income and will you speak to others about our needs?

After some words of praise for "such an able faculty" and for the support and encouragement of the board, "particularly the extraordinary interest and help afforded by Bishop Oxnam," Trott concluded: "Please put the Seminary and its future in your thoughts and prayers and make the circle large enough to include the faculty, student body, and I hope, the president-elect."

Graduate "organizations" had long been simply informal gatherings at the time of annual conference. Even in the Baltimore Conference, where Westminster graduates constituted the largest of such associations, there was little more than a fellowship dinner each year. Now these organizations discovered new energy, and the Alumni Association was reorganized in 1959. Changing its name in 1976 to the Association of Wesley Seminary Graduates, it has increased steadily in numbers and useful activities, and it continues to play a significant role in extending the seminary's influence throughout the church.

Most dramatic, and at the same time most important, was the quickly increased support from the denomination after 1956. Oxnam told the board of "the remarkable action of the General Conference regarding financial aid for Methodist Educational Institutions" and of the Baltimore Conference's agreement to go beyond the request of the General Conference in support of the seminary and The American University. Trott and Oxnam requested the Washington Area to approve a $500,000 capital needs campaign to be spread over three conferences (Baltimore, Peninsula, and Central Pennsylvania), and each of these conferences responded favorably. Yet Trott had to tell the board in June 1956 that he was still hard pressed for operating resources.

Even the purchase of a bed or mimeograph is a major item of consideration for us. Hence, you will find, we have overspent our budget in spots. One of the desperate and unattended needs not yet cared for is the replacement of dormitory beds. In all probability, there has not been a new mattress bought for a quarter of a century or more.

194

The schedule Trott announced in 1955 to move to the new campus in three years needed swift action on several fronts. Miraculously, as the months passed, there were few delays. From his Westminster office Trott sent long letters in all directions: to the architect already working on the plans; to Associated Engineers, Inc., about topographical surveys, aerial maps, boundaries, sewage disposal, and water supply; to The American University about heating, electrical, and air conditioning agreements; to Consolidated Engineering Company, Inc., about contracts, subcontracts, and cost-plus-fixed-fee contracts; to Wilberding Company, Inc., about designing the mechanical and electrical equipment for the new buildings; and to Bishop Oxnam cheerful letters reporting on everything.

Then there was the planning for Trott's inauguration. He had been technically president-elect since June 1955, though he exercised all the authority and received all the support of a fully installed president. He wanted his inauguration to dramatize most effectively the "shift" to Washington. It was first thought that the ceremony should be early in the fall of 1955, but after considering the distraction of school opening and the pressures of urgent administrative matters, Trott and Oxnam set 11 April 1956 as the inauguration date. This allowed more time to prepare a celebration of the magnitude and style they desired and the event deserved. The American University and the adjoining Metropolitan Memorial Methodist Church both offered everything needed for the day, including arrangements for lunch, and an Inaugural Committee got busy immediately. President Hurst Anderson of the university was chairman, and he designated S. H. Cassell, one of his administrative assistants, as coordinator. Twenty subcommittees sprang into life with responsibilities for invitations, luncheons, seating, procession, programs, traffic, ushering, academic regalia, reception, transportation, publicity, and much more.

Two luncheons began the festal day, one at Hamline Methodist Church for alumni and students, and another at the university's Clendenen Hall for delegates and official guests. Harold Hodgson, leader of the alumni, presided at the first and President Anderson at the second. Everything seemed to proceed in perfect order with all the "pomp and circumstance" anyone could want on such a notable occasion.

The academic procession included more than a hundred representatives from other seminaries, colleges, and universities; Westminster's Board of Governors and the trustees of The American University; bishops and district superintendents of The Methodist Church; delegates of learned societies and church boards; the Seminary Singers and faculty; and finally "the inaugural party." In the brightness of a blue and gold April day the line moved across the university campus into the Metropolitan Church sanctuary. Organist James McLain swept all into their appointed seats with Purvis's "Fantasia on *St. Anne*," Pastor Edward Latch called them to worship, Bishop Straughn prayed, Henry P. Van Dusen spoke on "Current Theological Education," Bishop Donald H. Tippett gave the charge to the new president, Bishop Oxnam read the Act of Inauguration, the seminary conferred honorary degrees on Van Dusen and Tippett, the Seminary Singers sang, Trott delivered his Inaugural Address, and Albert Day pronounced the benediction. A reception for President and Mrs. Trott followed in Clendenen Hall.

Out of all the day's proceedings the clearest picture of the seminary's future, its character and mission in the late 1950s, came from Norman Trott's Inaugural Address. "The times being propitious," he said, "these things by the grace of God we intend to do": 1) move to Washington, 2) build here a seminary of the first rank, 3) train men for the pastoral ministry (within only a few weeks the General Conference would take the historic step of approving the ordination of women, but if Trott foresaw that, his language did not reflect it), 4) nourish the ecumenical spirit, 5) develop a ministry of spiritual depth and social passion, 6) seek solutions for the many problems confronting Negroes ("black" was not yet the appropriate term), and 7) keep Christ and his cross at the center of the seminary.

It was a gratifying day, delightfully prophetic of things to come. The seminary community returned to Westminster and settled in for two final years of work on the old campus, their routine now enlivened, and sometimes happily interrupted, by transitional events.

7

Wesley in Washington

It is only fifty-four miles from Westminster, Maryland, to Washington, DC. For the little community comprising the Westminster Theological Seminary, the emotional distance was much greater. The move meant shifting from a rural to an urban environment, relating to a whole new array of institutions both educational and ecclesiastical, developing ways to utilize the vast resources of the nation's capital for the study and practice of ministry, and finding more adequate sources of support for the higher expectations of a broadening constituency. But the trauma of the physical move was more than offset by the joy of occupying a beautiful new campus, one that was sumptuous by comparison with the old and vastly richer in the symbols of the seminary's vocation.

A new name

The first action symbolizing the newness was a change of name, something that would also relieve a problem as old as the seminary. Many could remember how the old name "Westminster" confused many people. Somebody was always asking, "Are you Presbyterians?"—a query that would require the patient explanation that geography and not theology or history accounted for the seminary's name. Confusion was compounded when conservative Presbyterians withdrawing from Princeton during the Fundamentalist controversy of the 1920s appropriated the name "Westminster" for their new seminary in Philadelphia, even over President Elderdice's indignant protest.

When the Board of Governors met in McKinley Hall at The American University in June 1956, therefore, early on the agenda came a motion by Frank L. Shaffer to change the name of the school to "The Wesley Theological Seminary." John Hawley seconded, Bishop Straughn urged a favorable vote, and J. Leas Green requested "that it be made a matter of record that all those members of the Board who were of Methodist Protestant background were in favor of the change of name to Wesley." The motion would have passed then without further ado, but Albert Day countered with a suggestion that the new name be "The Seminary of the Wesleys." Hawley asked for a longer time to deliberate and to consider Day's proposal, but Green pointed out that the graduates had voted at their last meeting to support a change to "The Wesley Theological Seminary." Trott argued for Shaffer's original motion, Day withdrew his alternative, and the motion was adopted unanimously.[1] All agreed that as the seminary prepared to take on a new character in a new location, it was only fitting that it should have a distinctive new name.

Even more important was the implication that the seminary should remain a freestanding institution. Bishop Oxnam had often referred to the move as if the seminary would somehow become attached to The American University. But no structural connections were ever established—or for that matter, considered—and although the two schools developed mutually beneficial academic relationships at the graduate level, they both continued under separate administrations.

As a logical result of the decision to change the seminary's name, senior students at the seminary immediately petitioned the administration for the privilege of receiving their diplomas and degrees under the new name, even though they would still be graduated at Westminster. The board acceded to their request and also notified the alumni that they were now graduates of Wesley and that this fact "would be suitably inscribed and sent to each Alumnus on request, the printing to be so devised that it may be affixed to the graduate's diploma."[2] It came about, therefore, that at the next commencement, on 28 May 1957, thirty-eight students received the degree of Bachelor of Sacred Theology and three the Master of Sacred Theology in the name of Wesley Theological

Seminary. Trott had thoughtfully arranged that Bishop Oxnam should receive the very first Wesley degree, a Doctor of Sacred Theology, "conferred as a surprise by action of the Board and of the Faculty." Oxnam was not exactly rendered speechless (he had already been similarly honored by twenty other institutions), but it was a gracious gesture gracefully received.

The grant and the ground-breaking

Two memorable events earlier in 1957 rang up the curtain on the seminary's new beginning in Washington. The Kresge grant was approved on 20 January, and ground was broken for the first building on 5 April. Nearly four years had passed since Oxnam first wrote to Amos Gregory, secretary of the Kresge Foundation, appealing for "a grant of two million dollars for the purpose of locating the Seminary on the campus of The American University." Oxnam's letter, five pages of precise argument in the bishop's forceful style, described what such a gift would mean to the seminary, to the university, to The Methodist Church, to the city of Washington, and to the world.

1. It is of national and world-wide significance [and] will make certain that religion will dominate the life of the national university. . . .

2. Washington offers unique opportunities for the training of ministers. . . .

3. The Westminster Theological Seminary is an established Seminary which has full recognition by the American Association of Theological Schools, and thus precludes the necessity of traversing the trial years of tentative recognition accorded a new school. . . .

4. No Protestant Seminary is now located in Washington. [This was not true. The Howard University School of Religion had long been training black ministers, and the Virginia Theological Seminary (Episcopal) was just across the Potomac River in Alexandria.] . . .

5. [We have] a fundamental conviction [that] candidates for our ministry must be men of broad culture and intellectual attainment; but, more than that they must be men of vital religious experience . . . so trained that they may

become indeed "great preachers" . . . of such power that
the hearts of men are reached and changed.

This was language that the Kresges understood and liked.

Sebastian Kresge, founder of the S. S. Kresge Company, had
strong convictions about the church and the ministry. His son,
Stanley, was on the Official Board of the Metropolitan
Methodist Church in Detroit, and as a family they were warmly
evangelical, biblically oriented, and staunchly Methodist. Their
pastor in Detroit, Dr. Chester A. McPheeters, and the bishop
of the Michigan Area, Marshall Reed, both supported the
seminary's request. It seems that some unexpected help came
also from Dr. John L. Seaton, who had directed the damaging
survey of 1947 and who had long been suspected of being
no friend of the seminary. Some months after the grant was
approved, Seaton wrote Trott to offer congratulations. He
disclosed that for ten years he had been the educational
counselor for the Kresge Foundation, furnishing opinions
about various institutions. During all that time, he confided,
he had "urged a sizable grant to theological education." Seaton
continued:

> After the theological school survey in 1946-47, most of
> which I wrote, I was sure that for the good of the
> [Westminster] Seminary and Western Maryland College the
> Seminary would have to move. But certain changes had to
> take place with both the Seminary and American Univer-
> sity before I could conscientiously recommend a merge in
> Washington, though it was considered in 1946-47. For-
> tunately [the changes] were made and my final positive
> recommendation found the trustees of the Foundation in
> a receptive mood.*

Correspondence regarding the Kresge grant stretched over
four years of negotiation and waiting. In Trott's files are
numerous letters to and from Howard Baldwin, vice-president
and trustee of the foundation, Amos Gregory, secretary, and
the Kresges themselves, all evincing a high level of courtesy
and mutual respect which blossomed into real friendship.
Stanley Kresge recalled that his father had once said, "I had

PILGRIMAGE *of* FAITH

---

* *John L. Seaton to Norman L. Trott. 11 November 1957; in Trott Office File. This
revealing letter suggests what the survey team communicated privately to the
Board of Governors (above, p. 154) and also explains why Oxnam felt he had
to force Welliver to resign (above, p. 178).*

the right idea at the right time, and in the right place''; and Stanley added significantly, ''He also had saved $8,000 to implement his idea.'' It could have been a characterization of Norman Trott, for Trott's ideas always gave the sense of wise timing and sound financial planning. He fitted the Kresge mold, and that is why they got along so well together. In 1956 he impressed the Kresges by reducing his request from two million dollars to a million and a half, showing that the seminary could ''implement the idea'' substantially by securing other gifts. Foundation executives were also pleased with the careful plans and schedules for building the new campus, and when they saw Trott's convincing résumé of costs and his success at finding resources to match their grant, they were ready to approve the seminary's request. On 17 January 1957 Oxnam and Trott received the good news and immediately fired off a telegram to members of the Board of Governors:

Wesley in Washington

> We are happy to announce that the Kresge Foundation has granted the Westminster Seminary the sum of one million five hundred thousand dollars which will be made available in four annual grants, provided we raise one million five hundred thousand dollars to match the gift. This is in accordance with our own proposal to the Foundation. This will enable us to move steadily forward in our building program and complete the campus development by the end of 1960.

Methodist Information Service released the news in time to catch the Sunday papers of 20 January. Churches lifted grateful doxologies, congratulations poured in, and students expressed their own jubilation by singing ''I Found a Million-Dollar Baby in a Five and Ten Cent Store''—a bit of jollity that Trott enjoyed and used himself when the occasion suited. The first check for $250,000 arrived in due time, inscribed on the back, ''In the name and for the sake of Jesus Christ. Stanley Kresge.''

On 5 April, eleven weeks after the Kresge grant was assured, ground was broken for the first building on the Washington campus. It was a rainy Friday, but the ceremony went forward in good order and, as John Wesley might have said, ''with solemn joy.'' The guests assembled in the Glover Room of Hurst Hall at The American University. After a trumpet call to worship, Trott read a ''declaration'' and the people sang

Charles Wesley's hymn, "O For a Thousand Tongues to Sing." John Gross and Gerald McCulloh had come again from the Board of Education in Nashville, and the episcopacy was well represented in the presence of Bishops Oxnam, Straughn, Garber, and Ledden. Oxnam gave the main address of the day, describing John and Charles Wesley as models for the seminary's life and work. He spoke of "holy ground" for a "holy enterprise," rejoiced over the General Conference's recent affirmation that "theological education is the responsibility of the whole church," and noted the supporting presence of Gross, McCulloh, and the bishops. He pointed to Wesley Circle, where, by a curious coincidence (or providence?), the name already stood at the lower corner of the new campus where Tilden Street, 46th Street, and University Avenue intersect Massachusetts Avenue. Here, said Oxnam, the seminary would be associated with a rapidly developing institution appropriately named The American University, now under the dynamic leadership of Hurst Anderson. On the other side of the university campus a new School of International Service was taking shape with a distinguished scholar, Ernest E. Griffith, at its head. This fortuitous convergence, Oxnam declared, will demonstrate that "the political, social and economic institutions of the free society must be built upon religious foundations [and] the freedom of the Protestant tradition." Without a doubt the most pleasing part of the address was Oxnam's recognition of "the gift of Mr. Sebastian Kresge and of his son, Mr. Stanley S. Kresge, who, through the Kresge Foundation, have contributed $1,500,000 to this sacred undertaking . . . a revelation of Christian stewardship at its highest."

A silver-plated shovel was presented by Consolidated Engineering Company, the general contractor, and several guests used it for the symbolic act of beginning the first building. Trott wrote to Stanley Kresge: "We broke ground in the rain but it did not dampen our spirits. It just softened the ground."

To uphold the assurance given to the Kresge Foundation that the seminary could come up with funds to match the grant, Trott relied in part on the increased support for theological education from The Methodist Church. In 1956 the General Conference, upon recommendation of the Com-

The ground-breaking for the first building on the Washington campus took place in the rain on 5 April 1957. Trott, Oxnam, and Anderson (left to right) were the chief laborers.

mission on World Service and Finance, had raised the total annual contribution to Methodist theological schools from $800,000 to $1,250,000, an increase of 56 percent. The contributions to Wesley went from $10,000 to $65,000, a whopping percentage increase (550%) if one calculates on the basis of the pitifully small amount of pre-1956 allotments to little Westminster. Even so, the new amount fell far short of what the seminary needed for developing a new campus in Washington. Trott had much bigger plans. He soon started in Baltimore a quiet "special gifts" program with a committee of eighteen Baltimore business and professional people who agreed to sponsor a dinner meeting for "a select group of Methodists." The program would move next to Washington and then to other cities, in hope of raising at least $500,000 in special contributions within the quadrennium. He would request gifts for designated items in the building program and recognize various levels of giving as founder's shares, builder's shares, and chapel shares. The heart of the plan was Trott's concept of "a select group of Methodists"—not exactly a novel approach for such campaigns, but one he could exploit in the style he loved. He spurned conventional "potluck" or "covered dish" suppers in church basements, planning instead well-catered dinner meetings in prestigious places. An invitation was tantamount to public recognition of one's eminence or influence or wealth—perhaps all three—and human nature being what it is, the plan worked remarkably well.

Even more encouraging were the offers of cooperation and support which came from various annual conferences. Eight conferences reported campaigns under way by 1957, and the president said in May that "we have assurances of slightly more than $1,300,000 to date." The campaign in the Baltimore Conference soon achieved its goal of $300,000 in pledges payable over a period of twenty months. Many special gifts through individual churches put those churches well over their quotas.

There was a fine balance of faith and presumption in Trott's announcement that the seminary would move to the new campus in the fall of 1958, so soon after breaking ground in April 1957. The winter weather was dismal for building, and Consolidated Engineering told President Trott that for them it was the worst in sixteen years. But they put one hundred workers on the job and made the most of every day to keep the work going. Trott reassured readers of the *Seminary Bulletin* that the distinguished Baltimore firm had had a billion dollars worth of building experience, that they were engaged on a negotiated fee basis, and that "both of the top executive officers are Methodists and have more than a contractor's interest in the campus development." An additional reason for con-

John Hagenbucher (left) was superintendent for Consolidated Engineering Company, Inc., the builder of the Washington campus. During construction he not only conferred often with President Trott but was regarded as a regular member of "the seminary family."

fidence lay in the construction superintendent, John Hagenbucher. Experienced, capable, efficient, he watched over the project like a quiet hawk. Along with his technical expertise, Hagenbucher dispensed a folksy wisdom that endeared him to the whole seminary during his months of work on campus. He shared not only the company's pride but the school's joy when the building was completed very close to schedule.

Last months in Westminster

Two hot summers and a long academic year had to pass between the ground-breaking in April 1957 and the opening of school in Washington on 1 October 1958. But the routine work on Seminary Hill in Westminster was seasoned with joy and hope as daily reports streamed in from the new campus in the making. Particularly noteworthy was the comfortable relation with Western Maryland College now that each institution realized that it would soon be out of the way of the other's expansion plans. The seminary's use of college classrooms, chapel, dining hall, and parking lots caused little friction, a harmony fostered by courtesies natural to both presidents, Lowell Ensor and Norman Trott.

The seminary began its seventy-sixth year, its last in Westminster, with the admission of the largest first-year class in history and a total enrollment of 143. This was nearly a hundred more students than Elderdice had contemplated for his new building in 1920. The faculty now numbered ten full-time professors plus an equal number of visiting lecturers and assistants. For the record and in anticipation of curricular changes demanded nearly a decade later, the degree requirements at this point of transition should be noted. The Bachelor of Sacred Theology degree required ninety credit hours, of which fifty-seven comprised a "core" of specified courses in nine fields of study. Fifteen of the remaining thirty-three hours were "controlled electives," i.e., courses which had to be distributed among the fields of Old Testament, New Testament, Church History, Systematic Theology, Christian Education, and Missions. The Master of Sacred Theology degree required thirty credit hours of "B" or better work beyond the S.T.B. or its equivalent; four of these credits were allowed for a thesis and an oral examination. In addition, a reading knowledge of a "foreign language or languages usually associated with the field of study covered by the thesis may be required."

The seventy-first commencement, the last in Westminster, was held on 26 May 1958 in Alumni Hall at the college. Fred G. Holloway, a seminary graduate and former president of both the seminary and the college, now president of Drew University, gave the main address. His own career illustrated the origins and history of the seminary, and his address acknowledged the accomplishments of previous presidents and many other stalwarts of the past who had made the present possible. Thirty-four graduates received the Bachelor of Sacred Theology degree, among them Douglas Dillard (summa cum laude), Omro Todd (magna cum laude), and Lewis Robson and Gordon Stapleton (cum laude).

An assistant to the president came in June 1957, when J. Luther Neff accepted Trott's invitation to facilitate the move to Washington. A graduate of Dickinson College and Boston University School of Theology, Neff had recently retired from nearly forty years in the pastoral ministry, many of those years in or near Washington. His wife, Helen, was an alumna of Goucher College; an animated conversationalist and a charming hostess, she was active in many good causes. The Neffs took up residence near the new campus in the Berkshire Apartments, from which base they were able to supply counsel and assistance to reduce many of the frustrations of transition.

One of Neff's first assignments was to locate housing near the campus for the ten professors and their families who would be moving to Washington. Trott had recommended to the board in May 1957 that $200,000 be appropriated from the building fund for faculty housing. To faculty members wishing to build or purchase their own homes the seminary would offer financial aid in the form of a first mortgage at 4 percent, with 0.5 percent refunded for each of the first five years. For those desiring to rent, the seminary would purchase suitable houses and offer them to faculty families for $100 to $110 per month, depending on the type of house. A committee on faculty housing was appointed and given the details of purchasing, financing, renting or building "in time for the relocation of the faculty before the move." The procedure worked

J. Luther Neff was vice-president of the seminary from 1957 to 1961. His wife, Helen, was also a great asset to the seminary community.

very well. Neff located the houses, which were then inspected by Trott and Hagenbucher, and by a tactful interplay of choice and assignment, the houses were sold or rented to the various faculty families. In this way all professors were settled into their Washington homes before the fall semester of 1958. President and Mrs. Trott, however, stayed in Westminster a while longer because their new home on the campus would not be ready until April 1959.

Once the pressing business of faculty housing was settled, Neff's duties spread to other details like ordering furniture, arranging offices, overseeing the installation of equipment that seemed to arrive in a steady stream, scheduling preachers for the chapel services, and entertaining the many visitors and church tour groups who came to see the new campus. Trott expected to be consulted on all decisions, even the smallest, and Neff was careful to comply. Sometimes, he confessed, he felt as if he were "the vice-president in charge of waste-baskets." But the visitor load was heavy, and Neff served ably as a gracious host. In December 1959 he wrote: "Many of the leaders of the church . . . visit us: an amazing number of groups arrange with me for tours of the Seminary; and I have nothing but gratitude for the guidance that brought us, in these final years, into such a marvelous opportunity for growth and service." The seminary's gratitude in return was no less. By 1961 Neff was ready to "retire" again, which he did by becoming minister of visitation at the Towson Methodist Church for seven years. In 1968 the Neffs took up residence at the Methodist Manor House in Seaford, Delaware, where Luther died in 1980 and Helen in 1981.

The last summer school in Westminster went smoothly as the Supply Pastors School and the School for Town and Country Ministers finished their courses. Moving days drew on, and Westminster townspeople extended many thoughtful expressions of farewell and good will, while town organizations and church groups offered gracious reminders of pleasant associations and rewarding friendships. A dinner for the faculty in the home of Dorothy Elderdice recalled the heritage that all vowed would not be forgotten. Three quarters of a century of the seminary's life ended. A new era, livelier and richer yet, was about to begin.

Moving days

In spite of delays in building caused by the harsh winter, two cornerstones were placed on 29 April 1958, making that another day of "solemn joy." Mr. and Mrs. Stanley Kresge came for their second visit (they had made the first early in February). Trott wrote the litany, which was read by Bishop Oxnam. It concluded with the words: "For the training of a ministry that, in the language of John Wesley, will have 'such an earnest concern for the glory of God, and a thirst after the salvation of souls that [they are] ready to do anything, to lose anything, or to suffer anything, rather than one should perish for whom Christ died'—*We lay these cornerstones.*" On the stone for the administration building, which contained the chapel, five classrooms, and several offices, were engraved the words, "Other foundation can no man lay. First Corinthians 3:9-11." The cornerstone of the dormitory pressed Wesley's blunt question, "Dost thou love and serve God?"

In August the trucks began the fifty-four mile trek to Washington, transferring the seminary piece by piece to the new campus. By the first week of September President Trott could write jubilantly to the Board of Governors:

Every building on the Wesley campus has on its cornerstone some reminder of the seminary's purpose. The cornerstone of the Administration Building was laid with Bishop Oxnam troweling mortar while (left to right) Hurst R. Anderson, Stanley S. Kresge, Bishop James H. Straughn, Norman L. Trott, Gerald O. McCulloh, and Robert V. Fletcher watch.

Theodore M. McKeldin, governor of Maryland from 1951 to 1959, was a member of The Methodist Church, although he often attended Episcopal services. A friend of President Trott, he participated in the program at the laying of the cornerstone of the Administration Building.

Last Wednesday, September 3rd, we moved our offices from Westminster to Washington. We are in! I have been singing the Doxology every morning. It was no small job to thin down a 75-year accumulation of office files and miscellaneous materials (nothing had ever been discarded) and prepare for shipment.[3] Our new offices are beautifully equipped and once we get unpacked and straightened out I hope you will be in to see us.

It was feared that moving the library of nearly thirty thousand volumes would be most difficult. The movers supplied shelf-length boxes, and Roland Kircher, who had become assistant librarian and cataloguer the preceding February, had each box packed and marked in such a way that the entire library could be transferred shelf by shelf in proper order. After executing their move on 15 September, the library staff found it a simple matter to reshelve the books in time for the opening of the fall semester, even though they had to occupy temporary quarters in the dormitory until their own building was completed in 1959.

Meanwhile, the builders were hurrying to prepare the dormitory for occupancy. Bad weather had so delayed construction that furnishings could not be delivered until 15 September. Students arrived for a one-day orientation and registration on 30 September, but the dormitory was not fully ready until several days thereafter. Trott described the predicament in a letter of 7 October to Mr. and Mrs. Stanley Kresge: "Our dormitory was not ready, but neighbors and faculty members took students into their homes so we could start. By the end of this week, the dormitory is far enough along that the students can enter it." With many such makeshift arrangements, classes began on the first of October.

The first day of the first Washington semester began with a Eucharist celebrated by Bishop Oxnam. Lectures marking the opening of both Wesley Seminary and the new School of International Service at The American University were given by Herbert Butterfield, a distinguished historian from Cambridge University. As school got under way, construction surrounded chapel services, class lectures, study rooms, and offices. Trucks and tractors, backhoes and cranes—high-decibel machinery of all descriptions groaned and clanked and roared. Mud was everywhere, with planks to carry pedestrians safely across the waterholes. But no one seemed to mind. It was the noise of achievement, fulfillment, and the promise of a bright tomorrow. Professors paused in their lectures, waiting for the noise to subside, while chapel hymns and prayers seemed to rise above the din. Nothing could diminish the sheer joy of having individual faculty offices for the first time in the seminary's history.

The administration building and the dormitory were the only two buildings for all of that first year in Washington. The dormitory also housed the library on a floor that had been left without partitions. Construction continued for eight more

The seminary was moved "piece by piece" from Westminster to Washington, with all hands helping. Shown here are Professor J. Edward Moyer, Vice-President J. Luther Neff, public relations officer Bess S. Jones, library secretary Betty Cox, and President Norman L. Trott.

210

years on three additional buildings projected in the original design. The library was begun at once and completed in September 1959. Trott reported to the Board of Governors (a bit optimistically, perhaps) that the building had been planned "to accommodate 100,000 volumes and to provide maximum study-seating for 135 students at any one time." Oxnam had added to the seminary's holdings his entire personal library of over four thousand volumes; it included

Methodist historical materials of great value, such as "John Wesley's own Bible, two volumes of the Old Testament belonging to Francis Asbury, John Wesley's personal seal, and many rare first editions of Wesley's books and tracts." These made noteworthy additions to gifts received in Westminster days, collections like the Methodist Protestant Repository holdings from Pittsburgh, the Central Pennsylvania Theological Library, and the personal libraries of Charles E. Forlines, Charles Fellows Eggleston, Mrs. Arthur B. Bibbins, and Richard L. Shipley.

The dedication of the library on 26 October 1959 marked a high day, especially impressive because it brought to Wesley representatives of many other seminaries and universities in an atmosphere of academic conviviality. Amos N. Wilder of Harvard gave the dedicatory address, and at the appropriate

The first building to be completed on the new campus was the chapel and Administration Building, fronting on Massachusetts Avenue. The first semester in Washington began here in September 1958. The library building, completed in 1959, is at the left rear.

moment Roland E. Kircher was presented as the seminary's new librarian. This appointment had been some months in the making. In the preceding June, Trott had written to the Executive Committee of the Board of Governors about his desire to promote Kircher.

> Mr. Roland Kircher, who has been with us for a year and a half as Assistant Librarian, should now be given the status of Librarian. Mrs. Emily Chandler, who has been designated as Assistant Librarian, but who has been [the] responsible Library Officer, should be designated Circulation Librarian. She is eager to see Mr. Kircher have the position of Librarian. He has proved his worth and I feel that we may lose him if he is not tied to the Seminary more securely. I propose that these changes be made September 1st. They should be related to the opening of the new Library.

Kircher was a German, educated at the Eberhard-Ludwig Gymnasium in Stuttgart and at the University of Erlangen in the best traditions of European classicism and in German philosophy and theology. During World War II he served in the German Air Force, was captured in 1944, and spent the last year of the war as a prisoner of the Americans. When the war was over, he came to the United States for study at Westminster Seminary, graduating in 1951. After further studies at Boston University, he earned a master's degree in Library Science at The Catholic University of America and was duly appointed to his post at Wesley Seminary. Mrs. Chandler, having been seminary librarian since 1947, now wanted fewer responsibilities, and she was happy to see her choice of a successor approved.

Kircher brought to the library an added degree of professionalism and also what some students perceived as the strictness of German discipline. Once, when he was chastising a tardy student worker, the hapless student complained, "Mr. Kircher, you can't run the library like the German Air Force." Kircher, long aggravated by this student's perennially dilatory behavior, shot back in his heavy German accent, "No, but we don't run it like a kindergarten, either!" In any case, Kircher *ran* the library, and ran it well. The seminary had the honor of entertaining the American Theological Library Association at its annual meeting in June 1961, when some 150 theological school librarians gathered from all over the United States and Canada. Kircher's competence was recognized by his colleagues in the ATLA when they elected him president of the organization in 1975.

Getting the library out of its temporary quarters in the dormitory released a whole floor for more student rooms. Partitions were quickly installed, and the full occupancy of 150 students was possible by the second year in Washington. The dormitory was named in honor of Bishop James H. Straughn, a Methodist Protestant alumnus of the seminary, and was dedicated on 20 April 1960. On its most prominent corner was placed a bronze tablet commemorating the 1939 union of three denominations of Methodism. The plaque pictures Bishop Straughn, Bishop John M. Moore of the Methodist Episcopal Church, South, and Bishop Edwin Holt Hughes of the Methodist Episcopal Church (northern) with hands clasped symbolizing union. The caption reads, "Methodists are one people throughout the world."

Meanwhile, the classroom and refectory building was under construction. To the surprise of many, it was finished—or nearly so—by the fall of 1960. Trott had explained to the board that the steel strike of 1959 would occasion some delay.

The contract for the steel was placed well in advance of

Bishop G. Bromley Oxnam (right) bequeathed to the seminary many of his books and personal papers. Included in the collection were a Bible used by John Wesley and a bound volume of Wesley's letters. President Trott gratefully received the gift.

Roland E. Kircher (right), was appointed librarian at the dedication of the new library building in October 1959. He regularly urged upon the president (here, Trott) a strong acquisition program.

the strike (and in anticipation of it) and substantial savings were made. This was done, even though the contract for the building had not been placed, as a calculated risk to protect us. As a result we have steel stockpiled on the job, but in all probability we will suffer delay in the delivery of the main girders.

By early winter John Hagenbucher and Consolidated Engineering seemed confident of a spring completion, so the dedication date was announced for Saturday, 22 April 1961. Trott had decided to name the classroom building "The Kresge Academic Center," and he hoped the Kresges could be present for its dedication. After another warm and friendly exchange of letters, they happily accepted his invitation. Stanley Kresge often signed his messages to Trott, "We love you. Stan. Gal. 2:20c," a biblical reference to living by faith. When he came for the dedication of the Kresge building, Stanley Kresge inspected the whole campus and then confided to the president, "We think we have gotten more for our money at Wesley Seminary than anywhere else we have put it." Trott beamed, and the ceremony went on in the beauty of the April day. John Wesley Lord, new bishop of the

By 1962 the Washington campus was complete except for the apartment building, which would be built in 1965 at the south end of the parking lot (far right). The chapel, facing Massachusetts Avenue in the upper left corner, is attached to the L-shaped Administration Building. The library (right) and the Kresge Academic Center (with the refectory attached behind) complete the quadrangle. Straughn Dormitory is at the bottom.

Washington Area and now chairman of the Board of Governors, directed the program. At the door of the building facing the quadrangle was inscribed another verse of Holy Scripture: "Let this mind be in you which was in Christ Jesus. Philippians 2:5." A cornerstone had been brought from the old building at Westminster for placement at the other entrance to Kresge. Though damaged in transit, it still bore witness to the seminary's heritage, and its brokenness said something about the pain of all uprootings.

The fifth and last building planned for the new campus was the apartment house, or "married students' dormitory." Trott's first timetable called for its construction in 1961, but by 1960 the projected costs of the building program—even exclusive of the apartments—had shot up to three and a half million dollars, putting a stop to all building until more money could be found. Trott first approached the Kresge Foundation but "they were not interested since the initial gifts were exceptional for this Foundation."[4] Every year for five years Trott urged that the apartment building was "needed at once" because, as he often repeated, "70% of our students are married and at least 60% are married before they reach Seminary." Moreover, the new Master of Religious Education program had begun in 1959, and he expected about forty women students to enroll within the first four years. There would also be missionaries on study furlough who would need housing. Wesley, he pointed out, was far behind other seminaries in this matter. Happily for his peace of mind, Trott could not foresee the revolution about to sweep through many college and seminary campuses transforming the old men's dorms into co-ed residences. By retiring in 1967 he never had to consider this quick solution of the housing problem for single women.

It was not until October 1964 that ground was broken for a forty-apartment residence. Building superintendent John Hagenbucher and Robert Rote (the project manager) returned, and the campus was once more distracted by the roar of bulldozers, the intrusion of heavy trucks, and clouds of flying dust. The building took almost two years to complete. It was dedicated on 2 November 1966 with a dinner, a service in Oxnam Chapel, an "open house," and general rejoicing—a rerun of earlier days when such celebrations were almost

215

routine. The apartment residence was made possible by substantial help from two women's support groups. Epworth House, formerly the Washington Deaconess Board, invested their holdings of $40,000 in the building, paying for four apartments which they also furnished and planned to maintain for women students; and the Wesley Women's Guild provided furnishings for both entrance lounges. In 1972 the building was named Carroll Hall for Bishop Edward G. Carroll, in recognition of a gift of $200,000 from Mrs. Wilma H. Johnston of Silver Spring, Maryland, a member of Marvin Memorial United Methodist Church, where Bishop Carroll had been her pastor.

It seemed to some that apartments for married students should include some nursery space. The administration resisted this suggestion, and for the first dozen years only childless couples were permitted in the apartments. Trott defended the restriction by referring to an antiquated zoning ordinance for the neighborhood in which the seminary was located. But that regulation was eventually set aside; and after 1980, married residents with pre-school children were admitted to Carroll Hall, though adequate nursery space was still lacking.

Sermons in stone

The first year on the Washington campus was scarcely a time of ordered tranquillity. Whether the spring of 1959 brought some order or simply a tolerance of confusion is arguable, but unquestionably it did bring, along with the loveliness of a Washington April, many evidences of emerging campus beauty. The landscape architect, Boris Timchenko, by judicious pruning and thinning of old trees and planting of new ones, was largely responsible for enhancing the natural charm of the grounds. The buildings were skillfully tailored to their surroundings, and almost everywhere there was something to catch the eye and lift the soul. Trott saw to it that brick and stone were translated into silent sermons on the purposes of the seminary. The spiritual meanings in everything were described in dozens of handsome brochures

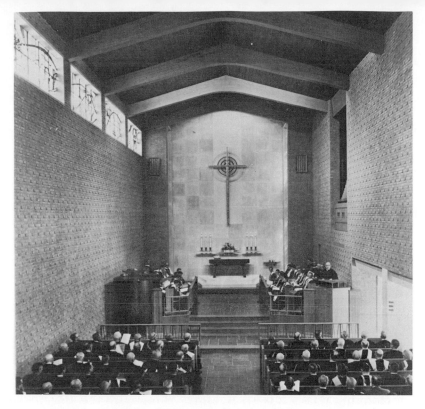

The left chapel wall, rising in solid brick to the clerestory windows, shuts out the world for the time of worship. But since total withdrawal is neither possible nor desirable, on the lower right (out of the picture) is a glass curtain through which worshippers can be aware of busy Massachusetts Avenue.

designed by experts and illustrated by professional artists and photographers. "Promotional literature" it was, but every page and picture preached eloquently on the meaning of the Christian ministry and the seminary's responsibility for ministerial education. As the president and many professors—especially Shroyer and Furgeson—often pointed out, work is sacred. The teaching of truth is not limited to lectern and pulpit but comes forth as well from the minds and hands of skilled architects, artisans, and builders.

The chapel was named for Bishop Oxnam, and when he died in 1963, his ashes were interred in the chancel. Here, at the heart of the seminary's life, religious symbolism proclaims the gospel wherever the eye turns. The cross, fifteen feet of olive wood bound in brass, stands against concentric circles symbolizing its radiating influence. The wood was obtained from Israel with the help of Maryland's governor, Theodore McKeldin, a Methodist and longtime friend of President Trott. From its high and solitary station above the Eucharistic table, also of olive wood, the cross at once arrests both eye and heart. Two chancel windows of conchoidally fractured glass in brilliant hues depict Christ's ministry and its extension in the world. Through the "I Am" window shine metaphors of the

The cross and communion table are of olive wood from Israel. The "Christian History" window, like the "I Am" window opposite it, is crafted of thick conchoidally fractured glass in brilliant colors. The chapel building is positioned approximately north and south; each chancel window catches direct sunlight, one in the morning and the other in the afternoon.

Christ: the good shepherd, the door, the light of the world, the living water, the bread of life, the branching vine, and the resurrection. On the opposite side of the chancel is the "Christian History" window, representing the continuing presence of Christ among the multitudes through the ages. The six clerestory windows above the nave portray functions of the ministry, drawn mainly from Ephesians 6:11-18, while the wooden choir screens are embellished with carved symbols of the twelve apostles. All the chapel furnishings clearly symbolize humanity's upward reach to God and God's reaching down to the world. Even structure translates into profound thought, for whereas a high massive wall of unbroken brick on one side excludes the noisy world from the congregation at prayer, on the other side is a glass curtain whose complete openness to the world destroys all illusions of withdrawing from human need.

Most striking is the figure of Christ on the exterior wall overlooking Massachusetts Avenue. Along with the architect, Hensel Fink, and the sculptor, Leo Friedlander, Trott wanted to portray a living Christ suggesting the message, "He beheld the multitudes and had compassion on them." A forty-ton block of Indiana limestone was imbedded in the masonry, and the figure was carved on the site. The work required nearly three years for modeling and completion, and fascinated observers often watched Paul Palumbo and Ed Ratti, carvers from the Washington Cathedral, create what ultimately proclaimed the seminary's reason for being.

But the "unorthodox" position of the hands as placed by the sculptor caused some to raise their eyebrows. A taxi driver who frequently passed the seminary commented, "I've seen a lot of statues of Christ, but that's the first one I ever saw with his left hand up in the air." Few knew how much discussion and correspondence had dealt with that issue during the early stages of the work. Oxnam thought the right hand, not the left, was the hand of blessing. He and Trott went to the sculptor's studio in New York City to discuss with him their reservations. Friedlander agreed to fashion another model with the hands reversed, and he did so, attempting to recreate the concept they all had in mind. But the reversed figure was not satisfactory; it did not "speak" or "live." The sculptor did

218

The figure of Christ emerged from a forty-ton block of Indiana limestone set into the outside wall of the chapel facing Massachusetts Avenue. Designed to suggest the text, "When Jesus beheld the multitudes, he had compassion on them," it was carved on location by Paul Palumbo (pictured) and Ed Ratti from the Washington Cathedral.

Sculptor Leo Friedlander checks the carving on the statue while architect A. Hensel Fink watches.

At night the Christ statue is illuminated by powerful floodlights. Interior lights glow through the "I Am" window.

not like it, and Trott could see the difference. They all finally agreed to stay with the original design: the left hand, nearest the heart, points to God while the right hand, the hand of service, reaches out to the multitudes. An apocryphal explanation for the position of the statue's hands circulated as campus wits observed that both Trott and Friedlander were left-handed. The finished statue was dedicated on 1 April 1960. When students wondered why the arms were so close to the body, Trott pointed out that limestone is very brittle, that an extended arm would soon break off, and that an artist always has to work within the limits of the material. "That," he concluded, "is what God has to do when working with you."

220

Artist Howard Frech puts finishing touches on the narthex mural, which depicts John Wesley preaching in the fields. Most of the characters represent 18th-century contemporaries of Wesley, but among the hearers are some modern figures; Norman Trott is clothed in black behind the rock (below).

There had to be a mural, of course, and a wall above the chapel narthex seemed made for it. John Wesley preaching to *his* multitudes was painted by Howard Frech, a Baltimore artist. The canvas includes Charles and Susanna Wesley, Thomas Maxfield, and several other probable figures among Wesley's auditors. Sharp-eyed viewers also discovered in the crowd the faces of a few contemporary Methodists, among them Norman Trott.

Many believe that the most beautiful spot on the Washington campus came into being on the lower corner at Wesley Circle, where Tilden and 46th streets converge at University and Massachusetts avenues. Some years of wishing, planning, and negotiating went into the proposal that a replica of the unique equestrian statue of John Wesley at Bristol, England, be cast and placed at Wesley Seminary. This seemed particularly appropriate since the seminary was at that time the only theological school in the western hemisphere bearing the name of the Wesleys. The statue was a gift on behalf of British Methodists from Lord J. Arthur Rank, a prominent Methodist layman who had long wished to strengthen the religious ties between his country and the United States. E. Benson Perkins, executive secretary of the World Methodist Council, helped

The John Wesley statue, an exact replica of the original at Bristol, England, was a gift to the seminary from J. Arthur Rank on behalf of British Methodists. Is the little book in Wesley's hand a Bible, a Book of Common Prayer, or some "tract of the times"?

to arrange the transaction, and the crated figure arrived in March 1961. Its emergence from the packing and its placement on the prepared base made for exciting times on campus as well as for wide public interest. The dedication, appropriately, was on 24 May, the anniversary of John Wesley's heart-warming experience at Aldersgate in 1738.[5] Senator Clinton P. Anderson of New Mexico, who lived directly across the street, liked the statue so well that he provided funds for landscaping the surrounding area. A Smithsonian guide to

Washington sculpture commented on "the artistic simplicity" of the piece:

> The contrast between the less-than-life-size statue of the famous founder of the Methodist Church, as opposed to the many greater-than-life-size statues of military men mounted on fiery chargers, expresses forcibly the differences between the commemoration of war and of peace. Wesley's gentle horse is carrying his master, the Bible open in one hand, toward the west to seek new opportunities for the word of Methodism.[6]

Wesley in Washington

Truly, in this stately bronze of John Wesley on his horse appear so much serene beauty and intensity of mission that the beholder not only is drawn into a great moment in history, but at the same time is prodded into thinking of his or her own calling in the present age.

At the center of the symbolic messages of the campus and marking the heart of the whole enterprise is the Elderkin Bell Tower, a 95-foot shaft of pre-cast stone pointing its white finger 140 feet above Massachusetts Avenue. Three messages go out with this symbol, as Trott explained in a descriptive brochure:

> *Belief in God.* Since the beginning of recorded time man has marked life's holy places with pillars of stone. Genesis 35:14 tells how Jacob set up a pillar of stone in the place where God spoke to him, naming it Bethel. The Bell Tower's slender shaft of stone, pointing heavenward, bears witness to our belief in the presence of God in this world and our witness to his presence on this campus. It marks our "Bethel."
>
> *Our Christian Faith.* The cruciform shape of the tower bears witness to the centrality of our Christian faith, for this cross marks the axis of our campus.
>
> *The Methodist Heritage*. . . . [The bells are] named for the Wesley parents (Samuel and Susanna) and Charles and John. . . . They strike the Westminster chimes throughout the day and [five minutes] after each hour the first eight notes of "O For a Thousand Tongues to Sing."

This last message has been frequently muted by mechanical problems, because mounting the bells in the open top of the tower made them vulnerable to the elements. An unexpected lesson emerged from the difficulties in casting and tuning the largest of the bells. This giant, weighing 1,300 pounds, was named for John Wesley and humorously referred to as "Big John." Three castings and many weeks of grinding were required to produce a satisfactory (if not perfect) "G" note. Trott observed that this was probably typical of John Wesley, a person of strong opinions and sometimes idiosyncratic behavior.

When the tower was dedicated in the afternoon of Monday, 14 October 1963, Bishop John Wesley Lord gratefully acknowledged it as the gift of Clarence E. Elderkin in memory of his wife, Ida Estelle Elderkin. The donor was chairman of the board of Consolidated Engineering Company, the general contractor for the whole campus, and he was present for the dedication ceremony. Although the Elderkins were Methodists, Mrs. Elderkin had died recently in a Roman Catholic hospital, where she won many friends. As a tribute to her, several nuns and priests, along with representatives from many other churches, attended the service dedicating the bell tower. They all stood in the quadrangle and sang with great gusto Charles Wesley's hymn, "O For a Thousand Tongues to Sing," thus confirming another of the seminary's sermons in stone, the figure of the good ship *Oikoumene,* symbol of the ecumenical movement carved at the front door of the Administration Building.

8

New occasions
and new duties

Upon moving to Washington in 1958, the seminary entered not only a new environment but also a new nexus of responsibilities and opportunities. The urban context required major readjustments in both the teaching approach of the faculty and the personal life styles of all members of the seminary community. Locating faculty residences in the city rather than on campus meant that the lives of faculty families revolved less around the school than they had in Westminster. Faculty spouses were now much better able to pursue professional careers of their own if they so desired, an opportunity that almost became a necessity because of rapidly rising living costs in the Washington metropolitan area. In the nation's capital, moreover, the seminary was much closer to the fast-moving changes that marked American life in the sixties and seventies, and along with most other educational institutions, it would experience the shock of unprecedented encounters with newly militant students. Wesley's new location, its new prominence in The Methodist Church, and its rising reputation as a graduate theological school attracted a student body whose numbers and diversity went far beyond what Westminster had ever known. The new campus was designed to accommodate 350 full-time students, and the administration expected to reach this figure some time in the middle or late seventies—an anticipation that materialized on schedule.

Managing the growth, however, proved to be something less than an exact science. Physical facilities were adequate enough. The seminary had gone from one to five buildings in less than a decade; and in 1967, when there came a change in the presidency, problems of an overcrowded library and insufficient office space were scarcely on the horizon. Immediate needs were faculty enlargement, curriculum modification, library development, enhanced academic standards, increased scholarship funds, and most important, an adequate endowment to undergird the whole enterprise. The seminary began to address these needs with energy and imagination, making the last two decades of its first century the most exciting years of its whole history.

Faculty growth and curriculum development

The most obvious need of the seminary in its new home was more teachers. In November 1959 President Trott told the board emphatically, "We must add three to five new faculty members by the fall of 1960 to match the student growth." He had already started anticipating this need before the move, for in June 1956 he announced the appointment of Haskell M. Miller in the field of Sociology and Social Ethics. Trott knew that Bible, Church History, and Systematic Theology would always be indispensable to any seminary's program, but he felt more and more the urgent necessity for critical study of Christian responsibility in society. He wanted to engage such problems as crime, delinquency, poverty, racism, welfare, economic justice, and urban blight; and all of these were Miller's concerns, both personally and professionally.

Haskell Miller (1910—), a native of Hubbard, Texas, was born to parents active in the Cumberland Presbyterian Church. Converted at the age of twelve and ordained at nineteen while at Bethel College in Tennessee, Miller went on to earn A.B. and M.A. degrees at Southern Methodist University and a Ph.D. in Sociology and Education at New York University. He transferred to The Methodist Church in 1944 partly because his views on evangelism and social action were more consonant with those of Methodists than of Cumberland Presbyterians. After serving briefly as vice-president and chaplain at Emory and Henry College in southwestern Virginia, he became head of the Department of Sociology and chaplain at what is now the University of Tennessee at Chattanooga. He came from there to Westminster, having first gained assurance that the seminary would be moving to Washington, where he could find wide opportunity not only for teaching but for demonstrating Christian social concern.

An author as well as an activist, Miller published several books whose titles illustrate the broad range of his interests: *Understanding and Preventing Juvenile Delinquency* (1958), *Barriers and Bridges to Brotherhood* (1962), *A Christian Critique of Culture* (1965), and *Social Welfare Ministries in a Time of Radical Social Change* (1969). In addition, his *Compassion and Community* (1961) is a book whose title characterizes the author exactly. Joining the faculty at a time when theological educators were emphasizing the essence of the church as ministering community rather than as object of professional ministry, Miller blended sociology, cultural anthropology, and Christian ethics to stress what many were beginning to call "an equipping ministry," that is, a clergy whose major task is to train church members for Christian service in the world.

Applied Christianity was for the parish as well as the classroom, as Miller demonstrated in two different situations. The first was his own pastorate at Buckeystown, Maryland, an appointment arranged by Trott, partly because there was no faculty housing available in Westminster and partly to satisfy Miller's ingrained need to be active in a parish. For two years he commuted daily to Westminster, a round trip of seventy miles, to meet his classes, while at Buckeystown he preached, made pastoral calls, and built a fellowship hall. In between these duties he wrote a book on juvenile delinquency—all "while struggling mightily," he said, "to transpose sociology into social ethics and sociology of religion. I wonder how I did it." Others wondered too, but somehow he managed, not only at Buckeystown but later in the considerably more difficult situation at Petworth Methodist Church in Washington. This second "laboratory" was a fifty-year-old church that at one time reported fifteen hundred members in a formerly white, middle-class neighborhood. As the Petworth community became more than 90 percent black, Miller

Haskell M. Miller joined the Westminster faculty after receiving assurance that the seminary would definitely move to Washington. Shown here on the new campus, he is planning another project of ministry in the inner city.

observed, the church "in tragically typical fashion, made no effort to minister to black people. Consequently, the congregation dwindled to a tiny handful of elderly people and its program declined to little more than the Sunday morning worship service."[1]

In 1966, under Miller's prompting, Wesley Seminary established the Wesley Institute of Urban Ministry, an experiment designed to bring the seminary "into vital direct encounter with realities of the church in the urban world." The institute focused on Petworth as its laboratory of learning, and Miller was appointed pastor of the church. This meant moving his family from the lawns and gardens of their suburban "white ghetto" to Petworth's crowded "black ghetto." Miller's wife, Ada, fully shared her husband's commitments, and her dedication became a mainstay of the whole enterprise. With her and a staff of students, along with a few faithful helpers from the remnant church, Miller began to test many possibilities of church renewal.

Although they did not accomplish all they wished, they did revitalize the parish. Miller's description of this venture, with its discouragements and mistakes, its achievements and joys, makes a poignant tale of extending ministerial education into an empirical context of human need. He expressed misgivings amounting almost to "frustration" about the prospects of success in putting "the social science emphasis into a proper relationship with the other elements of the [theological] curriculum." Miller was often dubious, if not downright pessimistic, about "trying to adapt everything. . . to theological and ecclesiastical tradition and to the interest of students in wanting to learn how to 'run a church.' " His colleagues, however, never shared this apprehension; they were gratified to see him establish in the seminary curriculum a permanent place of importance for Christian Social Ethics, a field which has continued to grow and serve a significant need. Miller retired in 1976 and with Ada took up residence in Rehoboth Beach, Delaware.

The next addition to the faculty, which brought an expansion of the curriculum as well, was a professor of Ecumenics. An ecumenical impulse had been present in the seminary from the beginning. Thomas Hamilton Lewis, the first president, was the champion ecumenist among Methodist Protestants, and he often prodded them to think seriously about closer relations with other mainline churches. Under his leadership they yearned for union with the two branches of Episcopal Methodism. In fact, Lewis could well be listed with prominent ecumenists like G. Bromley Oxnam and John R. Mott. Elderdicc and Forlines also were friendly toward church union movements, and at their invitation lecturers came annually to speak to the students on the subject. In the 1920s the Reverend Peter Ainslie of the Disciples Seminary House in Baltimore lectured at Westminster on "Progress toward Church Union." The seminary's first course on Ecumenics appeared in 1952, taught by Murray T. Titus in the Department of Missions and World Religions. In 1956 this course was handed over to a visiting professor, Ernest Lefever, and a year later James H. Pyke took the abandoned child back into the Department of Missions for another year of tenuous lodging.

New Occasions, Duties

When the seminary moved to Washington in 1958, Trott summoned John H. Satterwhite to what became a fifteen-year incumbency in Ecumenics, first as visiting lecturer and then as adjunct professor. Satterwhite was educated at Benedict College (A.B.), Oberlin Graduate School of Theology (B.D., S.T.M.), and Boston University School of Theology (Th.D.).

John H. Satterwhite (right) engages in ecumenical conversation with Henry Pitney van Dusen, president of Union Theological Seminary in New York, at the front door of the Administration Building.

Intimate involvement with the affairs of church union enterprises, especially the Consultation on Church Union (COCU), the World Council of Churches, and the World Methodist Council, was his meat and drink. As a minister of the African Methodist Episcopal Zion Church, Satterwhite insisted that true ecumenism had to be interracial. Speaking in 1966 to the Eleventh World Methodist Conference in London, he declared racism to be "the crisis in human relations from the point of view of the ecumenical movement" and urged Methodists to overcome the pattern of segregated churches whether white or black. As the first black addition to the faculty, Satterwhite raised the seminary's consciousness of racial issues and was influential in increasing the enrollment of black students.

In April 1962 Trott arranged for the seminary to join with the College of Preachers at the Washington Cathedral in playing host to the first annual meeting of the Consultation on Church Union. He shared in the drafting of the initial invitation and from 1962 to 1969 was a member of the Methodist delegation to COCU, which helped to keep ecumenical concerns before the seminary. In 1968 The Methodist Church joined with the Evangelical United Brethren to form The United Methodist Church, and the seminary welcomed without distinction students from E.U.B. backgrounds. Members of other denominations also came in increasing numbers to study at Wesley, while exchanges within the Washington Theological Consortium (organized in 1967) enabled professors, students, courses, credits, and ideas to circulate easily among the theological schools of the Washington area. With such relationships multiplying, the seminary would never find it possible, even should it so wish, to close its ears to the call for reuniting the broken church of Christ.

The size of the faculty took a quantum leap in 1960 when Trott announced the appointment of six new professors, five of them full-time with the sixth to become full-time the following year. The new additions learned only later that their appointments were made possible in part by a free decision of the existing faculty to forego much-needed raises in salary for another year. Joining the faculty in 1960 were Edward W. Bauman, George W. Buchanan, Tibor Chikes, Clarence C. Goen, W. Earl Ledden, and Harry M. Taylor.

230

Bauman, born in Illinois and reared in Ohio, was a graduate of DePauw University. Upon completing graduate study at Boston University School of Theology, he came to The American University as chaplain and assistant professor in the Department of Philosophy and Religion. In 1960 he was enjoying immense popularity through his recently developed "Bible Telecourse," an hour-long program broadcast live once a week, the first television course on religion ever offered for college credit. A film version, prepared later for the United States Armed Forces, was shown all over the world. At the seminary, where his dramatic talents attracted much student interest, Bauman's assignments were in Systematic Theology and Christian Ethics. He was as engaging in the pulpit as at the lectern and consequently was much sought after as a preacher. President Trott, somewhat distressed by Bauman's frequent absences to speak elsewhere, once remarked that his hardest job as president was "to keep the stars in their courses." The seminary gained some publicity through Bauman's widening reputation, while he in turn enjoyed the security of a stable institutional base at the seminary. In 1964 he became senior pastor of Foundry Methodist Church in Washington, though as adjunct professor he continued to offer each semester at Wesley a seminar on Contemporary Theology and the Parish.

George Wesley Buchanan, an Iowan, was educated at Simpson College, Garrett, Northwestern, and Drew. He had been a New Testament instructor at Drew and was appointed to teach in that field at Wesley on the eve of Shroyer's retirement. Buchanan did not confine his interests strictly to the New Testament. Having spent two years as a post-doctoral fellow at Hebrew Union College, he searched the rabbinic literature to find explanations for New Testament themes. To him, Christian origins, the historical Jesus, Paul, and the teaching of the apostles were understandable only in terms of their Jewish background. He studied with tireless energy and published copious expositions of his favorite arguments on biblical covenants, kingdom concepts, and revolutionary zealots. Happiest when debating, Buchanan sometimes made the Bible department a noisy battleground of disparate ideas.

The third addition to the faculty in 1960 was Tibor Chikes,

a Hungarian, who brought to the Department of Pastoral Theology his European university scholarship, clinical training at the University of Pennsylvania Medical School, and experience as minister of counseling at a church-sponsored center in Pittsburgh. His Calvinistic upbringing in the Hungarian Reformed Church, of which he was a minister, he described as "too strict and narrow even for John Calvin," and he rejoiced at the freedom afforded by his Methodist connection. Particularly precious was the freedom to retain his European perspectives along with the pursuit of American ways. In appointing him, President Trott agreed that Chikes might continue his private counseling practice while teaching at Wesley, and Chikes did so with a small but appreciative clientele, none of it from the seminary community. Chikes took over Pastoral Theology courses and gradually shifted his emphasis in the classroom from clinically oriented counseling to the comprehensive responsibilities of the pastoral office. He sought to help students relate to practitioners of the other helping professions, and one of his most popular courses came to be Medicine and Theology in Dialogue.

The search for a second professor of Church History brought Clarence C. Goen from Yale, where he had completed Ph.D. studies and was assisting Professor Sydney E. Ahlstrom on the manuscript of a new textbook in American religious history. A Texas Baptist with an early degree and some professional experience in electronic engineering, followed by theological degrees from Southwestern Baptist Seminary, Goen reinforced the Yale approach to the teaching of Church History at Wesley. He took over from Chandler courses in Reformation, Modern European, and American Church History, while offering other courses in Historical Theology. Although he was regarded as an engaging lecturer, Goen was also a demanding teacher. Students were often appalled at his expectations of them, and his electives were chosen only by the studious or the unwary. Yale University Press published his prize-winning dissertation, *Revivalism and Separatism in New England, 1740-1800* (1962) and his edition of the revival writings of Jonathan Edwards (1972). He served as president of the American Baptist Historical Society 1976-77 and as president of the American Society of Church History in 1982.

The Department of Preaching and Worship added two more professors in 1960. W. Earl Ledden had been bishop of the Syracuse Area of The Methodist Church since 1944 and had just retired. A graduate of Pennington Seminary (in organ), as well as of Dickinson College and Drew Theological Seminary, he was an accomplished musician, hymnologist, and liturgist with unusual gifts in preaching. Having been president of the Council of Bishops 1956-57, he was well known across the denomination. When Trott asked him to join the Wesley faculty, he welcomed the invitation as a providential opening and came from travel study in Africa, bringing not only his creative gifts to classes in Worship but also considerable episcopal prestige to the seminary. Ledden had been widowed many years. In 1964 he married Henrietta Gibson, an energetic executive of the Methodist Board of Global Missions, and together they added exceptional grace to seminary life. During the concert season in Washington the Leddens regularly invited students and faculty to share evenings with them at Constitution Hall and the Kennedy Center for the Performing Arts. He retired again in 1966, and he and Henrietta later moved into Asbury Village at Gaithersburg, Maryland, where she died in 1981. In 1978 the seminary celebrated with Bishop Ledden his ninetieth birthday, and he invited those present to join him for the hundredth—if they should still be alive then.

The faculty in 1962. Standing, l. to r.: R. Eugene Gilmore, Edward W. Bauman, President Trott, Lowell B. Hazzard, Roland E. Kircher, Robert R. Powell, Clarence C. Goen, W. Earl Ledden, Haskell M. Miller, and Emily M. Chandler. Seated: Mary Alice D. Edwards, Earl H. Furgeson, J. Edward Moyer, James H. Pyke, Montgomery J. Shroyer, George W. Buchanan, John H. Satterwhite, John B. Howes, Tibor Chikes, Douglas R. Chandler, and Ernest E. Bruder.

Harry M. Taylor's first year of teaching at Wesley required him to commute from Grace Methodist Church in Harrisburg, Pennsylvania, where he was the associate minister. After a year of part-time teaching, in 1961 he moved to Washington with his wife, Peg, and became professor of Preaching and Biblical Theology. Furgeson sorely needed to unload some of his burdens in Homiletics, and he greeted Taylor's coming with joy and relief. The two worked together in rare harmony. Taylor was a graduate of Lafayette College, the Teachers College at Columbia University, and Drew Theological Seminary, where his doctorate was earned under Edwin Lewis in Systematic Theology and Philosophy of Religion. He had taught many years at Drew before returning to the pastorate. Taylor distinguished between religion and theology, calling the first "experiences centered in relationship with God" and the latter "beliefs which derive from such relationships."

234

Theology he regarded as learned more from the "whole community of faith" rather than through a "hand-me-down" process or "getting the word from the Commander-in-Chief." A dramatic preacher with a wide range of literary resources, he offered a long-running series of seminars on Literature and Preaching, in which students rushed to enroll semester after semester. As a counselor-advisor trusted and respected by the students, he was the logical choice in 1965 to direct the "Lilly Project," an experimental attempt to discover better ways to deepen motivation for ministry. Taylor retired in 1974.

Peder Borgen from Norway, also a graduate of Drew, joined the faculty in 1962 as assistant professor of New Testament but remained only three years. In 1965 he returned to Drew to teach, but illness soon required his return to Norway. After Borgen resigned from Wesley, Dewey M. Beegle arrived to teach Old Testament, first as visiting professor for one year and then as a full-time member of the faculty. Born in Seattle, he came by way of Seattle Pacific College, Asbury Theological Seminary, and The Johns Hopkins University. Beegle brought to Wesley an evangelical faith nurtured in his early years in the Free Methodist Church and fifteen years of teaching experience at Biblical Seminary in New York City. In the conflict between older conservative views and modern critical ideas about the Bible, Beegle preferred the mediating point of view he saw in his Hopkins mentor, William F. Albright. He claimed a similarly moderate position as his own and exhibited it in his teaching as well as in his books: *The Inspiration of Scripture* (1963), *Moses the Servant of Yahweh* (1972), *Scripture, Tradition and Infallibility* (1973), and *Prophecy and Prediction* (1979). Beegle was also an experienced archaeologist, having dug at Shechem in 1964, Gezer in 1965, and Heshbon in 1968 and 1973. He gave his students some firsthand acquaintance with archaeological procedures in 1968 by directing them in a dig to determine the exact location of American Methodism's first college, Cokesbury, which opened in 1787 at Abingdon, Maryland, burned in 1795, and was never rebuilt. The students successfully located the foundation of the original building and discovered many interesting artifacts.[2]

The faculty continued to grow. Some of the more recent

additions are mentioned in other contexts, and though space limitations prohibit the full commentary that each deserves, the following should be listed here (with the schools at which they earned their graduate degrees): James T. Clemons (Duke) came in 1967 to teach New Testament, John D. Godsey (Basel) in 1968 as assistant dean and professor of Systematic Theology, Bruce C. Birch (Yale) in 1971 to teach Old Testament, Larry L. Rasmussen (Union, New York) in 1972 to teach Christian Social Ethics, Laurence H. Stookey (Princeton) in 1973 to teach Preaching and Worship, Joseph C. Weber (Boston) in 1973 to teach Biblical Theology and Ecumenics, Ellis L. Larsen (Northwestern) in 1976 as professor of Church Administration and director of Field Education, Geoffrey Simon (Catholic University) in 1977 to teach Church Music and direct the Seminary Singers, James M. Shopshire (Northwestern) in 1980 as associate dean and professor of Sociology of Religion, and William B. McClain (Boston) in 1981 to teach Preaching and Worship. Adjunct professors of recent years are too numerous to name here, but one deserves special mention. Charles I. Wallace, Jr., has regularly taught Methodist History since 1975; a graduate of Duke, Wallace is a grandson of Montgomery J. Shroyer and thus symbolizes an important link with the best of the seminary's heritage. Other adjunct faculty, readily available in the Washington area, regularly enrich the offerings with courses designed on the basis of their own special expertise, ranging from political science to film-making to world hunger.

Administration and staff

The burden of administrative detail about which Welliver complained did not appear to be too heavy for Trott. In the first place, Trott seemed to accept a heavy work load as a normal thing, for in reality he could perform on several levels at the same time. Furthermore, he enjoyed some blessings that Welliver never had: the excitement of a grand design, the admiration of his bishop, and the security of three million dollars. Yet it seemed both wise and feasible to have an assistant to share his work; and he turned first to J. Luther Neff, whose helpful assistance has already been described.

Neff retired in 1961 and was succeeded by William E. Smith, Jr., a graduate of Western Maryland College and Boston University School of Theology. Smith came directly from the University Methodist Church of College Park, Maryland, where he had been the pastor for six years. After a year on the job Smith described for the Board of Governors the gamut of his responsibilities: arranging accommodations for visitors to the campus, dispensing scholarship funds "in close conjunction with Miss Brewer [the treasurer] and the Scholarship Committee and with Dr. Trott," cultivating relationships with The American University, compiling the seminary catalog, counseling students, working with student committees (dormitory, chapel, orientation, spiritual life, and others), recruiting new students (he spent most of November, he said, visiting colleges in Michigan, Ohio, Pennsylvania, Tennessee, Virginia, Maryland, and Delaware), serving on various faculty committees, and teaching a seminar on Religion in Higher Education. The last was clearly his happiest duty. Smith carried a full portfolio, but every task was important and he worked at all of them cheerfully in his buoyant, gracious, and skillful manner. In 1964 he received a call to become the senior minister at North Broadway Methodist Church in Columbus, Ohio, and after careful consideration decided that he should return to the pastoral work he so much loved. At the time of his departure, L. Harold DeWolf of Boston University was considering Trott's invitation to become the seminary's first dean. According to a story that made the rounds then, DeWolf asked Smith privately if he had any advice about working with Trott. Smith urged DeWolf to accept the offer, but added: "Be sure you get your job description in writing."

During a brief interlude away from the pastorate, William E. Smith, Jr., was vice-president of the seminary from 1961 to 1964.

Trott tried once more to use a vice-president, this time turning to David J. Wynne, a graduate of Western Maryland College and of Westminster Seminary. Wynne had served several pastorates in the Western Pennsylvania Conference until Bishop Vernon Middleton arranged for him to become executive secretary of the Methodist Church Union in Pittsburgh. That included (among other things) managing two church homes, the Goodwill Industries, and some housing complexes for senior citizens, as well as involving himself in community work with the Housing Authority, the NAACP, Planned

David J. Wynne (left) spent six months in 1965 as the seminary's fourth vice-president. Here he is conferring with Bishop James H. Straughn, for whom the dormitory was named.

Parenthood, and the Urban League. Wynne clearly was a managerial type, able to take charge of things and act decisively on his own. He was a member of the seminary's Board of Governors and a long-time friend of Norman Trott. In 1964 Trott called, "Come down and help me," and Wynne came in February 1965. Those who knew both men shook their heads in apprehension. Bishop Middleton had doubts about the decision, and Wynne confessed later: "It was a mistake and I knew it in three months. There was just not enough for me to do and I wasn't ready for retirement. . . . To just sit and wait for Norman to throw me a bone was too hard to take." By the end of the summer Wynne was back in Pittsburgh.

Two incidents enlivened Wynne's brief stay at Wesley. The summer of 1965 witnessed the protest march from Selma to Montgomery, Alabama. Wynne recalled the situation:

> Selma found Norman out of the city and David in charge. A meeting with some faculty and a student meeting resulted in my authorizing Haskell Miller and ten students to make the trip. Since the Council of Churches plane was filled, my American Express card bought the tickets and off they went. Bess [Jones, public relations officer] was upset and gave me a bit of lip which I promptly returned. Needless to say, Bishop Ledden sparked the collection and I was repaid for the tickets. My only regret was that I didn't get to go along.

If Trott disapproved, he kept it to himself. The other incident was entirely local. Here is Wynne's account:

> I had purchased a new car and drove it to the Seminary. I came out and put the car in reverse—the gas pedal stuck—and I backed into a car parked in front of the [Straughn] dorm. It was knocked through the plate glass. Chrysler paid the damages and I got a new car. No one was hurt.

Wynne shattered more than glass in the few months he was on campus, but as he said of the car incident, no one was hurt. In August he resigned, effective 1 September, and Bishop Middleton welcomed him back to his old job in Pittsburgh. President Trott reported tersely to the Board of Governors, "For the present we are eliminating the office [of vice-president]." Wynne and Trott did not meet again until the Northeastern Jurisdictional Conference of 1972. "We met like old friends," reported Wynne, "hugged and cried and had dinner together. . . . He was a good administrator except when it came to delegating authority to his assistants."

Although it truly was not easy for Trott to delegate his administrative tasks, he soon saw in Bess S. Jones the qualities he thought would be most useful in public relations and development. During the seminary's first September in Washington he chose her to be his "assistant in charge of cultivation and promotion." She helped him set up the Development Office and supported his choice of Richard Hamilton in 1962 to direct it. After Hamilton returned in 1966 to pastoral duties in the Peninsula Conference, Trott appointed Jones as director of development. No one could have worked with the president more effectively in this office. She deftly implemented his ideas, modified them at times with her own, and introduced new ideas so tactfully that he thought they were his. Along with her professional expertise were a winsome personality and a gracious smile, all making clear why her efforts added so many names to the seminary's growing list of friends. Trott described her value in his report of October 1962 to the board, remarking that she was both charming and efficient. Jones guided the Development Office from its small beginning with gift records filed on three-by-five index cards into an impressive array of functions dealing with fund raising, public relations, and graduate organization affairs.

The seminary's adjustment to its wider world in Washington was made more orderly and pleasant by a small company of staff personnel who not only had the requisite skills but genuinely loved the school. Robert and Caroline Green came from Westminster with the seminary, Caroline having been secretary in the Admissions Office for a year before the move. Her detailed knowledge of degree requirements and of each student's progress toward meeting them evoked admiration and gratitude from all her colleagues, especially faculty advisors, who knew they could always get from her quick and correct answers to their questions. During Professor Moyer's leave in 1973, she directed the Registrar's Office with efficiency and grace. Bob, as everyone knew her husband, left his Westminster construction job to come along as superintendent of buildings and grounds. This was fortunate, for his constant walks about the campus not only ensured the necessary oversight but also supplied students with an ambulatory counseling service, replete with endless anecdotes. His pastoral care was instinctive and spontaneous. If his workers became delinquent or "got in trouble," as some occasionally did, he would not dismiss them until all second-mile patience and assistance had failed.

In 1973 John E. Bevan came as full-time registrar and director of admissions, relieving the faculty of these responsibilities that had intruded on their teaching time for so many years. As the holder of a theological degree himself (a Master of Theology from the School of Religion at the University of Southern California) and with eleven years prior experience as a university registrar, he brought to his post both professional competence and an understanding of seminary requirements. Bevan began to develop a systematic recruiting program to seek out capable college students and interest them in Wesley Seminary. His professional peers recognized his abilities by electing him president of the Middle States Association of Collegiate Registrars and Admissions Officers in 1976.

At the beginning of the Washington years, Virginia Hamner was employed as secretary to Vice-President Neff with an additional assignment to serve the faculty as needed. She had been secretary at Calvary Methodist Church in Washington, and there was never any doubt about her knowledge of The Methodist Church or her devotion to it. The seminary recognized her competence by regularly increasing her work load; she handled room assignments in the dormitory, managed the bookstore, operated the duplication services, distributed caps and gowns at commencement, and spent untold hours at her shorthand tablet and typewriter. Her "information service" processed up-to-the-minute data on

240

faculty, students, and graduates—their marriages, newborns, illnesses, emergencies, deaths—and extended to most things pertaining to Methodism throughout the world. She showed a keen interest in students from abroad, and after their graduation she visited many of them in their overseas homes.

The first officially designated treasurer for the seminary was Beulah Brewer. Her appointment in 1962 was a somewhat belated recognition of what she had been doing quietly as accountant for two years. The magnitude and complexity of the school's financial structure would have astounded any of the Westminster presidents, and it now involved an almost overwhelming mass of detail. Brewer, however, seemed to enjoy keeping the books, and she worried as much as the president when they didn't balance. There were some anxious moments after the Kresge grant was spent and many of the churches were contributing irregularly, if at all. Faculty members recalled times in the early 1960s when their biweekly meeting fell on payday (the fifteenth of the month). Around 11:00 A.M., when the morning mail arrived, Brewer would call Trott out of the meeting and together they would go through the letters to see if enough money had come in to allow them to release the payroll checks. But whatever the seminary's financial condition, one could always be sure that the books were in order, showing an accurate account of the state of affairs. Until she retired in 1978, Brewer graced her office with Maine speech and sparkling laughter, but she offered little tolerance of delinquent accounts. And the auditors were always pleased.

No doubt the most conspicuous person on the new campus was Margaret ("Peg") Harrison at the switchboard. Hers was the first voice heard by inquiring callers or visiting strangers, and her own "information bureau" became central to the school's life. Beloved and helpful, she was for twelve years (1958-70) the eyes and ears of all the offices. As for maintenance, the multiplied needs on the new campus could not have been imagined during the years at Westminster when Walter Sims cared for the building and grounds. There had been some talk, probably wishful thinking, about bringing the venerable Sims to Washington, but he would not even consider it. In 1961 Simmie Washington joined Bob Green's

241

staff and began a long period of faithful service, keeping the buildings clean and the flowers blooming. With his stolid dependability, pious devotion, and gift for gospel singing, he became a living symbol of the seminary's reason for being.

When Virginia Hamner's responsibilities grew too large for one person, Anne Jackson took over the management of the bookstore in 1968. She was unfortunately stricken with serious illness a year later and Nell Jernigan stepped in as her replacement. In 1972 Margaret ("Molly") Nash assumed responsibility

Faculty and staff worked together at the multitude of tasks necessary to keep the seminary running smoothly. Pictured in 1960 are: front row, left to right—Virginia Hamner, Gloria Thompson, Caroline Green, Margaret ("Peg") Harrison, Arlette Matthys, and Clara Reed; second row—Haskell M. Miller, Robert R. Powell, Beulah Brewer, Emily M. Chandler, and Douglas R. Chandler; third row—James H. Pyke, Chester Sheppard, Montgomery J. Shroyer, George W. Buchanan, Mary Alice D. Edwards, and Doretta Johnson; fourth row— Ernest E. Bruder, Earl H. Furgeson, Norman L. Trott, Roland E. Kircher, J. Luther Neff, John B. Howes, and Bess S. Jones; fifth row— Tibor Chikes, Lowell B. Hazzard, R. Eugene Gilmore, John H. Satterwhite, W. Earl Ledden, Clarence C. Goen, and J. Edward Moyer; sixth row— Edward W. Bauman, Robert (Bob) Green, George Williams, Roger Matthys, and Joseph Neale.

for the bookstore. Under her aggressive management the facility expanded from a small outlet supplying basic textbooks to a fully stocked religious bookstore serving churches of the surrounding area and the general public. An important by-product of the bookstore's growth is the Lay Resource Center, an ecumenical organization created in 1980 with faculty approval and support "to serve the needs of lay people and their congregations." As the vision of Molly Nash and four other laywomen connected with the seminary, the LRC offers continuing education courses for adults, resource materials for church programs, and a consulting service on lay ministry.

An academic dean, student unrest, and a new curriculum

When David Wynne left, Trott eliminated the office of vice-president and turned instead to a dean who could assume responsibility for the academic program. After consulting with various faculty members, he settled on L. Harold DeWolf, who had been teaching Philosophy, Theology, and Ethics at Boston University for thirty-one years. A Nebraskan by birth, DeWolf was educated at Nebraska Wesleyan, the University of Nebraska, and Boston University. He became dean of Wesley Seminary on 1 July 1965 and served until his retirement in 1972. In those seven years important changes in curriculum and degree programs were brought to completion. DeWolf's extraordinary abilities had already won him considerable prestige in American theological education. As the author of many books, among them a popular textbook entitled *A Theology of the Living Church* (2d ed., 1960), he was widely known and respected as an articulate spokesman for liberal evangelicalism. What was more, he possessed the sensitivities and insights needed for troubled times. In those revolutionary years he sometimes gave the impression that he himself was almost a revolutionary. The mentor of Martin Luther King, Jr., during King's doctoral studies at Boston, DeWolf was accustomed to applying his theological-ethical convictions to concrete strategies for social change. To the discomfort of a few more cautious members of the faculty, he seemed to welcome students bent on reform or even rebellion. He listened, reasoned patiently, yielded to some of their demands while firmly resisting others, added student representatives to nearly all faculty committees, and initiated various joint ventures and experiments.

The students, on their part, tinkered freely with all traditions, abandoning many and starting others. Coats and ties, long in disfavor, now disappeared, even in chapel. A new concept of freedom found expression in long hair, beards, blue jeans, T-shirts, sneakers and sandals, or no shoes at all. On one hot day a pair of bare feet wriggled comfortably during

New Occasions, Duties

a lecture on John Wesley—an unintentional reminder of that Anglican priest's barefoot appearance in his Georgia schoolroom to teach the children not to ridicule the poor among them but to be kind and generous. Seniors rebelled at commencement habits but were persuaded to keep gowns and hoods while discarding only the mortarboards. Chapel leaders abandoned traditional liturgies and experimented with guitars, folk music, liturgical dance, chancel drama, black bread for Eucharist, casual seating in the choir and about the chancel steps, and anything else that would break the pattern of customary formality. Much of this, when set against the turbulent events of the 1960s, can be discounted as relatively minor. With racial violence everywhere, protest marches on Washington, two Kennedys and Martin Luther King assassinated, the seemingly endless agony of Vietnam, and the new space program costing billions of dollars that many people thought could be better spent alleviating human misery, one might think that campus unrest should have been greater than it was.

In October 1961 the Soviet Union exploded a series of atomic superbombs (in the range of fifty megatons), provoking worldwide protests. On 31 October more than 100 Wesley students and faculty marched from the Soviet embassy to the White House urging a cessation of all nuclear testing.

For the most part, the really important and permanent changes associated with the seminary's new beginning in Washington were in the curriculum, and some of these were often extensions of revisions begun in Westminster. The critical survey of Methodist theological schools in 1947 had set forth minimum requirements for the seminary's accreditation and spurred the faculty to begin a decade of self-study and redirection. Faculty meetings devoted many hours to a close examination of the school's professional character, academic standards, admission requirements, grading, evaluation procedures, and responsibility for spiritual formation. When it was learned in 1953 that the seminary would be relocating on the campus of The American University, the curriculum was scrutinized again with university associations in mind. But compared to changes that would come in the 1960s, what was done before the move seems little more than a modest rearrangement of traditional features.

New Occasions, Duties

In 1963 President Trott reported to the Board of Governors that he had just proposed to the faculty "a radical shift in our concept of training, aiming the seminary teaching program at the mature student—with more freedom for him to mature." Speaking of the "tightly designed core curriculum and required class attendance [that marked the] spoon-feeding educational techniques" of Westminster days, he added: "We are now in a different age. It calls for more freedom on the one hand. It offers more promise on the other. Consequently we are dropping the cut [i.e., attendance] requirements, putting every man on his own." Trott assured the board that the faculty fully supported his proposals. The following April he reported that the first major steps in curriculum change had been instituted: compulsory class attendance abolished, an honors program instituted, and the rigid core "by-passed at points where the student's advanced college preparation parallels core requirements." In the fall of 1964 he repeated the charge that "a revolution in Seminary education is long overdue." By that time he was already talking about an academic dean, and when one came the following year, curriculum revision became the first priority.

L. Harold DeWolf was installed on 5 October 1965 as Wesley's first dean. His very coming was an unmistakable signal

L. Harold DeWolf came from Boston University School of Theology in 1965 as the seminary's first academic dean. During his seven-year tenure, the school modernized its curriculum in many ways.

of imminent change. In his Inaugural Address, "Theological Education for the Present Age," DeWolf bluntly laid out an agenda of the changes that would be necessary if the seminary were going to achieve "a new kind of theological education" for "a new ministry" in a "world on the brink of disaster." Work began immediately, with faculty committees spending long hours to construct a totally new degree program. The first step was to define four major areas of ministerial identity, learning, experience, and competence, which in turn became the major divisions of a new curriculum: 1) Development of the Person, 2) Interpretation of the Faith, 3) Encounter with the World, and 4) Ministries of the Church. Each area was set forth with carefully specified standards, and degrees were to be awarded not simply to those who had earned a certain number of course credits but to those who could positively demonstrate their readiness for ministry. There would be no core of required courses and no grades in the usual sense. Instead, a number of comprehensive examinations, other forms of evaluation, and systematic observation of each student's progress in academic studies, field education, and spiritual formation would provide the requisite evidence that a degree candidate was adequately prepared to be ordained and assume a ministerial vocation in the church. In recognition of the more rigorous requirements, the new program would lead to a more advanced degree, Master of Theology (M.Th.).

To launch the new program, the administration redesigned the catalog and printed descriptive brochures, long and detailed. Because he was expecting more students and because the program would require more intensive relationships between faculty and students, DeWolf obtained Trott's approval for the appointment of three new faculty members. In the fall of 1966 came James C. Logan in Systematic Theology, Charles W. Stewart in Pastoral Theology, and J. Philip Wogaman in Christian Social Ethics. All three held graduate degrees from Boston University, a circumstance that increased to nine the number on the faculty so educated and prompted some quips about Wesley becoming "a little Boston" or "Boston on the Potomac." DeWolf was unruffled. When asked about the "coincidence," he simply replied with a smile, "We wanted the best teachers we could find."

Wesley's pioneering attempt to offer a Master of Theology as the basic theological degree ran somewhat ahead of most other seminaries in the United States. But a trend toward some kind of master's degree soon developed, with the result that the American Association of Theological Schools (the primary accrediting agency for American seminaries) voted in 1968 to approve the Master of Divinity (M.Div.) as the basic degree to be awarded after three years of post-baccalaureate study in a graduate seminary. Wesley promptly announced that it would offer the M.Div. instead of the M.Th. But since the requirements of Wesley's M.Th. were more demanding than those of most M.Div. programs elsewhere, some adjustments became necessary. There were already some signs that expectations in the M.Th. program had been too high. Student enrollment was down, the attrition rate among M.Th. students was rising, more students than formerly were extending their stay at the seminary to four years or more, and many students were apprehensive about the rigors of the approaching comprehensive examinations. "These factors," the administrators concluded, "are beginning to operate against the Seminary's main purpose, which is to supply the church with as many well-trained ministers as possible." Accordingly in September 1968 the dean and president announced some modifications.

Abolishing the dreaded comprehensive examinations was hailed with general approval. In its place seniors were required to present a fifteen-thousand-word paper on "The Church and Its Ministry," written independently of any course and setting forth their most mature understandings in reference to the main areas of the curriculum, now defined as The Faith of the Church, The Church in the World, and The Ministries of the Church. This would give the students opportunity to integrate all of their learning experiences in a comprehensive statement explaining and defending their theological concepts, their understanding of the social context of the contemporary church, and their proposals for fulfilling the responsibilities of (usually ordained) ministry. The paper would be presented during the penultimate semester before graduation and would be evaluated by a cross-disciplinary team of two faculty readers. The C.I.M. paper (as it was called) thus stood as a kind of "senior thesis," except that instead of being a research paper, it required the prospective minister to think through in systematic fashion the knowledge, beliefs, methods, and commitments that had become his or her equipment for professional ministry.

The advisory system remained at the heart of the program. With no core of required courses, students needed careful academic counseling. Many students, moreover, were now coming to the seminary with an uncertain mixture of motives and purposes. Some were seeking clarification of their faith, or maybe even faith itself; some had little sense of any special "call" to ministry but were willing to investigate the feasibility of becoming ministers; some were avoiding the draft, and some were simply "professional students." In any event, most of them soon discovered that the experiences of seminary precipitated various crises—of faith, of vocational purpose, of pastoral identity and/or emotional health. Advisory groups became a forum in which a small group of students met with a professor for at least one hour each week to talk over whatever concerned them, whether it involved intellectual questions, a difficult situation in the parish or elsewhere, a struggle for faith, an attempt to clarify vocational goals, or some kind of personal problem. Although the groups were not intended to serve any formal therapeutic function, they did in many cases become prefigurations of the mutual support groups to which persons in ministry often belong, and in this way they filled a useful educational purpose in the total program of the seminary.

Another aspect of change in the sixties was the abandonment of the traditional system of letter grades in favor of "Pass" or "Unsatisfactory." To students worried that this kind of grading would not provide adequate support if they should wish later to apply to graduate school, the faculty offered the possibility of receiving a "P*" for superior work in a course. In awarding such a grade a professor would write a "citation for academic excellence" describing the student's accomplishments, and it was felt that a transcript accompanied by several such citations would impress graduate school admissions officers more than a bare string of undocumented "A's." A positive result of the "P/U" grading system was that many

248

students found themselves for the first time freed from the anxiety of competing for grades, and they worked instead for mastery of the material to be learned. In 1972, as such anxiety subsided (or returned?), more students wished to receive letter grades, and the faculty provided that option for them.

Spirituality and service

One of the most problematic tasks in educating men and women for effective ministry is spiritual formation. Nothing is more indispensable in the person of the minister than spiritual maturity, and at the same time nothing is more difficult to impart. President Trott often voiced the fear that amid the unaccustomed luxury of Wesley's new material facilities it would be easy to neglect spiritual development. He thought he saw a golden opportunity to develop a retreat center when in 1959 Joseph Himes of Washington unexpectedly deeded to the seminary his summer residence, an island with a forty-room house and several other buildings in the Thousand Islands area of the St. Lawrence River. Himes intended also to provide the basic costs of maintaining the place and its caretaker, but that part failed to materialize; and five years later Trott regretfully sold the property for $35,000. In the meantime, however, some of the faculty, students, staff, and their friends enjoyed several "retreats" to the place and lived briefly in a manner to which they probably would have liked to become accustomed.

The city of Washington offered libraries, museums, art galleries, historic churches, non-Christian religious centers, political activity, international diplomacy, and all the excitement of a great crossroads of the world. Students were exhorted regularly to experience as much of the city as they could. In addition to the "visitor's Washington," however, they soon discovered more poverty and pain than they had ever known existed. In the fall of 1961, with help from the Baltimore Conference Board of Missions, the seminary began a Washington Inner-City Project, more commonly known as "Shepherds of the Streets" (SOS). Clifford Ham, an urban sociologist who had been lecturing at Wesley on The Church in Urban Development, directed the project. It began with four students who spent several weeks in research, visitation, and fact-finding, and then it extended to adult group meetings, boys' and girls' clubs, a study hall, basketball games, crafts, "clean-ups," and a vacation Bible school, all in cooperation with churches in the precinct. A survey discovered 101 storefront and 44 "regular" churches in the area. Since the project was basically experimental and intentionally careful to avoid competition with already established churches and other groups with similar goals, its successes were limited. After a third year its work was discontinued, but its findings and the records of its experiments served to inform subsequent efforts in city missions by both the conference and the seminary.

A new venture—"an experimental project designed to deepen motivation for the Christian ministry"—was announced in December 1964. This was initially President Trott's idea, perhaps with some prompting from Elton Trueblood, the Quaker theologian, who visited the campus frequently in the early sixties. After the proposal had been refined by more than a year of faculty study, the seminary received an enabling grant from the Lilly Endowment and launched the "Lilly Project" with Harry Taylor as director. The experiment began in the fall of 1965 with a small group of first-year students who committed themselves to give priority to the spiritual rather than the academic or the psychological, "to seek spiritual maturity, to be strong in faith and seriously committed to the work of Christ." Taylor's report at the end of the first year described the way the experiment began and indirectly suggested something of its approach.

> We sent invitations to all our incoming class, ladies excepted. . . . Of some seventy invited twenty-three came and, after briefing, eighteen volunteered. From the eighteen, eleven were chosen by lot. . . . We decided to have eleven students and one faculty member constitute the twelve because we wished it to be clear that Jesus, not the faculty member, was to be the Person in charge.

The Lilly group's procedures included retreats, Monday field trips to various places in Washington, daily group meetings of at least an hour each Tuesday through Friday, service activities on campus by offering friendly assistance to fellow students and off campus by working ten hours a week without pay in some local church, interviews with psychologists (psychiatric therapy if needed), individual counseling with Taylor, and consultations with faculty advisors and members of the Project Committee. Although the group was unobtrusive enough on the campus, it could not escape some implications of elitism. There was also a lurking fear that such a program could jeopardize academic achievement. Some thought the goals of the project should be sought by all students and approached through the advisory groups already established under faculty supervision. When after two years the Lilly Endowment declined to renew the grant, the experiment ended.

Another experiment in the search for a different approach to seminary education was "Interact," a program adopted (perhaps "permitted" is more accurate) by the faculty for the year 1971-72. By this plan fifteen students pledged themselves to "a weekly minimum commitment" consisting of 1) twenty-five hours working at some kind of ministerial task in a local church, usually for compensation; 2) twenty-five hours of study on theological subjects, either in individual learning contracts or in regular courses at the seminary, or in a combination of these; and 3) ten hours in group discussion with a coordinator for reporting and mutual counsel. The Interact group chose as coordinator Tilden Edwards, an Episcopal priest with experience in spiritual direction and pastoral formation. The intent of this program was to address the "major unsolved problem of theological education, the adequate relating of classroom and library work to application in the field, that is, in ministry within the church and of the church in the world." Some interaction between study and ministry did occur, but at the end of the first year an evaluation showed more shortcomings than real values in the plan. Although the more mature and self-motivated students in the group profited by the experience, and although "Interact helped to strengthen Wesley's image publicly as a school that is open to experiment and change," the report concluded that, as with the Lilly Project, Interact's chief values were maintained by features of the curriculum already established. Even so, its will-

251

ingness to experiment in such ways showed that Wesley Seminary had no desire to be an ivory tower.

Minorities and women, graduates and support groups

Black students were few and therefore conspicuous on campus through much of the 1960s. The enrollment of two or three in Westminster led President Trott to recommend to the Board of Governors in November 1955 "the election to the Board of a distinguished Negro Methodist, looking forward to the time when in Washington there will be a reasonable number of well-qualified Negroes in training at the Seminary." The overtones of benevolence and the hint of a quota would have embarrassed Trott had they been pointed out to him, for he thought of himself as ahead of most of the church on racial issues. How would his "reasonable number" compare with twenty-eight, the maximum number of black students the seminary has yet enrolled in any one year? But he succeeded in getting blacks on the board—the first, J. Ernest Wilkins, in 1956—and in 1958 he appointed a black professor to the faculty. The seminary also worked vigorously to recruit black students, though not without some feelings of ambivalence. On the one hand, the school genuinely wanted to break with the WASP tradition; but on the other, it respected the work of the Howard University Divinity School and had no wish to compete with it for students.

Notwithstanding the seminary's desire to enroll black students and be responsive to their needs, the 1960s brought some tense days and a few angry confrontations. A black caucus organized, and it was critical and demanding, as it was meant to be. The faculty and administration tried to give it a sympathetic hearing, but genuine trust and acceptance developed slowly. Course offerings began to include black history, black theology, black biography, and black preaching. For fifteen years John Satterwhite was the only black professor, but in 1973 came Roy D. Morrison, a graduate of Howard University, Northern Baptist Seminary, and the University of Chicago. Morrison manifested exceptional brilliance in

Philosophical Theology and began to develop a series of courses in Black Philosophy of Culture and Religion that promised to make a distinctive original contribution to the study of the black experience in America. In 1974 theologian Manas Buthelezi came as a visiting professor from South Africa, even though at the time he was under the ban of his government; his courses on African Theology served to strengthen black awareness on the campus and to deepen understanding of Christianity in the Third World. By 1980, the number of black students had increased to twenty-eight, the black faculty to three, black staff members to five, and black board members to nine.

Although Methodist Protestants always accepted women into ministry and ordained a few, both the denomination and its one seminary shared an almost universal assumption that the Christian ministry was primarily for men. As noted earlier, President Elderdice revised his prejudices after hearing Maude Royden preach in London, and he set them aside entirely when the three women students who enrolled in the late twenties convinced him that their presence was a refining influence on male manners. Westminster had graduated its first woman candidate for the ministry in 1926, and she was promptly ordained in the Methodist Protestant Church. When Georgia Harkness from Boston and Bertha Paulson from Gettysburg lectured at Westminster, the campus had firsthand evidence that men held no monopoly on theological creativity. Yet by far the largest proportion of women students who came to the seminary before the 1960s were the dozen or so who enrolled in the M.R.E. program. Trott wanted women on the Board of Governors, and in 1964 he proudly introduced two new members, Mrs. Herminia H. Aiken and Mrs. Bernice D. Abrams. "For the first time," he said, "there are two ladies on the Board"—a boast somewhat diminished by his next announcement that "episcopal representation has been substantially expanded by the membership of eleven bishops," all male, of course.

The 1970s saw a rapid rise in the enrollment of women in most American seminaries. In 1970 there were 30 women at Wesley, a circumstance which can now be seen as the beginning of a trend, and by 1980 the number had climbed to 122, or 35 percent of the student body. Even more striking was the fact that most of these women were not interested in studying to be directors of Christian education. The vast majority of female seminary students were in the Master of Divinity program and were intending to seek ordination. Since there was no constitutional barrier to their purpose in The United Methodist Church, the main obstacle they had to overcome was cultural prejudice.

Faculty development at Wesley reflected the growing participation of women in theological education. When Douglas R. Chandler retired in 1973, Francine J. Cardman came from graduate studies at Yale to teach Church History. She was lured away to another seminary in 1979, and the following year Robin Darling arrived from the University of Chicago as her replacement. In addition to her impressive knowledge of the whole field (now called History of Christianity), Darling brought special strength in the history of Eastern Christianity, an area that had been neglected previously. When Robert R. Powell retired in 1979, Susan B. Thistlethwaite, a recent graduate of Duke, was appointed to teach Christian Education. After two years she moved to Boston with her husband, a research physician, and was replaced by Diedra H. Kriewald, a Vanderbilt graduate who had been serving as chaplain and professor of Religion at Shenandoah College. In 1979 Catherine A. Kapikian became artist-in-residence at the seminary and promptly began to develop a program in Religion and the Arts that has drawn nation-wide attention. Educated at Carnegie Mellon University, the University of Maryland, and Wesley Seminary, Kapikian attracted to her art studio a growing number of students intrigued by her assertion that "an artist is not a special kind of person; every person is a special kind of artist," and some of them professed to have learned as much history and theology in her courses as in their more direct address to those subjects. By the end of its first century, in 1982, the seminary had on its faculty six women, three of them in full-time tenured or tenure-track positions.

One of the most visible signs of prejudice against women has been the sexist language inherited from a long-lived patriarchal tradition. Hymnals and liturgical manuals were full of male-dominated language. Wesley women, with encourage-

254

ment and cooperation from most of the male students, faculty and administration, set about to remove the affront of language that excluded them. Pointing out that language not only symbolizes but powerfully conditions reality, they sought out new hymns and rewrote old ones, prepared new liturgies, and instructed visiting preachers to be sure to use inclusive language in chapel sermons. The Community Council mandated the preparation of a brochure entitled "The Use of Inclusive Language in the Worship of the Church." Written in 1979 by Laurence H. Stookey, professor of Preaching and Worship, the brochure attracted such a wide readership that thousands of copies were requested by church people from all over the country. A revised version with an updated bibliography was issued in 1982.

Some awareness of changing times and of the importance of inclusiveness in the seminary's life is also evident in the composition of the historic supporting groups. The corporate charter, as amended in 1975, requires a rotating Board of Governors with staggered terms of four years each. One-fourth of the board is to be elected annually, with each class composed of at least two blacks, two women, and two Wesley graduates. In 1972 Bradshaw Mintener, a Washington lawyer, became the first lay member to be elected chairman of the

Catherine A. Kapikian came as artist-in-residence in 1979. Her studio is always cheerfully cluttered with student projects in various stages of emerging creativity. "An artist is not a special kind of person," she tells them; "every person is a special kind of artist."

255

board, a belated recognition of the historic "mutual rights" of clergy and laity in the seminary's Methodist Protestant tradition.

The Development Office helped to organize a Women's Guild in May 1959. The group became a beehive of activity, supporting such projects as scholarship aid, Saturday evening meals for on-campus students, lounge furnishings, library funds, construction of a powder room in the refectory (a major oversight in the original plans), and a clothes closet to supply good used clothing for needy students. Although guild membership is concentrated in the Baltimore-Washington area, members are scattered across the United States and in at least one foreign country. A similar support group, Epworth House, brought the organization, work, and funds of the Baltimore Conference Deaconess Board to Wesley Seminary. During the seminary's early years in Washington, these women furnished apartments, subsidized the rent of women students on campus, and established several scholarships.

The Alumni Association, which in 1976 recognized the growing number of women graduates by changing its name to the Association of Wesley Seminary Graduates, became increasingly active after the move to Washington. In 1964 the group established the Society of John Wesley, electing ten charter members and proposing to elect two more each succeeding year. Based on "outstanding service to God, to the church, and to Wesley Theological Seminary," this is the highest honor the graduates can bestow on one of their colleagues. In the 1970s the association began to develop an annual Graduate Days program at the school. Activities of the graduates were coordinated through the Development Office. Bess Jones and her staff kept up-to-date files on the growing number of graduates, circulated a quarterly newsletter, and offered various supporting services to maintain an active and healthy organization.

Two more significant groups originated as President Trott's idea and were brought into being by the Development Office. In 1959 Trott sent to twenty-five "top ministers of our contiguous conferences" and to fifty "top-flight laymen" an invitation which began with the confession, "I need more wisdom." His invitation continued: "I am asking some particularly skilled, astute and wise colleagues to share with me their judgments, advice and interest in the developing Seminary program . . . to serve as a circle of advisors in cooperation with our Board of Governors." None could resist this kind of appeal, and in due course the Clergy Advisory Council and the Lay Advisory Council came into being. Both groups met regularly at the seminary, heard reports on recent developments, and offered the "wisdom" Trott had requested. Many members of these various groups became permanent good friends of the seminary and extended its influence further into the life of the church.

A change of presidents

President Trott planned his retirement and carried it out in his own typical style. At the close of the Board of Governors meeting on 29 March 1966 he requested the privilege of a personal statement. Now that the campus had been constructed and the expanded program put in place, he said, it was time to plan for "the next stage in the seminary's executive leadership—namely, the phasing out of the present President and the phasing in of the next one." He hoped a new president could assume office within a year because he wanted to "take a portion of a delayed sabbatical and assist in the transition . . . being available to keep firm the Seminary's supporting constituency." The board accepted his resignation with much regret, elected him president emeritus, and voted to name the administration building for him.

Back in 1960, while talking one day with a professor who was house hunting, Trott had said, "Take this place now. It's a good buy. And when you retire in a decade or so, I'll have your retirement home ready." Pursuing a plan that had been in the back of his mind for several years, he retired from the seminary to build a retirement home for others. In Gaithersburg, Maryland, around the nucleus of the old and well-established Asbury Methodist Home, he directed the erection of a magnificent complex of buildings called Asbury Methodist Village. When the first of the Village apartments was ready, he and his wife, Lillian, made it their home. There, suddenly, on Sunday, 16 November 1975, Trott died. As Wesley Seminary had done earlier, Asbury Village dedicated a building that bears his name and recalls his life.

The Board of Governors selected as Trott's successor John Lowden Knight, pastor of the First Methodist Church of Syracuse, New York. Knight grew up in Beverly, New Jersey, where he married Alice Kingston, his high school sweetheart, in 1941. After earning a liberal arts degree at Drew and a theological degree at Boston, he went to Vanderbilt for graduate studies. He served subsequently as professor of Church History at Willamette University in Oregon and president successively of Nebraska Wesleyan and Baldwin-Wallace colleges. Inaugurated as Wesley's eighth president on 30 October 1967, Knight would complete his term of office as the seminary ended its first century of existence. In Washington the Knights made their home a place of warm hospitality and gracious entertainment for all members of the seminary community, with the annual open house at "the Knights before Christmas" becoming especially memorable. Upon his retirement in 1982, they moved back to Beverly, New Jersey.

During Knight's first few years in office the turbulence of the decade reached a climax. It was fortunate, perhaps even providential, that the harsher aspects of student rebellions came not during Trott's last years but in Knight's early ones. Knight had an easygoing temperament that allowed angry dissidents to "blow off steam" until the pressure was well below the danger point. The very idea of confrontation was distasteful to him. He refused to be ruffled, to execute punitive measures, or to hold any kind of grudge. By his gentle (some would say permissive) style of administration, he kept protest within limits, and the seminary passed eventually into the quieter waters of the post-Vietnam era. Philip Wogaman, who was appointed dean upon DeWolf's retirement in 1972, described Knight's style in his own report to the Board of Governors, October 1977, as "steady, patient, wise, pastoral—always helping to maintain the conditions necessary for creativity by everybody in the seminary community. It has helped us move forward, secure in our roots and confident of our future."

By the time Knight arrived on campus, seminary life was already shifting to a more collegial mode of operation, well befitting the school's Methodist Protestant heritage. No longer were all decisions to be made in the front office and handed down by arbitrary fiat. A Community Organization was taking shape, not as a "student government" merely, but as a thoroughly representative body through which all segments of the seminary worked at their life together in the community. At its center was an elected Community Council whose members represented faculty, staff, administration, commuting students, dormitory residents, women, and minorities, so that no group on campus felt neglected. According to constitutional provision, the council had real decision-making power, dispensing its budget (derived from fees and contributions paid by all members of the community), forming committees to exercise responsibility for various aspects of campus life, and appointing student representatives to standing committees of the faculty. Especially important were the President's Committee, which dealt with administrative matters of concern to everyone (housing, food service, parking, campus regulations), and the Dean's Committee, which dealt with academic matters (degree requirements, curriculum changes, course evaluations, professors' expectations). Membership on these committees consisted of about half students, half faculty and administration, and through such structures the channels of communication remained open. Never did any controversy pass beyond the critical point at which dialogue was disrupted and opposing factions squared off in sharply polarized conflict.

John Lowden Knight came as the seminary's eighth president in 1967. He retired in 1982 as the school was completing its first century of existence.

Another evidence of Knight's collegial style may be seen in the way faculty appointments were made during his administration. All previous presidents had acted on their own to select professors, subject only to the approval of the Board of Governors, which was usually given pro forma. Trott usually made unilateral arrangements with prospective appointees and simply reported to the board what he had done. The selection of the seminary's first dean, however, was a step of such significance that Trott called together a small group of faculty members to consult with him on both the process of appointment and the prospective candidates. During the first year of Harold DeWolf's service as dean, it became feasible

259

to appoint a second professor of Old Testament to work alongside Lowell Hazzard. DeWolf joined Trott in taking counsel with certain faculty members, and as a result of this ad hoc procedure Dewey Beegle was appointed in 1965. These developments were the precursors of what became under President Knight the Faculty Personnel Committee. While it had no legal authority of appointment, its consultative role gave the faculty a strong voice in the selection of their future colleagues. The whole process matured into a collegial pattern which Knight found congenial, and it continued as "the established way of doing things."

A by-product of the faculty selection process was the manual on *Personnel Policies and Procedures,* which was issued first in 1968 with a section for the faculty and another for the staff. With the approval of the board, Knight stated precisely what the seminary's employees could expect in regard to such things as promotion, tenure, leaves, and benefits. For the first time every employee knew that he or she was being treated exactly as all the others. On its part, the faculty requested that all differences in pay within each professorial rank be abolished and

In the chancel of Metropolitan Memorial United Methodist Church are (left to right) Bradshaw Mintener, chairman of the Board of Governors 1972-78, the first layman to serve in this capacity; President Knight; J. Philip Wogaman, professor of Christian Social Ethics since 1966 and academic dean 1972-83; and Bishop W. Earl Ledden, professor of Christian Worship 1960-66.

that everybody in each rank be paid exactly the same. Knight carried this request to the Board of Governors with his support and dealt with their puzzled questions until they were ready to vote approval. The action did much to confirm the spirit of community among all the people who were investing their lives in the common enterprise of Wesley Seminary.

Since the students would be ministering in a pluralistic situation, it seemed to make good sense to provide their theological education in an ecumenical context. This thinking came to fruition in the Washington Theological Consortium, organized in November 1967. Member schools besides Wesley were the Virginia Theological School in Alexandria (Episcopal), the Howard University Divinity School (non-denominational), the School of Theology at The Catholic University of America, the Lutheran Theological Seminary at Gettysburg (which avoided long commuting by establishing a "house of studies" in Washington) and two coalitions of Roman Catholic seminaries now known as the Cluster of Independent Theological Schools and the Washington Theological Union. The multi-directional exchange of faculty, students, and courses among these schools, together with team-taught inter-confessional offerings by the consortium itself, opened up a new dimension of theological education in an ecumenical context. An interesting exchange occurred during the first year when Father Charles Curran taught Roman Catholic Ethics at Wesley and Douglas Chandler taught Methodist History at Catholic University. The consortium elected President Knight chairman of its Executive Committee for the years 1973-75.

The seminary began offering a program of advanced study leading to the Doctor of Sacred Theology degree (S.T.D.) as early as 1923, but ten years later decided that its limited resources should be concentrated on the Bachelor of Divinity program. The Master of Sacred Theology remained the only advanced degree for another quarter of a century, and it satisfied those who desired to study beyond the B.D. Following the move to Washington, several sporadic conversations were held with the faculty of the Department of Philosophy and Religion at The American University regarding the possibility of constructing a joint Ph.D. program in Religion. Although both faculties were always willing to move ahead

New Occasions, Duties

and at one point completed a detailed proposal for the program, the administration of neither school ever found the money to finance it. The proposal finally became a dead letter. Bilateral arrangements with the Department of Sociology and the School of Education at the university provided for joint Ph.D. programs in Sociology of Religion and Christian Education respectively, but neither program has attracted many students. The seminary and the university continue to offer full academic interchange at the graduate level, so that a student in either institution may cross-register for any course that is germane to his or her program of study.

When the basic theological degree was reconstituted in 1968 as a Master of Divinity, Wesley moved rapidly to upgrade its S.T.M. program to a Doctor of Ministry (D.Min.). As a new kind of degree, the D.Min. was not a research program modeled along the lines of a Ph.D. but a professional degree designed specifically for people committed to pastoral ministry. At the center of the program was an Advanced Seminar on the Ministry, an integrative, interdisciplinary, team-taught course using a modified case-study method and exploiting the students' own backgrounds of education and experience. The variety and maturity of these students, who represented not only many Protestant traditions but Roman Catholic and Jewish as well, made for a stimulating learning experience. Wesley inaugurated its Doctor of Ministry program in 1969, becoming one of the first American seminaries to do so, and it has continued to maintain the program's high academic standards and professional expectations in an effort to produce superior pastors of high promise in ministry.

In response to several requests for a two-year program of theological studies for people not intending to seek ordination but still desiring a seminary education, Wesley began in 1973 to offer a Master of Theological Studies degree (M.T.S.). Many of the men and women who enrolled in this program wanted to incorporate such studies into careers already established in law, social work, church administration, teaching, or various forms of lay ministry. The M.T.S. program has remained small but serves the purpose of providing theological understanding and vocational enrichment for people who are not professional ministers.

The National Capital Semester for Seminarians (NCSS) was developed by the faculty and first offered in the spring of 1978. It was designed, according to the catalog announcement, "to provide an opportunity for students of other seminaries to spend one semester of supervised study and interaction/reflection in Washington, D.C." The program affords a full semester of academic credit through meetings with public figures and church leaders in order to learn more about how public policy is made and to reflect on its theological ramifications. Some twenty-five seminaries across the continent became "participating institutions," and their students bring to Wesley each semester an added richness of diversity.

Illustrating further the seminary's maturing interest and involvement in Washington's national and international life was the establishment in 1977 of the Churches' Center for Theology and Public Policy. While not structurally a part of the seminary, its location on campus has become an appropriate symbol of Wesley's concern for the center's priorities: world peace, health care, minority rights, urban policy, economic justice, and the integrity of the political process. On all such issues the center addresses itself to a "critical examination of the structures, processes, and styles of policy-making in the United States." The director of the center, Alan Geyer, was accorded faculty status from the beginning, while Dean

New Occasions, Duties

Every Christmas during their years at the seminary, the Moyers (Ed and Frances) presented a unique program of carols from many times and places. At Westminster the listeners filled the central hall and ranged up the stairs; in Washington they sat or stood informally in the narthex of the chapel, as shown here. The annual event was a source of great delight and inspiration.

Wogaman was a charter member of its Board of Directors. The seminary has enjoyed the benefits of the center's program resources, including frequent contact with its steady parade of visiting fellows from many other institutions.

Facing the second century

The story of Wesley Seminary's first one hundred years is not completely unique. It exhibits, rather, many features common to the growth of most American institutions. Even the statistics, at first impressive, are recognized upon reflection to be not unusual: one proud graduate at the first commencement, 74 in 1982; a total of 5 students "packing to leave" in 1897, and 358 enrolled in the centennial year; an annual operating expense in the first decade of less than two thousand dollars, and a budget now of well over two million. Many such contrasts could be cited. But history is seldom told by the obvious. Hidden wonders, emotions, resolves, dreams, and duties done or shirked also make up the chronicle. The seminary is rooted deep in Methodist tradition, but it has often been critical of Methodist practice. It has been conservative in doctrine but liberal in application, devoted to scholarship but engaged in Christian action, denominationally committed but ecumenically involved. Its one continuing purpose is to supply the churches with ministers who have prepared themselves as whole persons to labor effectively for the increase among all people of love for God and love for neighbor.

Probably the most frequently quoted inscription on the campus is the one on the library building. Taken from one of Charles Wesley's hymns, it reads: "Unite the pair so long disjoined, knowledge and vital piety." The line speaks of the twofold emphasis on the trained head and the warm heart that has characterized the best of the Wesleyan tradition. During construction days its quaint language stood forth as a striking aphorism of the seminary's grand design. Even the physical layout of the campus witnesses to it, as chapel and library—the place of worship and the place of study—confront each other across the quadrangle, neither obscured from the other through the glass walls that enclose their facing sides. "Unite. . .knowledge and vital piety"—upon reflection the words lose their archaism. There are now (1982) more than two thousand living graduates who have carried this admonition into nearly every state of the Union and to eighteen foreign countries. Some are church administrators, some are missionaries and teachers, others serve in other ways; but more than 90 percent of them are in pastoral ministry.

At the seminary's first commencement in 1884, Thomas Hamilton Lewis, the first president, gave his Inaugural Address. Among other words of hope he said: "We have concluded our calculations, we have determined our bearings. We have made our chart. . .and our future is to work out our present plans." Now a second President Lewis[3] begins Wesley's second century, and although a hundred years have passed, there are still calculations to conclude, bearings to be determined, charts to be made—and a future to work out. If it is true that "what's past is prologue," it is not unreasonable to expect that "the best is yet to be." In this faith, the pilgrimage continues.

On the cornerstone of the library building are Charles Wesley's words urging a union of head and heart, faith and reason, in the service of God.

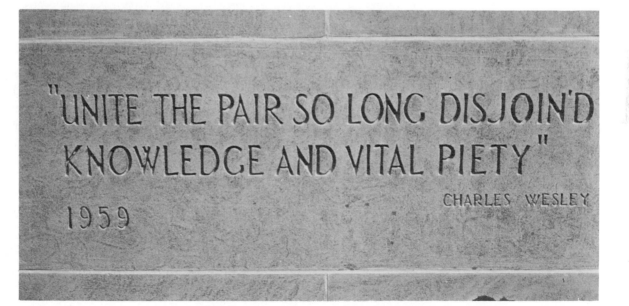

Notes

1 From Small Beginnings

1. To William McKendree, 5 August 1813; in *The Journal and Letters of Francis Asbury,* ed. Elmer T. Clark et al., 3 vols. (Nashville, 1958), 3:491.
2. *Works of the Rev. John Wesley*, ed. Thomas Jackson, 14 vols. (London, 1831), 6:274.
3. *The Journal and Letters of Francis Asbury*, entry for 3 September 1781; 1:411.
4. *Discipline of the Methodist Episcopal Church*, 1792, p. 58.
5. Jesse Lee, *A Short History of the Methodists* (Baltimore, 1810), p. 213.
6. Some of the material in this and the following seven paragraphs is adapted from my account of the Methodist Protestant Church in *The History of American Methodism,* ed. Emory S. Bucke, 3 vols. (Nashville, 1964), 1:669-70, 674; 2:405, 418. Used by permission.
7. Maryland Annual Conference of the Methodist Protestant Church, *Minutes*, 1882, pp. 28-29.
8. J. C. Berrier, "Historical Sketch of the Board of Ministerial Training of the Methodist Protestant Church" (1897), ms. in the library of Wesley Theological Seminary.
9. *The Western Methodist Protestant*, 26 July 1855 and subsequent issues.
10. .Samuel B. Schofield and Marjorie Cowles Crain, *Western Maryland College: The Formative Years, 1866-1947* (Westminster, MD, 1982), p. 31.
11. Maryland Annual Conference, *Minutes,* 1883, p. 33.
12. *The Methodist Protestant,* 17 May 1884, p. 1. The text of the address is printed in full.
13. [Fanny A. Hay, Ruth E. Cargo, and Harlan A. Feeman], *The Story of a Noble Devotion: A Short History of Adrian College, 1845-1945* (Adrian, MI, 1945), pp. 65-66.
14. This is the title of a book by Lewis published at Baltimore in 1905.
15. Thomas H. Lewis, *Methodist Protestant Principles* (Baltimore, 1899), p. 32.
16. Thomas H. Lewis, "Methodist Union Addresses," ed. by James H. Straughn, ms. in the library of Wesley Theological Seminary.

2 Miracle and Sacrifice

1. Reports of the Board of Governors for Elderdice's early years are in the Elderdice Office File in the library of Wesley Theological Seminary. Elderdice's correspondence is in separate file boxes, arranged in chronological order, with papers in each box in alphabetical order.
2. Hugh L. Elderdice to West Virginia University, 3 June 1911.
3. Board of Governors Minutes, 1916.
4. Paper in Elderdice File, 1918.
5. Ibid., 1919.
6. James W. Reese, a long-time professor at Western Maryland College who taught New Testament and Greek part-time at the seminary from 1886 to 1903, held a Ph.D. degree, the only faculty member to do so before Shroyer.
7. Dorothy Elderdice, "History of the Nativity Plays," ms. in the library of Wesley Theological Seminary.

3 Hugh Latimer Elderdice

1. Hugh L. Elderdice to W. M. Strayer, 3 March 1914.
2. Hugh L. Elderdice to G. E. Schott, 17 August 1914.
3. Hugh L. Elderdice to D. E. Vice, 1 September 1915.
4. Hugh L. Elderdice to R. A. Hunter, 23 June 1914.
5. Hugh L. Elderdice to Civil Service Commission, 6 May 1918.
6. Dorothy Elderdice, "Life of Hugh Latimer Elderdice," ms. in the library of Wesley Theological Seminary.
7. Hugh L. Elderdice to Jon Boetsma, 9 June 1919.

5 A Search for New Directions

1. Earl H. Furgeson, sermon in Oxnam Chapel at Wesley Theological Seminary on 27 September 1966, printed in the *Seminary Bulletin,* Fall 1966.
2. Frank Shaffer to Douglas R. Chandler, 18 May 1981.
3. *Zion's Herald,* 20 April 1949.

6 'On Our Way'

1. The Oxnam Papers in the Library of Congress include a large file (21 boxes) on "Un-American Activities and Related Material and Subjects." See also Ralph Lord Roy, *Communism and the Churches* (New York, 1960), pp. 233-35, 254-60.
2. W. Earl Ledden, "Memorial Address" (San Francisco, 16 April 1963), mimeographed copy in the library of Wesley Theological Seminary.
3. Report of the Study Committee, 25 April 1953.
4. Board of Governors Minutes, 2 June 1953.
5. Oxnam's accounts are apparently the only contemporary records that document the increasing difficulties at Westminster. It would be enlightening to have other perspectives, but unfortunately none of the other participants seems to have left any written account.
6. G. Bromley Oxnam to Norman L. Trott, 4 May 1954; in Board of Governors File.
7. Memorial tribute by W. Lynn Crowding, Central Pennsylvania Conference, *Minutes,* 1974, p. 433.
8. Oxnam File, library of The American University.
9. Biographical sketch of Norman L. Trott, ms. in the library of Wesley Theological Seminary.
10. Trott Office File; in library of Wesley Theological Seminary.

7 Wesley in Washington

1. Board of Governors Minutes, 11 June 1956.
2. Ibid., 28 May 1957.
3. John L. Seaton to Norman L. Trott, 11 November 1957; in Trott Office File.
4. This revealing letter suggests what the survey team communicated privately to
5. the Board of Governors (above, p. G120) and also explains why Oxnam felt
   he had to force Welliver to resign (above, p. G138).
   Fortunately the Elderdice File escaped this "thinning down."
   President's Report, 28 March 1960.
   John Wesley's journal for 24 May 1738 describes the experience in words that
   Methodists most love to quote: "In the evening I went very unwillingly to a
   society in Aldersgate Street [London], where one was reading Luther's preface
   to the *Epistle to the Romans*. About a quarter before nine, while he was describing the change which God works in the heart through faith in Christ, I felt my
   heart strangely warmed. I felt I did trust in Christ, Christ alone for my salvation; and an assurance was given me, that He had taken away *my* sins, even
   mine, and saved *me* from the law of sin and death."
6. James M. Goode, *The Outdoor Sculpture of Washington, DC* (Washington,
   1974), p. 312. I am grateful to John E. Bevan, the seminary's registrar and director
   of admissions, for calling this work to my attention. Bevan also pointed out
   that the Wesley figure is one of only two equestrian statues in Washington that
   are not of military heroes; the other is that of Francis Asbury, the first Methodist
   bishop in America.

8 New Occasions, New Duties

1. Haskell M. Miller, *Barricades or Bridges—Crisis in Community* (Nashville,
   1971), p. 16.
2. *Methodist History,* July 1969.
3. G. Douglass Lewis assumed office on 1 July 1982.

Appendices

1

Roster of the faculty

All presidents before 1943 taught full time in addition to their administrative duties, and some of these continued to teach after they had left the presidency. For the first half-century there was little specialization; most professors taught whatever subjects were needed at any given time, and the catalog descriptions of their responsibilities vary widely, especially in the cases of the longer-tenured faculty. For that reason, the fields specified beside each name below are only an approximate indication of what each professor taught. Most of the more durable part-time teachers are included in this roster, while many of the lecturers who came only for brief periods are omitted. The first list is chronological according to year of appointment, the second alphabetical. Much of the data is drawn from the seminary catalogs, however, and one should remember that a professor may have begun teaching the year prior to the appearance of his or her name in the catalog.

Faculty Roster: *chronological*

Lewis, Thomas Hamilton, 1882-1920: Biblical Theology, Historical Theology, Hebrew Language and Literature, Christian Evidences (president 1882-86)

Ward, James Thomas, 1882-96: Systematic Theology, Biblical Theology, Ecclesiastical History (president 1886-97)

Murray, Joshua Thomas, 1882, 1887-88: Pastoral Theology

Kinzer, John D., 1883-84, 1886: Pastoral Theology

Cralle, A. T., 1883: Historical Theology

Merrill, Austin H., 1884-86: Elocution

Spurrier, C. H., 1885-87: Vocal Music

Reese, James W., 1886-1903: New Testament Greek and Exegesis

Warfield, Edwin Alonzo, 1886-88: Hebrew, Ecclesiastical History

Mills, J. L., 1889: Pastoral Theology

Whaley, John B., 1889-94: English

Judefind, W. B., 1890-91: Vocal Music

Bates, Lawrence Webster, 1893-1901: Historical Theology, Pastoral Theology

Elderdice, Hugh Latimer, 1897-1938: Hebrew Language and Literature, Biblical Theology, Historical Theology, Practical Theology (president 1897-1932)

Benson, Benjamin Franklin, 1897-1902: Systematic Theology, Practical Theology, Historical Theology

Hering, Joshua Webster, 1898-1913: Preservation of Health

Cushing, Henry Caleb, 1903-08: Systematic Theology, Practical Theology

Douglas, Claude Cicero, 1903-14: Hebrew, Greek, New Testament, Biblical Theology, Historical Theology

Lease, Nannie Camille, 1905: Elocution

Forlines, Charles Edward, 1906-44: Theism, Systematic Theology, Historical Theology (president 1935-43)

Greenfield, David L., 1909-15: Pastoral Theology

Read, Edgar T., 1909-21: Literature and Religion, Pastoral Theology

Feeman, Harlan Luther, 1911-17: Biblical Theology, Practical Theology

Elderdice, Dorothy, 1915-54 (with some years out): Speech, Religious Drama

Hodges, Warren Hampton, 1914-19: New Testament Greek and Exegesis, Biblical Theology

Shroyer, Montgomery J., 1919-61: Greek, New Testament, Biblical Theology, Christian Sociology

Fraser, James, 1919-21: Greek, New Testament Exegesis

Stephens, Herbert Taylor, 1921-29: New Testament Exegesis, Theism, English Bible, Comparative Religion

Taylor, Walter P., 1922: Public Speaking

Crouse, Thomas O., 1925: Hymns and Bible Reading

Holloway, Fred Garrigus, 1928-41: Biblical Languages (president 1932-35)

Warner, Paul F., 1931, 1934-44: Modern Missions, Biblical Languages

Shipley, Richard Larkin, 1933-47: Christian Art

Cheyney, Harold Eglin, 1933: Christian Sociology

Weagley, Richard, 1935-36: Church Music

Hudgins, Herbert Eugene, 1936-38: New Testament Greek

Little, Lawrence Calvin, 1936-39: Religious Education

Richards, James Arthur, 1936-42: Church Music

Link, John Nicholas, 1938-45: Pastoral Theology

Chandler, Douglas Robson, 1939-73: Church History

DeLong, Alfred W., 1942-45: Church Music

Earp, James P., 1942-43: Christian Sociology

Depro, Frank Smith, 1943-48: Religious Education, Practical Theology, Systematic Theology

270

Van Pelt, John R., 1944-45: Systematic
  Theology
Schilling, Sylvester Paul, 1945-53,
  1970-73: Systematic Theology,
  Philosophy of Religion
Moyer, J. Edward, 1945-77: Church
  Music, Speech
Ashton, Eugene Samuel, 1946-47:
  Biblical Theology
Howes, John Baxter, 1947-79: Rural
  Church, Field Education
Hansen, Robert Emil, 1948-51: Old
  Testament
Furgeson, Earl Hubert, 1948-73:
  Preaching, Pastoral Theology,
  Worship
Schilling, Mary Albright, 1948-53:
  English, Christian Art
Bruder, Ernest E., 1949-76: Pastoral
  Counseling, Clinical Pastoral
  Education
Huber, Milton J., 1950-52: Social Ethics
Hazzard, Lowell B., 1951-70: Old
  Testament
Powell, Robert R., 1951-79: Christian
  Education, Psychology of Religion
Titus, Murray Thurston, 1951-55: Mis-
  sions, World Religions
Gilmore, Reuben Eugene, 1953-68:
  Systematic Theology, Philosophy
  of Religion
Furgeson, Edith B., 1953-73: English
Pyke, James Howell, 1955-83: Missions,
  World Religions
Miller, Haskell M., 1956-76: Sociology,
  Social Ethics
Kircher, Roland E., 1958— :
  Theological Bibliography (librarian
  1959—)
Satterwhite, John H., 1958-73:
  Ecumenics
Edwards, Mary Alice Douty, 1959-83:
  Christian Education
Ham, Clifford, 1958-61: The Church in
  Urban Development
Bauman, Edward W., 1960— :
  Systematic Theology, Christian
  Ethics (adjunct after 1964)
Buchanan, George Wesley, 1960— : New
  Testament
Chikes, Tibor, 1960-83: Pastoral Care,
  Counseling
Goen, Clarence C., 1960— : History of
  Christianity, American Religious
  Studies
Ledden, W. Earl (bishop), 1960-66:
  Christian Worship

Taylor, Harry M., 1960-74: Preaching,
  Biblical Theology
Smith, William E., Jr., 1961-64: Campus
  Ministry (also vice-president)
Borgen, Peder J., 1962-65: New
  Testament
DeWolf, L. Harold, 1965-72: Systematic
  Theology (also dean)
Beegle, Dewey M., 1965— : Old Testa-
  ment, Archaeology
Logan, James Cecil, 1966— : Systematic
  Theology
Stewart, Charles William, 1966— :
  Pastoral Theology
Wogaman, John Philip, 1966— : Chris-
  tian Social Ethics (dean 1972-83)
Clemons, James T., 1967— : New
  Testament
Godsey, John D., 1968— : Systematic
  Theology (associate dean 1968-71)
Stites, Raymond S., 1968-74: Religion
  and Art
Birch, Bruce Charles, 1971— : Old
  Testament
Miller, C. Ronald, 1971-78: Theological
  Bibliography (also assistant
  librarian)
Rasmussen, Larry L., 1972— : Christian
  Social Ethics
Stookey, Laurence Hull, 1973— :
  Preaching and Worship
Morrison, Roy D. II, 1973— :
  Philosophical Theology, Black
  Philosophy of Culture and Religion
Weber, Joseph C., 1973 — : Biblical
  Theology, Ecumenics
Cardman, Francine Jo, 1973-79: History
  of Christianity
Buthelezi, Manas, 1974: African
  Theology
Stith, Forrest, 1974— : Black Church
Poynter, R. Bruce, 1974— : Campus
  Ministry
Steimle, Edmund A., 1975-79:
  Preaching
Wallace, Charles I., Jr., 1975— : Church
  History
Larsen, Ellis A., 1976— : Church
  Administration, Field Education
McCabe, Kendall, 1976-79: Preaching
  and Worship
Jones, William A., 1976: Black
  Preaching
Geyer, Alan, 1977— : Political Ethics
Simon, Geoffrey, 1977-82: Church
  Music
Cleaver, Frances, 1977-81: Speech

Thistlethwaite, Susan B., 1979-81: Christian Education
Martin, Keith, 1979-81: Political Ethics
Kapikian, Catherine Andrews, 1979— : Artist in Residence
Darling, Robin, 1980— : History of Christianity
Shopshire, James M., 1980— : Sociology of Religion (associate dean 1980—)
McClain, William B., 1980— : Preaching and Worship
Wallace, Horace Lee, 1980— : Black Church History
Mathews, James K. (bishop), 1980— : World Christianity

Faulkner, Heather G., 1981— : English
Ferry, Henry, 1981— : Presbyterian History
Kriewald, Diedra Hanner, 1982— : Christian Education
McCan, Robert Lee, 1982— : Political Ethics
Harrison, Jean, 1982— : Speech
Maas, Robin, 1983— : Christian Education
Cleveland, J. Jefferson, 1983— : Church Music
Suchocki, Marjorie, 1984— : Theology (also dean)

Faculty Roster: *alphabetical*

Ashton, Eugene Samuel, 1946-47: Biblical Theology
Bates, Lawrence Webster, 1893-1901: Historical Theology, Pastoral Theology
Bauman, Edward W., 1960— : Systematic Theology, Christian Ethics (adjunct after 1964)
Beegle, Dewey M., 1965— : Old Testament, Archaeology
Benson, Benjamin Franklin, 1897-1902: Systematic Theology, Practical Theology, Historical Theology
Birch, Bruce Charles, 1971— : Old Testament
Borgen, Peder J., 1962-65: New Testament
Bruder, Ernest E., 1949-76: Pastoral Counseling, Clinical Pastoral Education
Buchanan, George Wesley, 1960—: New Testament
Buthelezi, Manas, 1974: African Theology
Cardman, Francine Jo, 1973-79: History of Christianity
Chandler, Douglas Robson, 1939-73: Church History
Cheyney, Harold Eglin, 1933: Christian Sociology
Chikes, Tibor, 1960-83: Pastoral Care, Counseling
Cleaver, Frances, 1977-81: Speech
Clemons, James T., 1967— : New Testament

Cleveland, J. Jefferson, 1983— : Church Music
Cralle, A. T., 1883: Historical Theology
Crouse, Thomas O., 1925: Hymns and Bible Reading
Cushing, Henry Caleb, 1903-08: Systematic Theology, Practical Theology
Darling, Robin, 1980— : History of Christianity
DeLong, Alfred W., 1942-45: Church Music
Depro, Frank Smith, 1943-48: Religious Education, Practical Theology, Systematic Theology
DeWolf, L. Harold, 1965-72: Systematic Theology (also dean)
Douglas, Claude Cicero, 1903-14: Hebrew, Greek, New Testament, Biblical Theology, Historical Theology
Earp, James P., 1942-43: Christian Sociology
Edwards, Mary Alice Douty, 1959-83: Christian Education
Elderdice, Dorothy, 1914-54 (with some years out): Speech, Religious Drama
Elderdice, Hugh Latimer, 1897-1938 : Hebrew Language and Literature, Biblical Theology, Historical Theology, Practical Theology (president 1897-1932)
Faulkner, Heather G., 1981-- : English
Feeman, Harlan Luther, 1911-17: Biblical Theology, Practical Theology

272

Ferry, Henry, 1981–– : Presbyterian History

Forlines, Charles Edward, 1906-44: Theism, Systematic Theology, Historical Theology (president 1935-43)

Fraser, James, 1919-21: Greek, New Testament Exegesis

Furgeson, Earl Hubert, 1948-73: Preaching, Pastoral Theology, Worship

Furgeson, Edith B., 1953-73: English

Geyer, Alan, 1977— : Political Ethics

Gilmore, Reuben Eugene, 1953-68: Systematic Theology, Philosophy of Religion

Godsey, John D., 1968— : Systematic Theology (associate dean 1968-71)

Goen, Clarence C., 1960— : History of Christianity, American Religious Studies

Greenfield, David L., 1909-15: Pastoral Theology

Ham, Clifford, 1958-61: The Church in Urban Development

Hansen, Robert Emil, 1948-51: Old Testament

Harrison, Jean, 1982— : Speech

Hazzard, Lowell B., 1951-70: Old Testament

Hering, Joshua Webster, 1898-1913: Preservation of Health

Hodges, Warren Hampton, 1914-19: New Testament Greek and Exegesis, Biblical Theology

Holloway, Fred Garrigus, 1928-41: Biblical Languages (president 1932-35)

Howes, John Baxter, 1947-79: Rural Church, Field Education

Huber, Milton J., 1950-52: Social Ethics

Hudgins, Herbert Eugene, 1936-38: New Testament Greek

Jones, William A., 1976: Black Preaching

Judefind, W. B., 1890-91: Vocal Music

Kapikian, Catherine Andrews, 1979— : Artist in Residence

Kinzer, John D., 1883-84, 1886: Pastoral Theology

Kircher, Roland E., 1958— : Theological Bibliography (librarian 1959—)

Kriewald, Diedra Hanner, 1982— : Christian Education

Larsen, Ellis A., 1976— : Church Administration, Field Education

Lease, Nannie Camille, 1905: Elocution

Ledden, W. Earl (bishop), 1960-66: Christian Worship

Lewis, Thomas Hamilton, 1882-1920: Biblical Theology, Historical Theology, Hebrew Language and Literature, Christian Evidences (president 1882-86)

Link, John Nicholas, 1938-45: Pastoral Theology

Little, Lawrence Calvin, 1936-39: Religious Education

Logan, James Cecil, 1966— : Systematic Theology

Maas, Robin, 1983— : Christian Education

Martin, Keith, 1979-81: Political Ethics

Mathews, James K. (bishop), 1980— : World Christianity

McCabe, Kendall, 1976-79: Preaching and Worship

McCan, Robert Lee, 1982— : Political Ethics

McClain, William B., 1980— : Preaching and Worship

Merrill, Austin H., 1884-86: Elocution

Miller, C. Ronald, 1971-78: Theological Bibliography (also assistant librarian)

Miller, Haskell M., 1956-76: Sociology, Social Ethics

Mills, J. L., 1889: Pastoral Theology

Morrison, Roy D. II, 1973— : Philosophical Theology, Black Philosophy of Culture and Religion

Moyer, J. Edward, 1945-77: Church Music, Speech

Murray, Joshua Thomas, 1882, 1887-88: Pastoral Theology

Powell, Robert R., 1951-79: Christian Education, Psychology of Religion

Poynter, R. Bruce, 1974— : Campus Ministry

Pyke, James Howell, 1955-83: Missions, World Religions

Rasmussen, Larry L., 1972— : Christian Social Ethics

Read, Edgar T., 1909-21: Literature and Religion, Pastoral Theology

Reese, James W., 1886-1903: New Testament Greek and Exegesis

Richards, James Arthur, 1936-42: Church Music

Satterwhite, John H., 1958-73: Ecumenics

Schilling, Mary Albright, 1948-53: English, Christian Art

273

Schilling, Sylvester Paul, 1945-53, 1970-73: Systematic Theology, Philosophy of Religion

Shipley, Richard Larkin, 1933-47: Christian Art

Shopshire, James M., 1980— : Sociology of Religion (associate dean 1980—)

Shroyer, Montgomery J., 1919-61: Greek, New Testament, Biblical Theology, Christian Sociology

Simon, Geoffrey, 1977-82: Church Music

Smith, William E., Jr., 1961-64: Campus Ministry (also vice-president)

Spurrier, C. H., 1885-87: Vocal Music

Steimle, Edmund A., 1975-79: Preaching

Stephens, Herbert Taylor, 1921-29: New Testament Exegesis, Theism, English Bible, Comparative Religion

Stewart, Charles William, 1966— : Pastoral Theology

Stites, Raymond S., 1968-74: Religion and Art

Stith, Forrest, 1974— : Black Church

Stookey, Laurence Hull, 1973— : Preaching and Worship

Suchocki, Marjorie, 1984— : Theology (also dean)

Taylor, Harry M., 1960-74: Preaching, Biblical Theology

Taylor, Walter P., 1922: Public Speaking

Thistlethwaite, Susan B., 1979-81: Christian Education

Titus, Murray Thurston, 1951-55: Missions, World Religions

Van Pelt, John R., 1944-45: Systematic Theology

Wallace, Charles I., Jr., 1975— : Church History

Wallace, Horace Lee, 1980— : Black Church History

Ward, James Thomas, 1882-96: Systematic Theology, Biblical Theology, Ecclesiastical History (president 1886-97)

Warfield, Edwin Alonzo, 1886-88: Hebrew, Ecclesiastical History

Warner, Paul F., 1931, 1934-44: Modern Missions, Biblical Languages

Weagley, Richard, 1935-36: Church Music

Weber, Joseph C., 1973— : Biblical Theology, Ecumenics

Whaley, John B., 1889-94: English

Wogaman, John Philip, 1966— : Christian Social Ethics (dean 1972-83)

274

2

Members of the
board of governors

No governors were elected the first year (1882) because the
founders thought they were establishing simply a Department
of Theology at Western Maryland College, a school which
already had its own trustees. But after the newly chosen principal, Thomas Hamilton Lewis, organized the seminary as a
separate institution, the Maryland Annual Conference of the
Methodist Protestant Church elected a five-member Board of
Governors for 1883 and requested the General Conference
to elect five additional members at its next meeting in 1884.
Half the board were clergy, half laity. This arrangement continued until the merger of Methodist Protestants with the northern and southern wings of Episcopal Methodism in 1939,
after which the board—now including bishops—slowly increased in size until the 1950s. President Norman L. Trott
(1955-67) added many leaders from business, government, the
professions, and the church, swelling the size of the board to
fifty-one in 1964. A reorganization in 1976 provided for a
twenty-member rotating board with four classes of five
members each.

The names of the governors are listed first chronologically
by year of election and then alphabetically. The dates of their
terms are derived from the seminary catalogs; the beginning
date is the year a name first appears and the ending date the
year it disappears. Because of delay in printing the catalog,
some of the dates may be off by as much as a year; it was not
possible to ascertain in every case precisely when a board
member retired, resigned, or died. An asterisk indicates a president of the seminary (member ex officio of the Board of Governors) and a cross indicates a bishop.

275

Board of governors: *chronological*

Bates, Lawrence Webster	1883-1901	Benson, F. Murray	1941-1964
Murray, Joshua Thomas	1883-1900	Culberson, George W.	1941-1972
Kinzer, John David	1883-1912	Holt, Thomas S.	1941-1949
Hering, Joshua Webster	1883-1913	Meeks, Benjamin W.	1941-1957
Dulany, William James		Scott, William C.	1941-1954
Clarke	1883-1901	Welliver, Lester Allen*	1940-1955
Henderson, Francis H. M.	1884-1888	Leonard, Adna Wright†	1943-1944
Stout, Benjamin	1884-1905	Hughes, Edwin Holt†	1944-1945
Crenshaw, Charles E.	1884-1897	Flint, Charles Wesley†	1945-1953
Roberts, John C.	1884-1897	Straughn, James Henry†	1945-1968
Lee, Thomas	1884-1888	Mowbray, Reginald G.	1945-1964
Lewis, Thomas Hamilton*	1884-1886	Shaffer, Frank L.	1947-1972
Stultz, J. D.	1888-1901	Corson, Fred Pierce†	1948-1969
Hull, J. W.	1888-1901	Colley, Thomas E.	1948-1956
Ward, James Thomas*	1888-1897	Harrison, Nathaniel M.	1948-1969
Harris, Fletcher R.	1897-1917	Lewis, E. Ralph	1948-1954
Wills, J. Norman	1897-1921	Porter, John J.	1948-1956
Elderdice, Hugh Latimer*	1897-1932	Robertson, J. Calloway	1948-1953
Gill, John M.	1900-1939	Sherwood, John W.	1948-1950
Sinkinson, Charles D.	1901-1925	Hawley, John W.	1950-1969
Drinkhouse, Edward J.	1901-1904	Oxnam, G. Bromley†	1952-1960
Searing, Walter T.	1901-1909	Garber, Paul N.†	1953-1969
Fisher, T. Pliny	1901-1932	Day, Albert E.	1953-1960
Mills, Joseph Levin	1904-1925	Hanifan, John E.	1953-1964
Queen, Crofford Lorentz	1905-1909	Luff, Ralph G.	1953-1956
Hess, Aubrey Franklin	1909-1917	Masland, Frank E., Jr.	1953-1970
Yingling, Charles J.	1909-1913	Ryman, Lynde H.	1953-1967
Kirk, Joseph W.	1912-1933	Trott, Norman Liebman*	1953-1967
Miller, Thomas C.	1913-1929	Watchorn, J. Vincent	1953-1972
Mather, T. W.	1915-1925	Amoss, Howard M.	1956-1960
Sheppard, C. E.	1917-1923	Anderson, Hurst K.	1956-1972
Cunningham, J. E.	1917-1935	Berkheimer, Charles	1956-1964
Harris, Fletcher R.	1921-1933	Camalier, Renah F.	1956-1972
Custis, Dwight L.	1923-1937	Chandler, George P.	1956-1972
Grimm, Perry E.	1925-1929	Green, J. Leas	1956-1970
Williams, John C.	1925-1933	McIntosh, James M.	1956-1969
Mather, George K.	1925-1948	McKeldin, Theodore M.	1956-1975
Bee, L. E.	1929-1947	Pullen, Thomas G.	1956-1969
Herrigel, Fred, Jr.	1932-1941	Shirkey, Albert P.	1956-1972
Scott, William C.	1933-1937	Wilkins, J. Ernest	1956-1959
Rosenberger, S. W.	1933-1941	Jones, John Bayley	1956-1960
Harrison, Nathaniel M.	1933-1941	Law, James B.	1956-1976
Shaw, Harry	1933-1934	Trott, Stanley B.	1957-1960
Holloway, Fred Garrigus*	1932-1935	Wicke, Lloyd C.†	1957-1972
Jacobs, Guy W.	1935-1941	Fisher, Lloyd E.	1960-1978
Forlines, Charles Edward*	1936-1944	Keese, William A.	1960-1972
Baker, John H.	1937-1955	Kesmodel, William P.	1960-1964
Shell, J. W.	1937-1941	Landis, Theodore E.	1960-1964
Hicks, J. B.	1937-1941	Latch, Edward G.	1960-1968
Nicholson, Reuben Young	1939-1948	Lord, John Wesley†	1960-1968

Love, Edgar A.†	1960-1968	Stetler, Roy H., Jr.	1972-1976
Mech, Karl F.	1960-1984	Stith, Forrest C.	1972-1985
Mintener, Bradshaw	1960-1978	Wagner, Ferd	1972-1986
Schooley, William E.	1960-1964	White, Raymon E.	1972-1975
Wynne, David J.	1960-1966	Williams, Frank L.	1972-1985
Abrams, Bernice D.	1964-1969	Allnutt, Marie C.	1972-1976
Aiken, Herminia H.	1964-1977	Carr, Larry A.	1972-1976
Beatty, W. Carroll	1964-1981	Handy, Doris M.	1972-1983
Budd, Henry G.	1964-1972	Johnston, Wilma Hollis	1972-1981
Chandler, Hartwell F.	1964-1972	McElwee, William C.	1972-1984
Elderkin, Clarence E.	1964-1966	Roe, Thomas C.	1972-1983
Harmon, Nolan B.†	1964-1968	Vaughan, Daniel	1972-1986
Henley, James W.	1964-1972	Wicklein, Helen	1972-1982
Hessey, John H.	1964-1969	Wurzbacher, A. F.	1972-1983
Hickman, Leon E.	1964-1970	Cuff, G. Wayne	1975-1983
Hoadley, Walter E.	1964-1969	Johnson, Charles A. II	1975-1984
Holloway, Fred G.†	1964-1968	Plummer, Kenneth H.	1975-1984
Hudgins, Herbert E.	1964-1969	Armour, Clifford A.	1976-1986
Jones, John Bayley	1964-1976	Kelley, Leontine T.	1976-1986
McKenney, W. Gibbs, Jr.	1964-1981	May, Felton E.	1976-1986
Middleton, W. Vernon†	1964-1966	Cooney, C. Douglas	1976-1983
Parlin, Charles C.	1964-1972	Yocum, Carol Cosens	1976-1984
Raver, W. Neal	1964-1972	Hutchins, Joshua, Jr.	1976-1984
Riddick, Roland P.	1964-1976	Cayce, Betty	1976-1982
Ward, W. Ralph†	1964-1976	Godfrey, Anne	1976-1980
Wayne, Edward A.	1964-1969	Crocker, Hugh D.	1977-1985
Wilson, Ernest S.	1964-1972	Duley, James L.	1977-1985
Taylor, Prince A., Jr.†	1966-1976	Smith, Helen	1977-1985
Knight, John Lowden*	1967-1982	Brooks, Viola	1978-1986
Sayre, Charles A.	1968-1977	Smithey, Wayne	1978-1986
Booth, Newell A.†	1968-1970	Graham, Bruce M.	1979-1984
Carroll, Edward G.†	1968-1976	Hensley, Basil	1979-1987
Cooke, R. Jervis	1968-1982	Berrier, Floyd L.	1980-1984
Dawson, John H.	1968-1976	Woodland, Helen M.	1980-1984
Drennan, Merrill W.	1968-1977	Wertz, D. Fred†	1980-1984
Hazzard, Walter E.	1968-1970	Donnelly, Robert J.	1981-1985
Van Brunt, F. Norman	1968-1984	Durrett, George M.	1981-1985
Holmes, Preston T.	1968-1979	Linn, LaVon P.	1981-1985
Massaglia, Edward J.	1968-1972	Rushing, Vaudra	1981-1985
Moore, A. Wallace, Jr.	1968-1986	Tull, Earl B.	1981-1985
Scarborough, Gilbert S., Jr.	1968-1987	Shockley, Olin J.	1982-1983
Weber, Walter O.	1968-1972	Rollins, John A.	1982-1986
Mathews, James K.†	1972-1980	Lewis, G. Douglass*	1982—
Andrews, David H.	1972-1983	Dillard, F. Douglas, Jr.	1983-1987
McCoy, Paul E.	1972-1975	Edmonds, Claude A., Jr.	1983-1987
Mick, Billee S.	1972-1979	Zimmerman, Elwood C.	1983-1987
Myers, Paul E.	1972-1981	Baker, Isham O.	1983-1987
Revelle, William H., Jr.	1972-1983	Kettler, Barbara	1983-1987
Sanders, Carl J.	1972-1976	Tingle, Norris W.	1983-1987
Smyth, Robert K.	1972-1980		

Board of Governors: *alphabetical*

Abrams, Bernice D.	1964-1969	Gill, John M.	1900-1939
Aiken, Herminia H.	1964-1977	Godfrey, Anne	1976-1980
Allnutt, Marie C.	1972-1976	Graham, Bruce M.	1979-1984
Amoss, Howard M.	1956-1960	Green, J. Leas	1956-1970
Anderson, Hurst R.	1956-1972	Grimm, Perry E.	1925-1929
Andrews, David H.	1972-1983	Handy, Doris M.	1972-1983
Armour, Clifford A.	1976-1986	Hanifan, John E.	1953-1964
Baker, Isham O.	1983-1987	Harmon, Nolan B. †	1964-1968
Baker, John H.	1937-1955	Harris, Fletcher R.	1897-1917
Bates, Lawrence Webster	1883-1901	Harris, Fletcher R.	1921-1933
Beatty, W. Carroll	1964-1981	Harrison, Nathaniel M.	1933-1941
Bee, L. E.	1929-1947	Harrison, Nathaniel M.	1948-1969
Benson, F. Murray	1941-1964	Hawley, John W.	1950-1969
Berkheimer, Charles	1956-1964	Hazzard, Walter E.	1968-1970
Berrier, Floyd L.	1980-1984	Henderson, Francis H. M.	1884-1888
Booth, Newell A. †	1968-1970	Henley, James W.	1964-1972
Brooks, Viola	1978-1986	Hensley, Basil	1979-1987
Budd, Henry G.	1964-1972	Hering, Joshua Webster	1883-1913
Camalier, Renah F.	1956-1972	Herrigel, Fred, Jr.	1932-1941
Carr, Larry A.	1972-1976	Hess, Aubrey Franklin	1909-1917
Carroll, Edward G. †	1968-1976	Hessey, John H.	1964-1969
Cayce, Betty	1976-1982	Hickman, Leon E.	1964-1970
Chandler, George P.	1956-1972	Hicks, J. B.	1937-1941
Chandler, Hartwell F.	1964-1972	Hoadley, Walter E.	1964-1969
Colley, Thomas E.	1948-1956	Holloway, Fred Garrigus *	1932-1935
Cooke, R. Jervis	1968-1982	Holloway, Fred Garrigus †	1964-1968
Cooney, C. Douglas	1976-1983	Holmes, Preston T.	1968-1979
Corson, Fred Pierce †	1948-1969	Holt, Thomas S.	1941-1949
Crenshaw, Charles E.	1884-1897	Hudgins, Herbert E.	1964-1969
Crocker, Hugh D.	1977-1985	Hughes, Edwin Holt †	1944-1945
Cuff, G. Wayne	1975-1983	Hull, J. W.	1888-1901
Culberson, George W.	1941-1972	Hutchins, Joshua, Jr.	1976-1984
Cunningham, J. E.	1917-1935	Jacobs, Guy W.	1935-1941
Custis, Dwight L.	1923-1937	Johnson, Charles A. II	1975-1984
Dawson, John H.	1968-1976	Johnston, Wilma Hollis	1972-1981
Day, Albert E.	1953-1960	Jones, John Bayley	1956-1960
Dillard, F. Douglas, Jr.	1983-1987	Jones, John Bayley	1964-1976
Donnelly, Robert J.	1981-1985	Keese, William A.	1960-1972
Drennan, Merrill W.	1968-1977	Kelley, Leontine T.	1976-1986
Drinkhouse, Edward J.	1901-1904	Kesmodel, William P.	1960-1964
Dulany, William James		Kettler, Barbara	1983-1987
Clarke	1883-1901	Kinzer, John David	1883-1912
Duley, James L.	1977-1985	Kirk, Joseph W.	1912-1933
Durrett, George M.	1981-1985	Knight, John Lowden *	1967-1982
Edmonds, Claude Λ., Jr.	1983-1987	Landis, Theodore E.	1960-1964
Elderdice, Hugh Latimer *	1897-1932	Latch, Edward G.	1960-1968
Elderkin, Clarence E.	1964-1966	Law, James B.	1956-1976
Fisher, Lloyd E.	1960-1978	Lee, Thomas	1884-1888
Fisher, T. Pliny	1901-1932	Leonard, Adna Wright †	1943-1944
Flint, Charles Wesley †	1945-1953	Lewis, E. Ralph	1948-1954
Forlines, Charles Edward *	1936-1944	Lewis, G. Douglass *	1982—
Garber, Paul N. †	1953-1969	Lewis, Thomas Hamilton *	1884-1886

Linn, LaVon P.	1981-1985	
Lord, John Wesley†	1960-1968	
Love, Edgar A.†	1960-1968	
Luff, Ralph G.	1953-1956	
McCoy, Paul E.	1972-1975	
McElwee, William C.	1972-1984	
McIntosh, James M.	1956-1969	
McKeldin, Theodore M.	1956-1975	
McKenney, W. Gibbs, Jr.	1964-1981	
Masland, Frank E., Jr.	1953-1970	
Massaglia, Edward J.	1968-1972	
Mather, George K.	1925-1948	
Mather, T. W.	1915-1925	
Mathews, James K.†	1972-1980	
May, Felton E.	1976-1986	
Mech, Karl F.	1960-1984	
Meeks, Benjamin W.	1941-1957	
Mick, Billee S.	1972-1979	
Middleton, W. Vernon†	1964-1966	
Miller, Thomas C.	1913-1929	
Mills, Joseph Levin	1904-1925	
Mintener, Bradshaw	1960-1978	
Moore, A. Wallace, Jr.	1968-1986	
Mowbray, Reginald G.	1945-1964	
Murray, Joshua Thomas	1883-1900	
Myers, Paul E.	1972-1981	
Nicholson, Reuben Young	1939-1948	
Oxnam, G. Bromley†	1952-1960	
Parlin, Charles C.	1964-1972	
Plummer, Kenneth H.	1975-1984	
Porter, John J.	1948-1956	
Pullen, Thomas G.	1956-1969	
Queen, Crofford Lorentz	1905-1909	
Raver, W. Neal	1964-1972	
Revelle, William H., Jr.	1972-1983	
Riddick, Roland P.	1964-1976	
Roberts, John C.	1884-1897	
Robertson, J. Calloway	1948-1953	
Roe, Thomas C.	1972-1983	
Rollins, John A.	1982-1986	
Rosenberger, S. W.	1933-1941	
Rushing, Vaudra	1981-1985	
Ryman, Lynde H.	1953-1967	
Sanders, Carl J.	1972-1976	
Sayre, Charles A.	1968-1977	
Scarborough, Gilbert S., Jr.	1968-1987	
Schooley, William E.	1960-1964	
Scott, William C.	1933-1937	
Scott, William C.	1941-1954	
Searing, Walter T.	1901-1909	
Shaffer, Frank L.	1947-1972	
Shaw, Harry	1933-1934	
Shell, J. W.	1937-1941	
Sheppard, C. E.	1917-1923	
Sherwood, John W.	1948-1950	
Shirkey, Albert P.	1956-1972	
Shockley, Olin J.	1982-1983	
Sinkinson, Charles D.	1901-1925	
Smith, Helen	1977-1985	
Smithey, Wayne	1978-1986	
Smyth, Robert K.	1972-1980	
Stetler, Roy H., Jr.	1972-1976	
Stith, Forrest C.	1972-1985	
Stout, Benjamin	1884-1905	
Straughn, James Henry†	1945-1968	
Stultz, J. D.	1888-1901	
Taylor, Prince A., Jr.†	1966-1976	
Tingle, Norris W.	1983-1987	
Trott, Norman Liebman*	1953-1967	
Trott, Stanley B.	1957-1960	
Tull, Earl B.	1981-1985	
Van Brunt, F. Norman	1968-1984	
Vaughan, Daniel	1972-1986	
Wagner, Ferd	1972-1986	
Ward, James Thomas*	1888-1897	
Ward, W. Ralph†	1964-1976	
Watchorn, J. Vincent	1953-1972	
Wayne, Edward A.	1964-1969	
Weber, Walter O.	1968-1972	
Welliver, Lester Allen*	1940-1955	
Wertz, D. Fred†	1980-1984	
White, Raymon E.	1972-1975	
Wicke, Lloyd C.†	1957-1972	
Wicklein, Helen	1972-1982	
Wilkins, J. Ernest	1956-1959	
Williams, Frank L.	1972-1985	
Williams, John C.	1925-1933	
Wills, J. Norman	1897-1921	
Wilson, Ernest S.	1964-1972	
Woodland, Helen M.	1980-1984	
Wurzbacher, A. F.	1972-1983	
Wynne, David J.	1960-1966	
Yingling, Charles J.	1909-1913	
Yocum, Carol Cosens	1976-1984	
Zimmerman, Elwood C.	1983-1987	

3

The Centennial Mace

The mace is a ceremonial staff carried in academic processions. The design of the Wesley Theological Seminary Centennial Mace symbolizes the first century of the seminary. The mace is 122 centimeters (48 inches) long overall and has on it a series of nine bands. The distance from the first to the ninth is one hundred centimeters (one meter), representing the years 1882-1982, while the distance between the bands represents the term of office of each of the eight presidents of the seminary. They are listed here in reverse order as they appear from top to bottom on the mace:

John Lowden Knight	1967-1982
Norman Liebman Trott	1955-1967
Lester Allen Welliver	1943-1955
Charles Edward Forlines	1935-1943
Fred Garrigus Holloway	1932-1935
Hugh Latimer Elderdice	1897-1932
James Thomas Ward	1886-1897
Thomas Hamilton Lewis	1882-1886

Below the bottom band, the mace spreads outward like roots, thus acknowledging the years of discussion and planning prior to the school's founding. Above the top ring, the mace is slightly rounded and is surmounted by a cross, indicating the future of the seminary as it moves by faith into its second century. In the center of the cross is the seal of the seminary; the arms of the cross are enameled copper inlay. The colors of the cross and seal are purple and white, the official seminary colors.

Maces have their origins in primitive clubs and hence grow wider from bottom to top. The swelling of the Centennial

Mace indicates the growth by merger of the denomination with which the seminary is affiliated. The bottom half of the mace represents the Methodist Protestant Church. The staff becomes larger during the presidency of Charles E. Forlines, symbolizing the merger in 1939 of that denomination with the Methodist Episcopal Church (northern) and the Methodist Episcopal Church, South, to form The Methodist Church. The mace again widens just after the beginning of President Knight's term, to indicate the merger in 1968 of The Methodist Church and the Evangelical United Brethren to form The United Methodist Church.

The Centennial Mace was used for the first time on 10 November 1982, when G. Douglass Lewis was inaugurated as the ninth president of the seminary. The service took place in the sanctuary of Metropolitan Memorial United Methodist Church, and Professor Laurence H. Stookey served as marshall of the academic procession.

The section of the mace representing the presidency of Norman L. Trott contains a thin inlaid band of light wood to indicate the change of the name of the seminary from Westminster to Wesley and its move from Westminster, Maryland, to Washington, DC.

Designed by Laurence H. Stookey, '62, professor of Preaching and Worship, the mace was a gift from the Peninsula Annual Conference chapter of the Graduates Association. The staff was made of walnut with holly inlay by Ronald W. Starnes, '59, a member of that conference who teaches in the Department of Religion at Wesley College in Dover, Delaware. The sterling silver cross was made by George Black of Pitman, New Jersey, father of Kathleen M. Black, '80.

4

The Seminary Hymn

The seminary hymn was written in 1950 by S. Paul Schilling, professor of Systematic Theology and Philosophy of Religion at Westminster Theological Seminary 1945-53. He had been attending a retreat at the Kirkridge Center in Pennsylvania, which centered his attention on the theme of the church in the world. At Westminster he formed the Fellowship of the Covenant, a prayer cell which met weekly in the tower of the seminary building. From that tower, he could look out over the college, the town, and the Carroll County countryside, all of which impressed him with the diversity of the context in which his students would be called to minister. Out of such experiences came the inspiration for the hymn, the only one he ever wrote. The music is an original composition by his son, Robert A. Schilling, who had just graduated from high school and was entering DePauw University; he became a professional musician and a minister of music serving Methodist churches in the Midwest.

SEMINARY HILL. 10. 10. 10. 10.

S. Paul Schilling

Robert A. Schilling

1. E - ter - nal God, to us in Christ re - vealed,
2. We thank Thee for this min - is - try we share,
3. In days of stud - y, Lord, with us a - bide;
4. For stead - fast zeal to teach and live Thy way,

In grace re - deem - ing hast Thou from a - bove
Thy call to serve 'mid sor - row, sin, and strife.
Re - new our minds, and make us whol - ly Thine.
For shep - herd heart to guide the wan - d'rer home,

Com - mis - sioned men, in boat and mart and field,
We heed the voice which bids us to de - clare
From hill - top school o'er town and coun - try - side
For power to preach Thy Word we hum - bly pray.

To build Thy church, and man - i - fest Thy love.
To bur - dened souls the way, the truth, the life.
Through-out this dark-ened earth let Thy light shine.
In us, through us, O God, Thy king - dom come! A - MEN.

Index

Names on the Faculty Roster and Board of Governors list are not indexed here; see the alphabetical sections in Appendices 1 and 2 (pp. 269-79). Italicized page numbers below refer to pictures and illustrations.

seminary graduates in, 194;
supports seminary, 194, 204;
Board of Missions of,
249-50;
Deaconess Board of, 216,
256
Bangs, Nathan, 7
Baptists, 53, 232
Barrows, Elijah Porter, 25, 92
Bassett, A. H., 73
Bates, Lawrence Webster, 14,
26, 40, 43
Bates, Lucius, 22
Bauman, Edward W., 230, 231,
234, 242
Baxter, Richard, 73
Beach, Robert, 135, 175, 176
Bee, L. E., 93, 115
Beegle, Dewey M., 235, 260
Bell, George, 81
Bell tower, 223-24
Benedict College, 229
Bennett, William Henry, 73
Benson, Benjamin Franklin, 9,
33, 35, 41, 43
Benson, F. Murray, 114, 168,
182
Benton, John K., 153
Bethel College, 226
Bevan, John E., 240, 268 n.7:6
Beyschlag, Willibald, 73
Biblical languages requirement,
24-25, 30-32, 37, 108
Biblical Seminary, 235
Billingslea, Charles, 14-15, 40
Binney, Amos, 8, 25
Birch, Bruce C., 236
Black, George, 281
Black, Kathleen M., 281
Blacks, 156, 184-85, 230,
252-53
Blair, Hugh, 7
Blizzard, Helen M., *156*
Bluefield (WV) Methodist
Church, 174
Board of Education of The
Methodist Church, 152,
154, 159, 163, 166, 182,
202
Board of Global Missions of
The Methodist Church,
233

Board of Governors:
composition of, 16, 39, 255,
275;
supports President Elderdice,
33-36, 39, 81;
elected by General Con-
ference, 16 (1884), 65
(1922), 93-94 (1932),
114-115 (1940);
includes bishops, 115, 253;
approves Forward Movement
Program, 124-35, 152;
responds to Survey of 1947,
152-54;
includes graduates, 159, 193;
elects Oxnam chairman,
162, 165;
decides to move seminary,
169-70;
changes name of seminary,
198;
first women members, 253;
first lay chairman, 255-56,
260;
historical sketch, 275;
list of members, 276-79
Board of Ministerial Education:
of Ohio Annual Conference,
9;
of Maryland Annual Con-
ference, 13;
of the Methodist Protestant
Church, 13, 27-28,
76-77, 88, 97
Bollinger, Hattie, 87
Book of Discipline:
in Methodist usage, ix;
of Methodist Episcopal
Church, 3, 7;
of Methodist Protestant
Church, 6, 7, 11, 25, 63;
of The Methodist Church,
12 n., 113, 115
Bookstore, seminary, 242
Borgen, Peder, 235
Bosley, Harold, 132
Boston University (including
School of Theology), 91,
114, 124, 128, 129, 130,
136, 138, 151, 162, 206,
212, 229, 231, 236, 237,
243, 258;

DeWolf on, 246-47
Bowers, Herbert, 185
Brastow, Lewis Orsmond, 74
Brewer, Beulah, 241, *242*
Brightman, Edgar Sheffield, 91,
151
Broadus, John A., 26, 74
Broadway Methodist Protestant
Church (Baltimore), 14,
34, 35
Brookeville Academy, 28
Brookland Methodist Church
(Washington), 127
Brown, Charles Reynolds, 74
Brown, John, 185
Browning, Robert, 98
Brown's *Philosophy,* 7
Bruder, Ernest E., *141-42, 234,*
242
Brunswick (MD) First
Methodist Church, 184
Bryn Mawr College, 148, 163
Buchanan, George Wesley,
230, 231, *234, 242*
Bucke, Emory Stevens, 156,
176
Buckingham School, 156
Budget: *see* Finances, seminary
Buildings, seminary:
in 1882, *22,* 27, 33;
president's home, 36, 64-65,
69-71, *70,* 207;
in 1887 and 1907, *65;*
faculty residences, 65-66, *71;*
in 1920, 66-69, *70;*
in 1932, 95;
Welliver's plans for, 155-59,
180;
in Washington, 201-02,
204-05, 209-11, *211,*
213-16, *214*
Burns, Robert, 84
Buthelezi, Manas, 253
Butler, Joseph, 6, 8, 25, 28
Butterfield, Herbert, 210

C

Calvary Methodist Church
(Washington), 240
Cambridge University, 210

285

McNurlan, Dorothy, 107
McPheeters, Chester A., 200
Magee, William Connor, 7
Magee Carpet Company, 187
Maintenance, buildings and grounds, 36, 40, 81, 115, 241-42
Married students, 27, 80, 169, 215-16
Marvin Memorial United Methodist Church, 216
Maryland Annual Conference, 7, 8, 20, 26, 40, 69, 73; theological education in, 13-17, 25; supports seminary, 35-36, 63-64, 68
Masland, Frank E., 170, 187
Mason, John, 2
Master of Divinity degree (M.Div.), 247-49, 261-62
Master of Religious Education degree (M.R.E.), 147, 215, 253
Master of Sacred Theology degree (S.T.M.), 38, 98, 126, 205-06, 262
Master of Theological Studies degree (M.T.S.), 262
Master of Theology degree (M.Th.), 246-47
Mather, George K., 40, 94, 115
Mather, T. W., 40, 67
Matthys, Arlette and Roger, *242*
Maxfield, Thomas, 221
Mayer, Milton, 176
Maynard, James H., 8
Meeks, Benjamin W., 114, 116, 127, 158, 165, 166, 177
Melvin, A. D., 26
Mengers, Randolph, 184
Mennonites, 131
Methodist Church, 1, 96, 109, 114-15, 121, 281; *see also* General Conference of The Methodist Church
Methodist Church Union (Pittsburgh), 237
Methodist Episcopal Church, 1,

2, 68, 106, 113, 213, 281; polity, ix, 19
Methodist Episcopal Church, South, 113-14, 213, 281
Methodist Information Service, 201
Methodist Protestant (at times *Methodist Protestant Recorder*), 4, 5-6, 11, 13, 20, 48, 72, 82, 84, 92, 93, 100
Methodist Protestant Book Concern, 127
Methodist Protestant Church, vii, 33, 108, 113, 281; organization and early history, 1-6; theological education in, 12-15; principles of, 19; and Methodist union, 113-14, 213, 229; and women, 253
Methodist Protestant Repository, 211
Methodist union (1939), 106, 112, 123, 213, 281; Thomas Hamilton Lewis on, 19; effect on seminary, 113-15
Metropolitan Memorial (United) Methodist Church (Washington), 192, 195, 196, 281
Metropolitan Methodist Church (Detroit), 200
Meyer, Frederick Brotherton, 73, 74
Meyer, Heinrich A. W., 73
Miami University, 5
Middle States Association of Collegiate Registrars and Admissions Officers, 240
Middler class, origin of, 37-38
Middleton, Vernon, 237, 238, 239
Miley, John, 26, 73, 91, 92
Miller, Ada, 228
Miller, George H., 88
Miller, Haskell M., 226-28, *227, 234, 242*

Miller, Samuel, 11, 26, 79
Mills, J. L., 43
Milton, John, 6, 72, 86
Milton Avenue Methodist Church (Baltimore), 184
Mintener, Bradshaw, 255-56, *260*
Missions, Christian, 101, 148-52
Mondol, Shot K., 189
Moody, Dwight L., 90
Moody Bible Institute, 89
Moore, Hannah, 6
Moore, John M., 213
Moral Rearmament, 151
Morgan, G. Campbell, 73, 91
Morrison, Roy D., 252-53
Mosheim, Johann Lorenz von, 6, 11, 26
Mott, John R., 229
Motto of the seminary, 90, 93
Mt. Lebanon Church, 27
Mt. Tabor Church, 83
Mount Union College, 145
Mount Vernon Place Methodist Church (Baltimore), 131, 189
Mowbray, Reginald G., 158
Moyer, Frances Apple, 131, *263*
Moyer, J. Edward, 131-34, *132, 133,* 146, *150,* 172, *210, 234,* 240, *242, 263*
Mural, 221
Murray, Joshua Thomas, 14-15, 20, 22, 26, *31,* 43, 73
Music, 109-10, 131-33, 236
Mutual Rights, 4

N

Nash, Margaret, 242
National Capital Semester for Seminarians, 263
Nativity Pageant, 52, 56-57
Nazarenes, 130
Neale, Joseph, *242*
Neander, Johann A. W., 73
Nebraska Wesleyan University, 243
Neff, Helen, *206,* 207

293

166, 200 n., 245
Syracuse Area of The
   Methodist Church, 233
Syracuse First Methodist
   Church, 258
Systematic Theology, 127-31,
   231, 236, 246

T

Tanimoto, Kiyoshi, 176
Taylor, Harry M., 230, 234-35,
   250-51
Taylor, Peg, 234
Temple University, 131
Testing and counseling,
   140-41, 180, 187-88
Textbooks:
   in 19th-century Course of
     Study, 6-8;
   assigned by Webster, 11;
   required at Westminster,
     25-26;
   cost of, 27, 62;
   recommended by Elderdice,
     72-74
Theological education,
   Methodist:
   schools, 114, 124, 152-54;
   financial support, 159, 175,
     194, 202-03;
   see also Association of
     Methodist Theological
     Schools, Commission on
     Theological Education,
     Department of
     Theological Schools
Thesis requirements:
   for first seminary degree,
     37-39, 98, 247-48;
   for advanced seminary
     degree, 38, 126, 205-06
Thistlethwaite, Susan B., 254
Thomas à Kempis, 73
Thompson, Gloria, *242*
Thompson, William J., 97
Thousand Islands Retreat, 249
Thurman, Howard, 117, 176
Tillich, Paul, 139
Timchenko, Boris, 216
Tippett, Donald H., 196

Titus, Murray Thurston, 101,
   149-*50, 229*
Titus, Olive, 150
Tobacco, 9, 63-64
Todd, Omro, 206
Tower room, *68,* 282
Town and Country Ministers,
   School for, 136-37, 175,
   207
Trott, Lillian Durfee, 184, 207,
   257
Trott, Norman Liebman:
   acting president, 171-73;
   elected president, 182;
   sketch, 183-84;
   style of leadership, 186-92;
   inauguration, 189, 193,
     195-96;
   plans for moving seminary,
     191-92;
   raises funds, 193, 201,
     203-04;
   relations with Kresge,
     200-01, 214-15;
   moves seminary to
     Washington, 208-10;
   on the Christ statue, 218-20;
   on the bell tower, 223-24;
   and his vice-presidents,
     206-07, 236-39;
   ecumenical activities, 230;
   enlarges faculty,147, 230-35;
   urges new curriculum, 245;
   enlists support groups,
     256-57;
   retirement and death,
     257-58;
   mentioned, 161, 165, 166,
     170, *173,* 177, 181, *183,*
     185, 203, 204, 208, 210,
     213, 221, 231, *234, 242,*
     280, 281
Trueblood, Elton, 250
Tufts College, 143
Tuition: *see* Student costs

U

Union College, 136
Union Theological Seminary
   (New York), 110, 135,
   147, 151, 175, 184, 189,

   236
Unitarians, 5, 86
United Brethren, 106
United Church of Christ, 131
United Methodist Church, vii,
   230, 281
United States Congress, 5, 162
United States Department of
   Agriculture, 137
Universalists, 5
University Methodist Church
   (College Park, MD), 237
University of Basel, 236
University of Berlin, 128
University of Chicago, 130,
   252, 254
University of Edinburgh, 143
University of Erlangen, 212
University of Manitoba, 141
University of Maryland, 254
University of Nebraska, 243
University of North Carolina,
   134
University of Pennsylvania
   Medical School, 232
University of Pittsburgh, 145
University of Southern Califor-
   nia, 44, 114, 240
University of Tennessee, 227
University of West Virginia, 44
University Senate of The
   Methodist Church, 118,
   153, 166
Urban church, 227-28, 249-50

V

Vanderbilt University, 153,
   254, 258
Van Dusen, Henry Pitney, 189,
   196
van Leeuwen, Arend Theodor,
   151-52
Van Pelt, John R., 127
Veterans Administration, 125,
   155
Vietnam, 53, 57, 244
Virginia Annual Conference,
   108
Virginia Theological Seminary,
   199, 261

W

cornerstone at Wesley, 215
Wicke, Lloyd, 189
Wilberding Company, Inc., 195
Wilder, Amos N., 211
Wilkins, J. Ernest, 191, 252
Willamette University, 150, 258
Williams, George *242*
Williams, J. D., 8
Williams, James R., 7
Williams, John, 93
Williamsport, PA, 122, 178, 181
Wills, J. Norman, 148
Wilson, P. L., 14-15
Wilson College, 131
Wogaman, J. Philip, 246, 258, 263-64, *260*
Women:
    at Western Maryland College, 21, 77-79;
    at Westminster Seminary, 79, 94, 253;
    in school for supply pastors, 137;

begin wives' meetings, 169;
    approved for ordination, 196, 253;
    at Wesley Seminary, 253-55
Women's Guild, 216, 256
Women's International League for Peace and Freedom, 57, 117
Wooden and Benson, 115, 156
World Council of Churches, 163, 184, 230;
    see also Faith and Order Conference, Life and Work Conference
World events, noted at seminary, 48, 53, 57, 86, 97, 102, 116-18, 184, 244
World Methodist Conference, 184, 230
World Methodist Council, 221, 230
World Service and Finance: Committee of the Baltimore Conference, 158;

Commission of The Methodist Church, 163, 202-03
World War I, 46, 48-49, 66
World War II, 116-18, 123
World's Convention of Christian Protestant Ministers, 5
Wynne, David, Jr., 237-39, *238, 243*

Y

Yadkin College, 10, 103
Yale Divinity School, 12, 13, 32, 34, 91, 190
Yale University, 23, 51, 71, 89, 112, 232, 236, 254
Yenching University, 151
Y.M.C.A., 48, 49, 78, 101

Z

Zepp, Ira, 148
Zion's Herald, 156-57